Expansions
Volume One

The Purpose of Creation

By
Imam Fode Drame

Tasleem Publications
Vancouver, BC

TASLEEM PUBLICATIONS
www.expansions.ca

EXPANSIONS VOLUME ONE
Copyright 2012 © Tasleem Publications.
All Rights Reserved. No part of this book may be reproduced in any form or by any means, electronic or mechanical, including photocopying, recording, or by any information storage and retrieval system, without permission in writing from the publisher.

First Tasleem Publications edition published 2012.

Library of Congress Cataloging-in-Publication Data
Expansions Volume One – *The Purpose of Creation* by Imam Fode Drame
Vancouver, Canada: Tasleem Publications, 2012.

ISBN 978-0-9880860-0-5
I. Spirituality II. Personal Development

Notes on Translation

In most cases we have attempted to transliterate Arabic words as they are pronounced. Throughout this book, references to the Qur'an are in brackets. These refer to the name of the chapter (*surah*), the chapter number, and then the verse number (*ayah*) for easy reference. When the Prophet Muhammadﷺ is mentioned in a paragraph, his mention is followed by the calligraphic symbol for *salla Allahu alayhi wa sallam*, which means, "May the peace and blessings of Allah be upon him."

Table of Contents

PREFACE	8
UNITY AND DIFFERENCE	11
Yaqeen (Certitude): The Peak	20
Unity	22
The Double Vision and the Two Domains	27
The Two Names	29
Difference (*Khilaf*) and Disagreement (*Firqah*)	33
TRUTH BY THE TRUTH	34
The Ascension (*'Uruj*)	35
The Parallel Between the Sun and the Spirit	37
The Soul, the Spirit, and the Sun in the Story of Dhul Qarnain	39
The Story of Moses and the Guide	41
Building Spaces	47
The Wisdom (*Hikmah*) of Prophet Joseph (*Yusuf*)	48
THE REWARDS OF GRATITUDE	50
I: The Hoopoe (*Hudhud*)	52
II: The Jinni	54
III: Man with Knowledge of the Book	56
IV: Queen of Sheba	60
The Angel, the Jinn, the Human (Children of Adam)	64
The Rule of Joseph (*Yusuf*)	71
The Sun, the Moon, the Star	72
Six Days of Creation	79
The One Day	83
Conclusion	84

COUNTER-SPINNING THE SOLAR SYSTEM	**89**
Finding a Way Out of the Heavens and the Earth	93
Clockwise and Anti-Clockwise	94
I: Stillness (*Sukoon*)	94
II: Counterclockwise Movement	97
Conflict Between Seeing and Hearing	101
Physiological Positions of the Eyes and the Ears	102
The Reordering of Seeing and Hearing	103
Certainty (*Yaqeen*) and the Stage After	107
The Three Categories of Certainty (*Yaqeen*)	108
Unveiling (*Kashf*) and Certainty (*Yaqeen*)	109
THE STORY OF KING SOLOMON	**111**
Islam	111
The Throne (*'Arsh*)	113
Book	114
Gratitude (*Shukr*) and Ingratitude (*Kufr*)	117
Prostration (*Sujud*)	120
Genuflexion or Bowing Down (*Ruku*)	121
Categories of Knowledge (*'Ilm*)	123
Six Components of the Kingdom of God	124
Ifrit (*Jinn*)	130
Man with Knowledge of the Book	131
Guidance (*Hidayah*)	134
Book and Faith	142
Belief (*Iman*) and Submission (*Tasleem*)	143
Two, Three, Four	146
The Twos in the Story	147
Things that Come in Threes	147
Things that Come in Fours	149

Knowledge (*'Ilm*) to Differentiate	151
Positive Thinking and Respect (*Ta'dheem*)	152
Charity and Justice	155
Well-Thinking and Excellence	156
Common Ground	160
MERCY AND KNOWLEDGE	**169**
The Perfect Teaching	171
The Two Forms of Existence	173
Mercy (*Rahmah*) and Safe-Guarding (*Taqwa*)	175
The Twin Fruits of *Taqwa*	177
Tranquility and Mercy	178
Three Modes of Divine Communication	182
The Double Measures of Mercy (*Rahmah*)	183
The Double Measure of Knowledge (*'Ilm*)	185
God is Odd and Loves Odd	187
Communion Between Odds	189
The Two Hundreds	192
The Two Greatest Names of God	193
The Two Universal Needs	193
THE EXALTED COMPANY	**197**
The Seventh Day	203
Outer Expansion	204
Iman and *Islah*	209
Birr and *Taqwa*	211
The Exalted Company and the Messenger	211
Wisdom and Balance	223
Wisdom (*Hikmah*) and Supplication (*Du'a*)	225
THE PROHIBITED TREE	**239**

First Choice	240
The Second Choice	240
The Third Choice	241
The True and the False	243
Distinction and Separation	243
The Three Methods in the Story of Moses and the Guide	247
Land, Sea and the Boundary	248
The Three Methods in the Story of Dhul Qarnain	249
The Three Steps in the Story of Ibrahim	253
The Three Steps in the Creation of the Universe	253
The Two Extensions	256

GLOSSARY OF TERMS — 257

Preface

When God created the heavens and the earth, He established His presence in two domains: the domain of creation and the domain of commandment. As God says in the Qur'an:

> "Your Lord indeed is the One God, Who created the heavens and the earth in six periods, then He established His presence over the throne. He causes the night to cover the day following it in swift pursuit and (He created) the sun and the moon, and the stars subservient through His commandment. Lo! for Him is the creation and the commandment. Bounteous is The One God the Lord of the Worlds."
> [*Surah Al A'raf* (The Heights) 7:54]

The domain of creation spans from the East to the West and is commonly referred to in these volumes as the horizontal dimension. The domain of commandment spans from the heavens to the earth and is referred to as the vertical dimension.

When God created the human being and made him His vicegerent on this earth, He gave him four entities; a faculty of hearing, a faculty of sight, a Soul that belongs to the domain of creation and a Spirit that belongs to the domain of commandment and He also gave the human being a heart that is connected to all four as a moderator.

Each being exists within its own space (*sadar*) along these entities and an expansion of the heart gives a being more exposure in that dimension. The domains of commandment and creation are not mutually exclusive but are different from each other and the human being is required to bring a harmony between the two without bias towards one or the other. If he succeeds in doing so, he is considered to have fulfilled the purpose of his creation as a being who faithfully reflects all the qualities of his Creator and hence being a true vicegerent (*khalifah*) of his Creator. This series of volumes is about expansions of the heart and the means to attain expansion and the benefits that follow.

As for the means and ends of an expansion, the first means is 'tranquility' that expands the heart horizontally in the domain of creation and increases a being in life. The second means is 'peace' that expands the heart vertically in the domain of commandment and increases a being in light.

God, in the Qur'an, mentions the expansion of the heart a few times. Reference is made to the following verses in the Qur'an, which are about the horizontal expansion:

"Have we not expanded your heart for you and as a result we took your heavy load off you that was weighing on your back and then we raised up your remembrance for you."
[Surah Ash Sharh (The Expansion) 94:1-5]

The above verse is referring to Prophet Muhammad ﷺ and the next verse relates how Prophet Moses, peace be upon him, asked God for an expansion of the heart in a similar way:

"He [Moses] said: "O my Lord expand my heart for me and make easy my command for me and untie my tongue so they fully comprehend my speech."
[Surah TaHa (TaHa) 20:25]

And the vertical expansion is also mentioned in the Qur'an in the following verses:

"And whomsoever Allah wills to guide, his heart He expands wide with willingness towards self-submission [Tasleem]; and whomsoever He wills to go astray, his heart He causes to be tight and constricted, as if he is climbing into the space."
[Surah Al An'am (The Cattle) 6:125]

"And whomsoever Allah expands his heart for self-submission, will soon get a light from his Lord."
[Surah Az Zumur (The Crowds) 39:22]

When peace is in our heart the immediate effect is that our heart expands vertically and this vertical expansion gives us an opening into the world of commandment while tranquility (*sukoon*) produces a different effect. When it enters our hearts, it causes our hearts to expand not vertically but horizontally giving us an opening unto the world of creation. Each time we experience any of these two kinds of expansions, some of the following results will follow:

1. A deep feeling of safety and security and the total absence of fear: horizontal expansion

2. The complete absence of any form of grief and a deep feeling of contentment: vertical expansion

3. An overwhelming feeling of compassion and love for all creation without discrimination: horizontal expansion

4. A sense of detachment from everything as part of witnessing supremacy of God above all things: vertical expansion

The first volume of *The Expansions* explores the place of the human being in relation to his Creator on the one hand and the creation on the other. In order for the human being to fulfill the purpose for which God created him and to attain the prize, which is written for him, he must know his true self and the role assigned to him by his Creator within the order of the creation.

Imam Fode Drame
Vancouver, BC

Unity and Difference

It is evident that there are differences in the world. For example, we see different colors, races, tongues, genders, and tastes. The existence of these differences was not accidental nor was it purposeless, rather, they came to be by God's design and they serve a purpose. With regards to the creation of different genders, male and female, God says:

> "Out of everything we created pairs so that you may remember (dhikr)."
> [Surah Adh Dhariyat (The Winds That Scatter) 51:49]

The purpose here is remembrance (dhikr). Similarly, with regards to the creation of genders, God says:

> "A sign among His signs is that He created out of your souls a partner that you may find rest in them and between you He established a bond of sentiment and compassion in these there are signs for those who reflect."
> [Surah Ar Rum (The Romans) 30:21]

The purpose here is self-reflection and introspection (fikr). With regards to difference of colors, God says:

> "Among His signs is the creation of the heavens (firmaments) and earth and differences in your tongues (languages) and your colors (complexions). In these are signs for those who are knowers."
> [Surah Ar Rum (The Romans) 30:22]

The purpose here is knowledge ('ilm). Furthermore, with regards to differences in colors, God says:

> "Have you not observed that Allah has sent down rain from above, thereby He brought forth fruits of different colors, among the mountains are those with lines (stripes) of different colors white, red and black (pitch). So as well among humans, and cattle

(livestock) all in different colors; indeed only the knowers are servile to Allah among His slaves, indeed Allah is mighty and forgiving."
[Surah Fatir (The Originator of Creation) 35:27-28]

Here again knowledge is evoked as the purpose and the outcome. Conversely, sometimes differences in color may not lead to knowledge (*'ilm*) but rather to reflection (*fikr*). God says to the bees:

"Then eat from all kinds of produce and then travel through the ways of your Lord which are smooth. From their bellies comes out a drink of various colors, in it is a healing for the human beings. Verily in that is truly a sign for a people who reflect."
[Surah An Nahl (The Bee) 16:69]

Here again the result or the purpose is introspection or self-reflection (*fikr*). With regards to differences in taste God says:

"On the earth are tracts of land that share boundaries and gardens of grapes, crops, dates, trees identical and dissimilar all watered with a single water, yet we make ones excel over the others in taste, in that there are signs for these who understand."
[Surah Ar Ra'd (The Thunder) 13:4]

Here the purpose is understanding (*'aql*). With all the foregoing verses we observe that God has created differences for a genuine end and not for anything else; sometimes it is meant to produce remembrance, or introspection and reflection or knowledge or understanding. From the difference in gender we gain remembrance (*dhikr*). From the difference in color and tongue we gain knowledge (*'ilm*). From differences in gender or color we derive reflection and introspection (*fikr*); from differences in taste we derive understanding (*'aql*). Remembrance, reflection, knowledge and understanding; these are the outstanding qualities of human beings and among them some stand out more than others; that is they are different from others. This kind of difference is a very constructive difference and it leads to a healthy competition, whereby each competitor wants to stand out more than others in remembrance (*dhikr*), in reflection (*fikr*), in knowledge (*'ilm*), and in understanding (*'aql*) and it is to these good ends that God created differences.

> "For each among you we've appointed a direction where they must turn their face. Then strive together (as in a race) towards all that is good. Wheresoever you are, Allah will bring you together. For Allah has power over all things."
> [Surah Al Baqarah (The Cow) 2:148]

> "And vie with one another to attain to your Sustainer's forgiveness and to a paradise as vast as the heavens and the earth, which has been readied for those who revere Allah."
> [Surah Al Imran (The Family of Imran) 3:133]

> "Vie, then, with one another in doing good works! Unto God you all must return; and then He will inform you about all that on which you used to differ."
> [Surah Al Ma'idah (The Table Spread) 5:48]

> "Race with one another to forgiveness from your Lord and to Paradise which is as large as the heavens and the earth kept in store for those who have belief in Allah and His messengers, that indeed is the grace of God and He gives it to whosoever He pleases, and Allah is the Lord of the magnificent grace."
> [Surah Al Hadid (The Iron) 57:21]

> "They are given to drink from a pure extracted wine sealed with musk, for the sake of that let those who compete, compete."
> [Surah Al Mutaffifin (The Defrauders) 83:26]

From the study of these we come to the conclusion that God does encourage human beings to compete with one another and to race with one another in things that are noble and heroic. Namely, it is the noble and heroic acts that earn us God's deliverance from the burden of our sins. Once we are delivered from our burdens, fetters and chains then we stand free and light. The lighter one becomes, the faster he or she can race. Therefore, God says:

"Go forth light or heavy and strive with your property and your lives in the way of Allah. That is best for you if you (but) knew."
[Surah At Tawbah (The Repentance) 9:41]

As we see from this verse, the racers are of different conditions; some are light and some are heavy and surely those who are light get ahead of the heavy ones. The light ones being those who have less worldly burdens to encumber them on their journey; if they earn wealth they quickly get rid of it by spending it in the way of God or for that matter any other possessions so that they only keep what suffices as provisions of the way. For the lesser you own the lesser your accountability. For that reason, those who travel light get into paradise long before the heavy travellers for having so much to account for, which causes them delay to set into the kingdom of God. Thereby, the saying of Jesus:

"*It is harder for a rich man to enter the kingdom of God than the camel to go through the eye of a needle.*"
[Matthew 19:23-24, Mark 10:24-25 and Luke 18:24-25]

This statement is in reference to the rich who holds back from spending, not the one who earns and spends in the way of God. Indeed the one who earns and spends in the way of God is better than the one who does not earn nor spend in the way of God. There is a saying by the Prophet Muhammad:

"*Envy is allowed only in two circumstances: 1) to envy someone whom God has blessed with wealth and he/she spends it privately and publicly in the way of God, 2) to envy someone whom God has blessed with knowledge of the book (Qur'an) and he or she is engaged in its study day and night.*"

Such an envy, that incites one to emulate in good causes, is a healthy envy. It is the type of envy that motivates people to reach higher up and to shake off their inertia. A nation seeks to emulate another, a tribe seeks to emulate another, so does a clan to another clan, a race to another race, a family to another family, a school to another school, a system to another system and so on. If there were no differences there would be no envy and if there were no envy there would be no motivation to emulate and to surpass. The outcome of this would be self-complacency, which causes stagnation and decay. Therefore, differences are a blessing for it generates the motive for progress.

On the other hand, uniformity breeds a lack of motivation and kills the human spirit for distinction and excellence. The difference that serves as a catalyst for excellence is a good difference and it is this kind of difference that serves the purpose of creation in the way God has designed it. God created differences so that we may excel in good actions, and the Prophet Muhammad is reported as saying:

"The difference of my Nation (ummah) is a blessing."

This means that through one's differences will they try to surpass one another in good deeds especially in the four major areas of excellence."

1) Remembrance (*dhikr*)
2) Reflection, introspection (*fikr*)
3) Intelligence/understanding (*'aql*)
4) Knowledge (*'ilm*)

For this reason we see different schools of thought (*madhhab*) like *Shafai, Hanafi, Hanbali* and *Maliki*. Because of this difference of schools, the Islamic thought in different fields of learning progressed immensely. Besides that, we have schools of hadith as well as schools of spirituality (*tariqas*) like *Shadhaliyya, Tijania, Naqshabandiya* and others. Out of all these healthy differences, *Islam*, as a whole, came out rich and the sole winner. It is this kind of difference that the Prophet ﷺ meant to convey in his saying:

> *"To differ in pursuit of truth not for the mere sake of being different."*

One spiritual master puts it aptly by saying:

> *"The people of tasawwuf will stay well (khayr) as long as they differ, while their differences motivate them to excel, their concurrence will reduce them to be mutually complacent thereby extinguishing the spirit of competition and race to reach new limits."*

Life, be it spiritual or mundane, is a drama and there is no drama without conflict, as Shaw puts it. However, conflict for the sake of truth is praiseworthy. The one who gets it right is rewarded twice and the one who gets it wrong is rewarded once. When the Prophet ﷺ migrated to the city of Madinah he found that the two major clans of the city, the Aws and the Khazraj, had a bitter rivalry among them that led them at times to bloody confrontations. Once they embraced Islam, that negative rivalry between them turned into a positive rivalry to the benefit of Islam. They continued to rival in serving Islam with their possessions and their lives such that each time a man from the Aws clan would perform an excellent service for Islam, a man from the Khazraj would try to match it. In the process, the cause of Islam was thus advanced:

> *"Lo! Those who go in awe for fear of their Lord. And those who believe in the revelations of their Lord, And those who ascribe not partners unto their Lord, And those who give that which they give with hearts afraid because they are about to return unto their Lord, these race for the good things, and they shall win them in the race."*
> [Surah Al Muminun (The Believers) 23:57-61]

It is for similar purposes that God created differences beginning with the difference of death and life. God says:

"He created death and life to put you to test as to who would excel in deeds."
[*Surah Al Mulk* (The Dominion) 67:2]

This means that if there were no death in sight, human beings would definitely be mediocre in their performance since they have no death to challenge them. It is the challenge of death that compels humans to bring the best out of themselves and without the challenge of death there would be no civilization.

As humans race with death, trying to out race death, they reach such levels of excellence in performance that they indeed outrace death. For if your deeds survive your death, then you are not dead, you are indeed alive and though you are not present in flesh you are present in deeds, which is all that matters. Only those are considered dead whose mention does not survive them because they have no deeds left behind to survive them and hence they are not remembered through their excellent deeds.

Death indeed is created for the sake of life; that is, it is a means to life and those who are most aware of death among us are the ones who excel in life. The certainty of death impresses upon them the urgency to act and to act fast and with determination and out of certainty of death, the certainty of life is born.

Those who lack the certainty of death are the ones who perform poorly in life, for there is no excellence without certainty. Though most humans know they will die, they lack certainty about it, for if they have certainty about it, they would certainly enter a race with it and in the course of that race with death we come to exert ourselves and rise to a higher and better life.

"And call not those who are slain in the way of Allah 'dead'. Nay, they are living, only ye perceive not."
[Surah Al Baqarah (The Cow) 2:154]

"Think not of those, who are slain in the way of Allah, as dead. Nay, they are living. With their Lord they have provision."
[Surah Al Imran (The Family of Imran) 3:169]

For this reason the word certainty (*yaqeen*) is correlated with the word death (*mawt*) in the Qur'anic exegesis (*tafsir*):

"Worship your Lord till certainty (death) comes upon you."
[Surah Al Hijr (The Rocky Tract) 15:99]

Therefore, anyone who has attained the certainty about death is a martyr even though he is alive on earth. For the word martyr (*shahid*) comes from the word to witness (*shahada*), meaning someone who has witnessed the truth. The witnessing of truth at the moment of death can be attained prior to that moment by reaching the certainty about death while one is alive. The proof of that is that such a person is actively engaged in the race with death by trying to bring the best out of him before death comes upon him. Once he or she reaches the peak of his or her potential then onwards real life is born and death is defeated. It is also reported from the Prophet Muhammadﷺ:

"The person who remembers death ten times a day earns equal ranks to someone who falls as a martyr."

In fact, the word remembrance is closely connected to the idea of death and life. Whenever God says in the Qur'an, that you may remember, it means that you may remember death, which, if you do, will increase you in certainty and which if you do, it would increase you in excellent deeds and which if you do, it would increase your life. And increasing in life means an increase in hearing, seeing and understanding which all amounts to an increase in knowledge and an increase in knowledge should lead to further expression of gratitude by deeds, not by words. And gratitude leads to the ultimate quest, which is to attain the pleasure of God (*Ridwan*). God says:

> "*Remember Me and I will remember you and be grateful to Me and do not be ungrateful.*"
> [Surah Al Baqarah (The Cow) 2:152]

To remember God is to remember death first, which, if you do then you will come to the beginning when you were nothing (dead) and then God brought you to life:

> "*Was there ever a time when the human being was a thing not remembered?*"
> [Surah Al Insan (The Human Being) 76:1]

That time was when they were in the darkness of death and then by God's mercy they were brought forth into life. So any remembrance not including death is incomplete. So each time the human being goes back in remembrance -- to the beginning -- he comes back with a new life with an increased level of hearing, seeing and understanding. These new tools are given to him to employ in rendering gratitude towards God with a new level of performance:

> "*... He made for you the hearing and the [degrees of] sights and the hearts so that perhaps you may offer gratitude.*"
> [Surah An Nahl (The Bee) 16:78;
> Surah As Sajdah (The Prostration) 32:9]

That expression of gratitude leads to further increase in life:

> "*... if you offer gratitude I will give you increase...*"
> [Surah Ibrahim (Abraham) 14:7]

> "*Say, my Lord increase me in knowledge.*"
> [Surah TaHa (TaHa) 20:114]

It is through this movement back and forth between death and life that one finally reaches his peak; the peak of their potential after which continuing to live physically has no meaning:

> "You cause the night to enter into the day, and you cause the day to enter into the night; You bring the Living out of the dead, and you bring the dead out of the Living; and You give sustenance to whom You please, without measure."
> [Surah Al Imran (The Family of Imran) 3:27; Surah Ar Rum (The Romans) 30:19]

With each return to death and each rise to life there is an increase in life's potential, meaning the dynamics of life like hearing, sight, and understanding.

Yaqeen (Certitude): The Peak

Yaqeen, the word for certitude (certainty), etymologically in Arabic means the top of a mountain where normally some amount of rainwater collects. Therefore, the word peak and *yaqeen* have the same lexical significance. It signifies that certainty is attained only when we reach the peak, the farthest boundary, and that is exactly what death is. Death is the peak where one comes to an absolute standstill. It is when the heart reaches this point of absolute standstill that it is said to have known certainty. In life, few reach that point but at death everyone does. It is when the heart reaches this point of absolute standstill that it can see God and that is certainty (*yaqeen*), the peak. That is the level of excellence to worship God as though you see Him and know that you will not see your Lord till you die. So when Moses asked God to see God, He said to Moses:

> "You cannot see Me, except that if the mountain stands still in its position then you can perhaps see Me."
> [Surah Al A'raf (The Heights) 7:143]

God set an example by the mountain to spare the feelings of Moses, but the allusion was made to his heart; if your heart reaches its point of absolute stand still then you can see God. With regards to the revolutions of the sun, God says:

> "And the Sun is on its course as till a point of absolute standstill for it."
> [Surah Ya Seen (Ya Seen) 36:38]

Every soul is on its course till it reaches its final destination (*mus'taqarr*), its point of *yaqeen*/peak/certainty.

> "It is God who made you out of one soul then assigned it it's final station and its temporary stations."
> [Surah Al An'am (The Cattle) 6:98]

> "There is no creature that moves in the earth but surely its sustenance is binding upon Allah and He knows its place and time of rest and its place and time of motion..."
> [Surah Al Hud (Hud) 11:6]

Their final abode is when they come to absolute stillness and then certitude is also attained. This certitude, *yaqeen*, while everyone reaches it at death and on the Day of Judgment is attained only by a few in this life. Among those few was Abraham (*Ibrahim*), as God says:

> "Thus did We show Abraham the inner kingdom of the heavens and the earth that he might be of those possessing certitude."
> [Surah Al An'am (The Cattle) 6:75]

The non-believers on the Day of Judgment claim the same certitude as they make their prostrations to God:

> "O our Lord we have seen and have heard, send us back (into the world) that we may worship you in excellence for we are of those with certitude."
> [Surah As Sajdah (The Prostration) 32:12]

As we can see they have experienced death before they could come to this certainty. This certainty is known as the greatest remembrance, the remembrance of God:

"Indeed this is the reality of certainty; do your glorification with your Lord's Great Name."
[Surah Al Waqiah (The Inevitable Event) 56:95-96; Surah Al Haqqah (The Reality) 69:51-52]

Unity

Behind all these visible differences lies a unity and the wise man (*hakeem*) is the one who sees with two eyes. With one he sees the differences; with the other he sees the unity. With this fine balance between differentiation and unity one is able to pursue his or her individual quest for excellence (*ihsan*) while he or she also pursues the collective welfare. Even though excellence induces a feeling of superiority, that feeling of elevation above others must be kept in check by keeping in view the common origin of the indifferent source from which all the differences emerged. By keeping this balanced view we see ourselves as low and high, humble and elevated, without running the risk of getting into either extremes. Every extreme is a prelude to a fall:

"Eat of the good things We have provided for your sustenance, but commit no excess therein, lest My Wrath should justly descend on you: and those on whom descends My Wrath do perish indeed."
[Surah TaHa (TaHa) 20:81]

"Thus be upright as you have been commanded, you and those who have turned back with you to Allah in repentance and do not transgress. For He verily is a seer of all that you do."
[Surah Hud (Hud) 11:112]

"Go thou to Pharaoh, for he has indeed transgressed all bounds."
[Surah TaHa (TaHa) 20:24]

So while the extreme feeling of superiority will lead to arrogance (*kibr*), on the contrary an extreme sense of self-abnegation will surely lead to degrading abjectness. The greatest man is the one who is given a double vision, the one who senses his strength and his weakness at the same time. The sense of his strength will motivate him to pursue further excellence while the sense of weakness will allow him to lower himself to the level of his fellow humans in humility, gentleness and suavity. The latter attitude allows for strengthening our unity, while the earlier allows for progress and excellence in knowledge (*'ilm*), so that the one who is the most knowing is the most excellent.

On the other hand, the principle that underlies indifferentiation and which allows for unity or uniformity is called *rahmah* (mercy). The marriage between these two principles, knowledge and mercy, makes a perfect balance and the whole truth. Any divorce between these two will lead to a disequilibrium either at a personal level or communal level leading to one extreme or to another; either to the murky darkness of ignorance in the West or to the incandescent blazing of knowing in the East. Each side represents a one-eyed vision, with the West being the right eye (the eye of mercy) and the East being the left eye (the eye of distinction) -- one synthesizes and one analysizes. However the Light of God is neither Easterly nor Westerly and it is only perceivable by those with two eyes:

"Allah is the Light of the heavens and the earth. The Parable of His Light is as if there were a niche and within it a lamp: the lamp enclosed in glass: the glass as it were a brilliant star: Lit from a blessed tree, an olive, neither of the east nor of the west, whose oil is well-nigh luminous, though fire scarce touched it: Light upon Light! Allah doth guide whom He wills to His Light: Allah doth set forth parables for men: and Allah doth know all things."
[*Surah An Nur* (The Light) 24:35]

For that matter the anti-Christ is described by the Prophet Muhammadﷺ as having one eye, that is the left eye. He is missing the right eye which is the one with which we perceive mercy. The emphasis of the anti-Christ is on the differences with no room for mercy. Christ, on the other hand, endowed with the two visions, will strike a balance between mercy and knowledge unifying the entire humankind into one nation where individuals will still find room to pursue their quest for fulfillment.

In *Surah Al Kahf* (The Cave), the man who acted as guide for Moses was characterized as a man who was given mercy from God and endowed with knowledge:

"Then found they one of Our slaves, unto whom We had given mercy from Us, and had taught him knowledge from Our presence."
[*Surah Al Kahf* (The Cave) 18:65]

This man was equipped with double visions and that is the description of a perfect teacher and guide. The perfect guide blends the lenience and flexibility of mercy with the rigor and exactitude of knowledge. The guide mercifully forgives, pardons and accepts repentance of the fallen. At the same time he is upright, demanding and strict to help bring the best out of the disciple. He pardons and he chastises. We find this double vision best exemplified on the character of the Prophet Muhammadﷺ:

"And it was by God's grace that thou [O Prophet] didst deal gently with thy followers: for if thou hadst been harsh and hard of heart, they would indeed have broken away from thee. Pardon them, then, and pray that they be forgiven. And take counsel with them in all affairs; then, And when thou art resolved, place thy trust in God: for, verily, God loves those who place their trust in Him."
[*Surah Al Imran* (The Family of Imran) 3:159]

"There hath come unto you a messenger, (one) of yourselves, unto whom aught that ye are overburdened is grievous, full of concern for you (and) for the believers full of tenderness, merciful."
[Surah At Tawbah (The Repentance) 9:128]

In both these verses God emphasizes to the Prophet ﷺ, the importance of being lenient and soft towards his companions and that an attitude of haughtiness, caused by intellectual superiority, is bound to scatter them away. However, God commands him to pursue more knowledge:

"Then exalted be Allah, the True King! And hasten not (O Muhammad) with the Qur'an before its revelation hath been perfected unto thee, and say: My Lord! Increase me in knowledge."
[Surah TaHa (TaHa) 20:114]

His companions inherited this double vision that the Prophet ﷺ had. For even though they were many and they each had their specific personality, it was through the medium of mercy they were kept together in unison:

"Muhammad is the messenger of Allah. And those with him are hard against the disbelievers and merciful among themselves. Thou (O Muhammad) seest them bowing and falling prostrate (in worship), seeking bounty from Allah and (His) acceptance. The mark of them is on their foreheads from the traces of prostration. Such is their likeness in the Torah and their likeness in the Gospel - like as sown corn that sends forth its shoot and strengthens it and rises firm upon its stalk, delighting the sowers - that He may enrage the disbelievers with (the sight of) them. Allah hath promised those among them who believe and do righteous deeds, forgiveness, and a great Reward."
[Surah Al Fath (The Victory) 48:29]

"O ye who believe! Whoso of you turn back from his religion, very soon Allah will bring a people whom He loveth and who love Him, humble toward believers, firm toward disbelievers, striving in the way of Allah, and fearing not the blame of any blamer. Such is the

favor of Allah, which He giveth unto whom He will. Allah is All-Encompassing, All-Knowing."
[*Surah Al Ma'idah* (The Table Spread) 5:54]

As they continued to practice mercy among them they continued to reflect the qualities of mercy like humbleness, generosity, suavity and kindness. They continued to keep their unity. No sooner did those qualities disappear then strife and fury began among them. The two visions were divorced. One group continued espousing the principle of knowledge and repudiated the principle of mercy. The other group continued embracing the principle of mercy to the exclusion of knowledge. In the former group we find pride, arrogance, conceit, and hard heartedness, and in the latter we find humility, compassion, gentleness, and self-abnegation. The latter group however is described by the Prophet ﷺ as *Ghurabaa* (Westerners or strangers), referring to their anonymity and lowness that makes them unnoticed by people around them.

With reference to this group the Prophet ﷺ said, "*Tuba belongs to the Ghurabaa.*" Tuba is either a tree in paradise or simply bliss. The term *Ghurabaa* came to be known later under other names like *faqir, fuqaraa,* or the destitute, still referring to their humble conditions. In a prophetic tradition, the Prophet ﷺ says:

"The religion started as a stranger it will end as a stranger; Tuba belongs to the strangers."

All those who joined Islam while still in its humble beginnings fall under the title of *Ghurabaa* before it finally found a home. In a like manner it will come to pass at the end that Islam will be a stranger again on the earth and those who adhere to it will be strangers and *Tuba* belongs to the strangers.

The Double Vision and the Two Domains

God is the Light of the heavens and the earth that can be perceived only by those who have a double vision. Those with a single vision have a fragmented vision of the Divine Light. To behold the Light, God created two eyes for the human being and to speak with Light, God created for them two lips and a tongue like a needle between the two as a balance and then God showed him or her the two ways:

"Have We not made for him a pair of eyes? And a tongue, and a pair of lips? And shown him the two ways?"
[*Surah Al Balad* (The City) 90:8-10]

Hence he or she is endowed with double Light, *Nur ala Nur*, Light upon Light, the Light of Mercy (*Rahmah*) and the Light of Knowledge (*'Ilm*). With these two lights he is able to perceive the Light of God, which is Light upon Light. Similarly, God made two realms exist, the realm of *khalq* and the realm of *'amr*:

"Indeed to Him belong the khalq and 'amr."
[*Surah Al A'raf* (The Heights) 7:54]

Khalq is the realm of Creation and *'Amr* is the realm of Commandment, respectively, the Universe of Mercy and the Universe of Knowledge. In this way, God's Mercy and Knowledge encompasses everything:

"Those who bear the Throne, and all who are round about it, hymn the praises of their Lord and believe in Him and ask forgiveness for those who believe (saying): Our Lord! Thou encompass all things in mercy and knowledge, therefore forgive those who repent and follow Thy way. Ward off from them the punishment of hell."
[*Surah Ghafir* (The Forgiver) 40:7]

"And ordain for us in this world that which is good, and in the Hereafter (that which is good), Lo! We have turned unto Thee. He

said: I smite with My punishment whom I will, and My mercy encompasses all things, but I shall ordain it for those who revere (Me) and pay the purifying dues, and those through our signs attain to belief."
[*Surah Al A'raf* (The Heights) 7:156]

Therefore, we see that these are the two most comprehensive names or qualities of God; Mercy (*Rahmah*) and Knowledge (*'Ilm*). His Mercy encompasses everything as well as His Knowledge and His other names and qualities all derive from these two domains - that of creation (Mercy) and that of commandment (Knowledge). The realm of Creation (Mercy) form the quarry for the material from whence the ones that are selected are lifted up to the realm of Commandment:

"And your Lord creates what He pleases and selects."
[*Surah Al Qasas* (The Narrations) 28:68]

While they are all equal at the creation level, they differ by selection. Ones selected above others by the Divine Will. None can select himself; only God is the one to select you and lift you out of the level of indifference to the horizon of distinction. Both the domain of creation and the domain of selection exist by the names of God and as one makes his journey up from the creation to commandment he rises from level to level and there is no end to that rising.

Reference to this rising through the stages is mentioned in few Qur'anic verses starting with the first revealed chapter of Qur'an, *Surah Al Alaq* and the first Commandment came to the Prophet to read, "*Iqra*", and these letters can form another word "*Irqa*", meaning rise, for indeed, as you read you rise: God increase me in knowledge and for that the one who has the Qur'an in his heart, it is said to him on the day of rewarding, with the evidence from a Prophetic hadith we read:

"Step on the ladder and read and you will stop rising where your reading stops."

This is one of the miracles of Qur'an that the word for read is also the word to rise. To add to that, the word *Iqr* in *Suriani* means excellent; to read and to rise means to excel.

The Two Names

The first commandment with the first revelation came in connection with two names:

"Read (rise) by the name of your Lord who created (out of Mercy) He created the human being out of a drop of blood."
[*Surah Al Alaq* (The Congealed Blood) 96:1-2]

Creator (*Khaliq*) is the first name of God; His name of Mercy by which He created the world of creation, therefore, reading and rising must begin by that name and that is His name of Mercy. Next comes the second name with the next level. When someone enters this new level he must use the appropriate name that is His name of Knowledge. We do notice a big difference in usage of the preposition in the first level and in the second level. In the first, the rising takes place by the means of the name. That name is like a rope, the rope of mercy by which the reader holds unto and as he reads he rises. Here the name or the rope stands between the reader and God. This name is called the rope of God and God commands all the believers to hold unto the rope of God, which is His Mercy. It is through holding unto Mercy that they will stand united.

In the second level, however, the *Wa*, meaning "and" signifies a greater closeness between the reader and God. God's person seems to be put into focus rather than His names and the verse reads:

"Read and (wa) your Lord the most bountiful."
[*Surah Al Alaq* (The Congealed Blood) 96:3]

Here one is moving along *with* God, not towards Him.

The journey towards Him, by the means of His names, is completed now. The journey is over and the traveller is *with* God, and now, he or she reads and rises with his or her Lord, thereby, increasing in knowledge:

"The One who taught by the pen and taught man what he knew not before."
[Surah Al Alaq (The Congealed Blood) 96:4-5]

Now the traveller is part of *mal ul ala*, the settlers of the high, known as the exalted company, *Ar Rafiq ul Ala*. As long as he or she observes the etiquette of this company he or she maintains his or her place and rises with it forever. Before he or she was travelling *to* God, now he or she is travelling *with* God. Before the traveller held onto the rope (name) of God and that rope is a veil between him and God:

"And hold fast, all of you together, to the cable of Allah, and do not fall in disunity. And remember Allah's favour unto you: How ye were enemies and He made friendship between your hearts so that ye became as brothers by His grace; and (how) ye were upon the brink of an abyss of fire, and He did save you from it. Thus Allah makes clear His signs unto you, so that ye may be guided."
[Surah Al Imran (The Family of Imran) 3:103]

Here the traveller is holding unto something other than the person of God, like Moses held onto his staff. Once the traveller enters the Kingdom of commandment, God tells him or her to let go of his or her staff and he or she lets go of the staff and now stands only by God himself or herself without depending on anything in between. Some who get to this level may be sent back by God to bring others and to these He will say:

"Take it back."
[Surah TaHa (TaHa) 20:21]

In earning the staff and taking it back it returns to its former state. The staff when it turns into a serpent signifies that whatever we hold onto besides God potentially is a serpent. The serpent symbolizes the absence of uprightness, form, strength, elevation, and upliftment as it symbolizes down-to-earthness, abjectness, low desires and obsequious passions. When God was lifting Moses to the high level, He told him to throw away the stick, which was in fact a snake. When He sent him back into the lower domain then He commanded him to take the staff back. Had God not commanded back, Moses would never have taken it back and the fact that he ran away from it, he took the best course of action for that is how the human should flee.

As Joseph fled from the passion of Zuleikha so Moses fled from the passion of this world symbolized by a snake. But how many of us are carrying this snake with us without knowing it? How many are reluctant to throw it away even though its poison is deadly? To all of us indeed God says "flee" as Moses fled and to all of us He says "flee" as Joseph fled:

"Therefore flee unto Allah; lo! I am a plain warner unto you from him."
[*Surah Adh Dhariyat* (The Winds that Scatter) 51:50]

"And they both raced to the door and she tore his shirt from behind and they both found her master [husband] at the door. She said, "What is the reward of someone who harbours evil at your family if not imprisonment or a painful punishment?"
[*Surah Yusuf* (Joseph) 12:25]

Moses fled from this world that was symbolized with the snake towards God, as Joseph fled from this world in the form of Zuleikha's passion, towards God. When Moses, in terror from this world, sought refuge with God, God welcomed him saying, "Come along O Moses, do not be afraid, you are safe."

"Throw down thy staff. And when he saw it writhing as it had

been a demon, he turned to flee headlong, (and it was said unto him): O Moses! Draw nigh and fear not. Lo! Thou art of those who are secure."
[Surah Al Qasas (The Narrations) 28:31]

"And throw down thy staff! But when he saw it writhing as it were a demon, he turned to flee headlong; (but it was said unto him): O Moses! Fear not! The emissaries fear not in My presence."
[Surah Al Naml (The Ant) 27:10]

After God gave him the assurance of safety and security then He showed him how hollow and fake the world is, how it has nothing to offer to those who expect anything from it, and their hope is in vain, and those who fear the world, they are fearing a mere shadow, a toy snake, if only they could rub their eyes harder to find that it was all a mere trick of the eye. When Moses picked the staff again he had already demystified it, he had neither fear nor hope in it. He carried it merely for one purpose, the world must be fought with its own tools, plan for plan, and trick for trick:

"They planned, God planned and God is the Best Planner."
[Surah Al Imran (The Family of Imran) 3:54]

Moses to his credit found that this snake was harmless and so it must be subjected to his service. For, if you serve God the world will serve you. The world in the form of snake is now serving Moses. Joseph on the other hand did not feel so confident, he rather preferred to keep his distance from it and chose the prison. However, Moses had the confidence and the strength to take it back, by the permission of God. At the juncture, God commands the slave to throw away the stick, which symbolizes the different dependencies that one secures for oneself in this life. If he or she had the courage to throw it away then he or she has relinquished the world in its entirety and there onward immediately he or she stands in God's presence in the station of excellence.

As Moses and Muhammadﷺ enter in to this presence, Moses, peace be upon him, is commanded to get rid of the stick before he could be allowed to go up on the ladder. However, Muhammadﷺ had no attachment, he was commanded to start right away, "*Iqra,*" read and rise.

Difference (*Khilaf*) and Disagreement (*Firqah*)

While difference out of unity is productive, disunity is counter-productive. The difference is known as *ikhtilaf*:

"And if thy Lord had willed, He verily would have made mankind one nation, yet they cease not differing, save him on whom thy Lord hath mercy; and for that He did create them. And the Word of thy Lord hath been fulfilled: Verily I shall fill hell with the jinns and mankind together."
[*Surah Hud* (Hud) 11:118-119]

In this verse God states that he had out of design made humankind into different nations that they may seek excellence through their differences but not for the purpose of disagreement, which comes from lack of mercy (*rahmah*). Those with mercy are exempted from breaking up into factions (*tafriq*):

"And hold fast, all of you together, to the cable of Allah, and do not break up into factions. And remember Allah's favour unto you: How ye were enemies and He made friendship between your hearts so that ye became as brothers by His grace; and (how) ye were upon the brink of an abyss of fire, and He did save you from it. Thus Allah maketh clear His revelations unto you, that ye may be guided."
[*Surah Al Imran* (The Family of Imran) 3:103]

God commands the nation of the faithful to hold together unto the rope of God, His Mercy, and not to disagree.

Truth by the Truth

In order to reach the truth you must seek it with another truth, for like attracts like, and so truth is only reachable by the means of another truth. Therefore, a truth in the heavens can only be attracted down to the earth through the means of another truth in the earth.

For further clarification, we ought to know that overall God's dominion extends over two main domains known as creation (*khalq*) and commandment (*'amr*). The soul (*nafs*) and the body (*dhat*) belong to the domain of creation (*khalq*), while the spirit (*ruh*) alone belongs to the domain of the commandment (*'amr*).

> "Indeed unto Him (God) belong the creation and the commandment."
> [*Surah Al A'raf* (The Heights) (7:54]

It follows therefore that the spirit (*ruh*), body and soul are also true as long as they retain the sound disposition (*fitrah*) in which God first disposed them. This conditional statement does not apply to the spirit (*ruh*) since by nature it is inalienable. By nature we mean that it is single (pairless) and things that are by nature single (odd) do not change at all. However, change and alienation does occur at the level of creation (*khalq*), thus, they occur to the body and the soul.

Therefore, when the body and soul undergo alteration, they instantly lose their true disposition and consequently fall out of accord with the spirit (*ruh*), which for its part has remained true. In this particular case, the harmony between creation (*khalq*) and commandment (*'amr*) is broken. In order to re-establish that harmonious rapport between creation (body and soul) and commandment (spirit), it is the body and the soul that need to be reinstated into their true disposition.

As soon as they are returned to their *fitrah* in truth, the corresponding truth (i.e. the spirit) will descend from the commandment to reconnect with the body and soul. This harmonious marriage between the two is known as peace (*salam/Islam*). And, with peace comes light.

"And when souls are reunited."
[*Surah At Takwir* (The Roll Up) 81:7]

"By the Soul, and the proportion and order given to it."
[*Surah Ash Shams* (The Sun) 91:7]

The Ascension (*'Uruj*)

"The angels and the spirit ascend unto Him in a Day the measure whereof the span is fifty thousand years."
[*Surah Al Ma'arij* (The Ladder Steps) 70:4]

The descent of the spirit (*ruh*) into the domain of creation (*khalq*) is only for the purpose of assisting the soul to ascend into the commandment. This ascension of the spirit with the soul up into the domain of commandment (*'amr*) is known as the ascension (*miraj*). Without the guidance of the spirit, the soul and the body cannot undertake such a journey that transcends the boundaries of the earth and the seven heavens:

*"O you assembly of Jinns and men! If it be that you can pass beyond the zones of the heavens and the earth then pass through. Not without authority (sultan) shall you be able to pass! Which is it of the favours of your Lord that you deny? On you will be sent (O you evil ones twain!) a flame of fire (to burn) and a smoke (to choke):
no defense will you have."*
[*Surah Ar Rahman* (The Most Gracious) 55:33-35]

The final ascent takes place at death when the spirit descends (*nazlah*) upon the soul and then ascends with it into the commandment. This occurs if the soul is in its true disposition.

> *"(To the righteous soul will be said) O soul, in (complete) rest and satisfaction! Come back to your Lord - well pleased (to yourself), and well-pleasing unto Him! Enter then, among My devotees! Yea, enter thou My Heaven!"*
> [Surah Al Fajr (The Break of Day) 89:27-30]

If the soul is not in its true disposition however, it is barred from entry into the commandment to be confined within the domain of creation until the Day of Resurrection.

> *"To those who reject Our signs and treat them with arrogance, no opening will there be of the gates of heaven, nor will they enter the garden, until the camel can pass through the eye of the needle. Such is Our reward for those in sin."*
> [Surah Al A'raf (The Heights) 7:40]

From the foregoing, we can discern the respective roles of the soul and the body on the one hand, and the spirit on the other. The role of the spirit is to guide whereas the role of the soul and body is to follow; the spirit commands and the soul obeys. If this relationship between soul and spirit is maintained appropriately, the life of that human being is a well-guided and peaceful life.

If, God forbid, the soul seeks to overtake the spirit, or pretends to lead the spirit, nothing except misguidance and dissension would come out of it. The reason being that it is the spirit that truly hears, sees and knows; the soul on its own does not see, hear or know except through the intermediary of the spirit. Therefore, to walk under the command of the soul is like walking without light neither hearing, nor seeing or understanding. That indeed is what is known as misguidance.

However, even though the spirit is appointed as guide and leader over the soul, it is still not permitted to exercise an excessive authority on the soul. If that happens, the spirit would totally eclipse the soul and the body, and consume them. The same would happen if the sun were allowed to have an immediate impact on the moon or the earth it would certainly burn them down completely.

The similitude for the spirit is the sun, for the soul is the moon and for the body is the earth. As the sun is the source of light for both moon and earth, even more so the spirit is the light for both the soul and the body. Similarly, as the sun provides light for the moon and the earth from a safe distance, likewise the spirit illumines the soul and the body from a safe distance. The closer the spirit gets to the soul and the body, the stronger the illumination (*ishraq*), it generates in them. The absolute illumination takes place at death, which leads to the absolute consumption of the soul and the body by the absolute immediate contact of the spirit with them.

"And a Sign for them is the Night: We withdraw there from the Day, and behold they are plunged in darkness; and the sun runs his course for a period determined for him: that is the decree of (Him), the Exalted in Might, the All-Knowing. And the Moon - We have measured for her mansions (to traverse) till she returns like the old (and withered) lower part of a date-stalk. It is not permitted to the Sun to catch up the Moon, nor can the Night outstrip the Day: Each (just) swims along in (its own) orbit (according to Law)."
[*Surah Ya Seen* (Ya Seen) 36:37-40]

The Parallel Between the Sun and the Spirit

God draws a parallel between the sun and the spirit in many places in the Qur'an. This is because their roles in the system of the world are identical. The term *"tadhally,"* which means to 'lower down,' is used in reference to both sun and spirit. *"Tadhally"* refers to a situation whereby the sun or the spirit lowers itself down upon a particular body, generating in it a brightened level of energy. The volume of energy generated depends on the degree of closeness between the two: sun and body, or spirit and body. On the contrary, the farther they are apart, the weaker the energy flows from one to the other.

The *tadhally* of the spirit is mentioned with regards to the occasion of the Prophet Muhammad's ﷺ nightly journey and ascension. On that occasion, the Prophet, in body and soul, drew so near to the spirit they were as close as the angle between a bow and its string, or even closer. In that instance of extreme closeness, the spirit communicated to the Prophet ﷺ the revelations of God.

"He was taught by one Mighty in Power, endued with Wisdom: for he appeared (in stately form) while he was in the highest part of the horizon. Then he approached and came closer, and was at a distance of but two bow-lengths or (even) nearer So did (Allah) convey the inspiration to His Servant - (conveyed) what He (meant) to convey."
[*Surah An Najm* (The Star) 53:5-10]

As for the *tadhally* of the sun, it is mentioned in *Surah Furqan* with regards to the soul. The soul is described in terms of a shadow because it is like a shadow continuously shifting from side to side, restless and unstable. However, whenever God so wills, He causes the soul to become still. When it is in stillness, He allows the sun to lower itself (*tadhally*) upon the soul, allowing the solar energy to directly flow into that soul. After that, God lifts the soul up to Himself.

*"Have you not turned your vision to your Lord? How He prolongs the shadow! If He willed, He could make it stationary! Then do We make the sun its guide; then We draw it in towards Ourselves,
a contraction by easy stages."*
[*Surah Al Furqan* (The Criterion) 25:45-46]

The Soul, the Spirit, and the Sun in the Story of Dhul Qarnain

God relates to us the travels of Dhul Qarnain in *Surah Al Kahf* verses 83-98. The first part of his journey led him to the murky water (*aynin hamiah*) water mixed with clay. This murky water constitutes the substance out of which the body and the soul were created. We can therefore conclude that this first part of his journey was within the domain of creation (*khalq*).

Here in the creation, Dhul Qarnain found people with a great deal of diversity in colour, tongue, forms and gender. He also noticed that they were in different states of being; some were in their true disposition with a sound soul and body, but some were not. Those who were in their true disposition he gave them glad tidings whereas those who were not, he warned them:

"They ask thee concerning Dhul Qarnain. Say, I will rehearse to you something of his story." Verily We established his power on earth, and We gave him the ways and the means to all ends. And he followed a road until, when he reached the setting of the sun, he found it set in a spring of murky water. Near it he found a People: We said: 'O Dhul Qarnain! (you have authority,) either to punish them, or to treat them with kindness." He said: "Whoever does wrong, him shall we punish; then shall he be sent back to his Lord; and He will punish him with a punishment unheard-of (before). But whoever believes, and works righteousness, he shall have a goodly reward, and easy will be his task as We order it by our Command."
[*Surah Al Kahf* (The Cave) 18:83-88]

We can also assume that when Dhul Qarnain reached the murky water, it was getting dark and the night was sinking because he saw that at this time, the sun was setting into the murky water. This coincidence between his arrival at the murky water and the sun's setting therein further points to the fact that keeping the remembrance of God at night is the way of maintaining one's sound disposition (*fitrah*), and on the other hand those who fail to keep remembrance of God at night are deprived of the self-renewal that occurs every night.

> "O you who have wrapped up in your garments! Stand (to prayer) by night, but not all night; Half of it, or a little less or a little more; and recite the Qur'an in slow, measured rhythmic tones."
> [Surah Al Muzzammil (Folded in Garments) 73:1-4]

The second part of his journey took him to the domain of commandment (*'amr*) where he found the sun rising in the glory of day. Here as well he found people who were directly exposed to the radiance of the sun without any veil between them and the sun. Since this is the domain of commandment (*'amr*), we must conclude that the people here refer to the spirits, which have similar characteristics as the sun. They can come into direct contact with the sun without suffering from its splendor or intense heat. Another common feature between the sun and the spirit is the absence of any shadow. The sun has no shadow, and in a similar manner, the spirit (*ruh*) also has no shadow. The shadow that we see with human beings comes from their bodies and souls. In the world of commandment, the domain of spirits, there are no shadows.

> "Then followed he (another) way until, when he came to the rising of the sun, he found it rising on a people for whom We had provided no covering protection against the sun. (He left them) as they were: We completely understood what was before him."
> [Surah Al Kahf (The Cave) 18:89-91]

Then Dhul Qarnain continued his journey from the commandment to what would be a middle place (*barzakh*) between creation and commandment. Here as well he found people and these people are described as being nearly deprived of the power of understanding speech. They complained to him of the havoc wreaked by Gog and Magog (*Yajuj and Majuj*), and therefore requested him to build for them a wall that would keep them away. This third place seems to be neither Easterly nor Westerly whereby the human being is neither body and soul alone nor spirit alone, but well-balanced combinations of both.

The mention of Gog and Magog appears at this third level which points out the fact that they are neither spiritual nor human beings, but rather curious misfits who make it their duty to interpose between souls and the corresponding spirits. Thus, they interfere with the connection between souls and their spiritual mates - the souls in creation and the spirits in commandment. Dhul Qarnain built the wall, which was meant to keep Gog and Magog in check and allow the free unhindered communication between creation and commandment.

"Then he followed (another) way until, when he reached (a tract) between two mountains, he found beneath them, a people who scarcely understood a word. They said: O Dhul Qarnain! The Gog and Magog do great mischief on earth: shall we then render you tribute in order that you might erect a barrier between us and them? He said: (The power) in which my Lord has established me is better (than tribute): help me therefore with strength (and labour): I will erect a strong barrier between you and them: Bring me blocks of iron. At length, when he had filled up the space between the two steep mountain-sides, He said, Blow (with your bellows) Then, when he had made it (red) as fire, he said; Bring me, that I may pour over it, molten lead. Thus were they made powerless to scale it or to dig through it."
[Surah Al Kahf (The Cave) 18:92-97]

The Story of Moses and the Guide

The story of Moses (*Musa*), peace be upon him, and the guide in *Surah Al Kahf* (18:65-82) is another example of how the relationship between the soul, body and spirits works. The guide in the story represents the spirit, and Moses, peace be upon him, represents the body and soul. In order to accept Moses to follow him, the guide lays certain conditions upon Moses: 1) to be patient; and 2) not to ask any questions, but rather wait for the explanation. The guide decided to lead Moses on a journey that would extend from creation to commandment and finally to the wall which represents the boundary (*barzakh*).

> *"So they found one of Our servants, on whom We had bestowed Mercy from Ourselves and whom We had taught knowledge from Our own Presence. Moses said to him; May I follow you, on the footing that you teach me something of the (Higher) Truth, which you have been taught? He said: Surely you cannot have patience with me. And how can you have patience about things of which your understanding is not complete? Moses said: You will find me, if Allah so will, (truly) patient: nor shall I disobey you in anything. The other said: If then you follow me, ask me no questions about anything until I myself speak to you concerning it."*
> [*Surah Al Kahf* (The Cave) 18:65-70]

In this first part of the story, they went aboard a ship and as they sailed, the guide took an axe and made a crack in the ship, to which Moses, peace be upon him, objected. This objection was a breach of the agreement to be patient and silent.

> *"So the two set out till, when they were in the ship, he made a hole therein. (Moses) said: Have you made a hole therein to drown the folk thereof? Verily you have done a dreadful thing. He said: Did I not tell you that you could not bear patiently with me? (Moses) said: Be not wroth with me that I forgot, and be not hard upon me for my fault."*
> [*Surah Al Kahf* (The Cave) 18:71-73]

This first part of the story corresponds to the first part of the story of Dhul Qarnain, which means that it also took place in the domain of creation at the murky water where the sun sets. The crack in the ship was a gesture opening into a space - to allow the space to expand by letting in the light of God. That light allows the life in that space to grow and improve as much as the light of the sun is essential for the continuity of life on earth. In other words, the life in the space is the soul, and the light from God is the spirit. For the spirit to enlighten the soul, the space in which the soul is placed must have an opening. It means then that the soul that has no opening in its space is a soul that is deprived of enlightenment, or in other words, deprived of a spiritual life, a life that is not lived under the guidance of the spirit. However, in order to crack the space of a soul, patience and silence are mandatory, both of which are included under the common term of *"tasleem"* (unconditional submission to Gods will).

> *"Those whom Allah (in His plan) wills to guide - He opens their breast to Islam; those whom He wills to leave straying - He makes their breast closed and constricted, as if they had to climb up to the skies: thus does Allah (heap) the penalty on those who refuse to believe."*
> [*Surah Al An'am* (The Cattle) 6:125]

> *"Is one whose heart Allah has opened to Islam, so that he has received Enlightenment from Allah, (no better than one hard-hearted)? Woe to those whose hearts are hardened against celebrating the praises of Allah! They are manifestly wandering (in error)!"*
> [*Surah Az Zumar* (The Crowds) 39:22]

In the second part of the story, the guide went on with Moses on their journey until they met a boy whom the guide seized and slew. This act once again elicited a protest from Moses:

> *"So they twain journeyed on till, when they met a lad, he slew him. (Moses) said: What! Have you killed an innocent soul who has killed no man? Verily you have done a horrid thing. He said: Did I not tell you that you could not bear patiently with me? (Moses) said: If I ask you after this concerning anything, keep not company with me. You have received an excuse from me."*
> [*Surah Al Kahf* (The Cave) 18:74-76]

This second part of their journey matches with the second part of Dhul Qarnain's journey when he travelled until he reached the rising place of the sun where he found a people receiving the sunlight without any veil between them and the sun. As we already mentioned, the people here refer to spirits that were under the full glare of the sunlight, completely stripped of any veil between them. The difference between the souls in the first part and those of the second part of both these stories is that the souls in the former place received the light only through a crack, but in the latter place, they were under the full impact of the light signified by the total absence of the veils.

The story again illustrates the two kinds of relationship between the soul and the spirit. In the first instance, the soul (*nafs*) and spirit (*ruh*) are far apart, yet the light of the spirit comes in upon the soul through a crack that allows only a beam of light. This beam of light serves as a line of connection between the soul and the spirit. It is strong enough to raise the soul that was dead before into a new life, the life of faith (*iman*). This new faith infused into the soul by beam of light from the spirit is enough to guide the soul from darkness towards light, from creation towards commandment. The soul and spirit keep on drawing nearer to each other until all veils between them are removed and the radiance of the spirit comes upon the soul with full impact. This full impact of the spirit's radiance on the soul effectively kills the soul with its light beams, which are sharper than well-sharpened iron. Killing the soul with iron as an instrument means a forcible removal of the lustful desires (*shahawaat*) that choke the soul and hinder it's growth.

It is this killing of the soul by the spirit that is signified by the guide killing the boy. The boy represents the soul and it's vain desires (*shahawaat*) and the guide represents the spirit. When the spirit consumes the soul, it is at this point at which the transformation from faith (*iman*) to certainty (*yaqeen*) takes place. The soul indeed has now attained certainty (*yaqeen*).

"And serve your Lord until there come unto you the Hour that is Certain."
[*Surah Al Hijr* (The Rocky Tract) 15:99]

After the attainment of certainty (*yaqeen*) comes the third part of the story, which consists of walking among men and doing the good works of God (*islah*), also known acts of gratitude (*shukr*). In order to fulfill their mission in the midst of human beings:

"Moses and the guide went into a town (city). Since they were hungry and thirsty, they begged for food from the townspeople but were turned down. As they walked in the town, they found a wall that was about to collapse. The guide went up to the wall and raised it back up. However Moses, peace be upon him, commented saying, Had you wished, you could have asked for a pay for your service."
[*Surah Al Kahf* (The Cave) 18:77]

This third part of the story contains four guidelines for those who, by the will of God, are designated to undertake the mission of doing God's good works on earth:

1. Take taqwa as their provision and not be concerned if they are deprived of food, water and shelter

2. Seek only the face of Allah (*Ridwan*) for what they are doing

3. Make no discrimination between people while rendering them services

4. Expect no reward from people for the good works they do, for every slave expects reward from his master; and whoever is a slave of people expects his reward from people, and whoever is a slave of God expects his reward from God. And indeed God's reward is the best.

Here again we find striking similarity between this third

episode and the third part of Dhul Qarnain's story. That is, when he arrived at the boundary he was requested by the people he found there to build a wall between them and Gog and Magog (*Yajuj and Majuj*). They offered to pay for his services, which he declined because he was working only for the face of God (*Ridwan*). Also, he raised a wall like the guide raised a wall in the story of Moses (*Musa*), peace be upon him. Raising a wall is about founding a foundation. The wall in the story of Moses is said to have a treasure underneath. This treasure in reality is referring to the foundation of the wall. That treasure which is the foundation of the wall is called *taqwa*. This word is the combination of wisdom (*hikmah*) and knowledge (*'ilm*). Also by means of these two principles, wisdom (*hikmah*) and knowledge (*'ilm*), Dhul Qarnain built the wall against Gog and Magog. Any wall that is built on the foundation of knowledge and wisdom (*taqwa*), that wall is destined to remain standing till the end of the world. Each time the wall is on the verge of collapsing, God Almighty would raise someone righteous who would raise it up again, thus preventing mal-appropriation of the treasure buried underneath the wall.

"There is a Masjid whose foundation was laid from the first day on piety (taqwa); it is more worthy of the standing forth (for prayer) therein. In it are men who love to be purified; and Allah loves those who make themselves pure. Which then is best? - He that lays his foundation on piety to Allah (Taqwa) and His good pleasure (Ridwan)? - Or he that lays his foundation on an undermined sand-cliff ready to crumble to pieces? And it crumbles to pieces with him, into the fire of Hell. And Allah guides not people that do wrong."
[*Surah At Tawbah* (The Repentance) 9:108-109]

This wall is supposed to be a place of refuge for those who are seeking refuge from the sedition (*fitnah*) that is prevalent abroad. It is supposed to be a sanctuary for those who are seeking God's mercy. It is supposed to be like a beehive that welcomes all sorts of produce in order to produce a health-giving honey that is sweet to the taste and pleasant to the eye because of its multifarious colours.

Building Spaces

The best term to describe those people who walk about in the earth doing the good work of God among men is "builder." They are God's builders of spaces on the earth and in the hearts of men. However, anyone who aspires to become a qualified builder working for God must possess two kinds of instruments that are necessary for building spaces that endure the wear and tear of time and remain standing till the end. The first instrument is called knowledge (*'ilm*), also known as certainty (*yaqeen*). The second one is known as wisdom (*hikmah*) and is also known as the balance (*mizan*) and still known under a third name called intelligence (*'aql*). Every true builder working for God must be in possession of these two sets of instruments in order to build whatever he builds in the most perfect manner.

Every space must consist of two major dimensions, namely the vertical dimension which goes from bottom-top, or in other words from earth to heaven, and the horizontal dimension which stretches from right to left or from West to East. In order to establish the vertical dimension of our space, we require certainty (knowledge), since it is the instrument that is well suited to things that run up-down or down-up. In other words, it suits things that are single because things that are single by nature stand upright.

On the other hand, in order to establish the horizontal dimension of our space, we need to apply the instrument of wisdom, which is also called the balance (*mizan*) or intelligence (*'aql*). This requires matching well between the pairs so that none supersedes the other or transgresses upon the other. What is in the West is well balanced with what is in the East. When all these rules are applied in building the space of God, that space is guaranteed to last as long as the earth and the heavens last since it is founded on the same principles that the earth and the heavens were founded on. Verily, God built the earth and the heavens with knowledge and wisdom, and truly anything that is built by knowledge and wisdom will last as long as the earth and heavens last. In a dialogue between Moses, peace be upon him, and Pharaoh:

> *"Pharaoh asked Moses, Who is the Lord of the Worlds? Moses replied, the Lord of the heavens and the earth and all that is in between them, if you had certainty (muqineen). When Pharaoh seemed to not understand, Moses further said, Lord of the east and the west, and everything in between if you had any understanding ('aqI)."*
> [Surah Ash Shu'ara (The Poets) 26:23-27]

In these verses we see that Moses related certainty (*yaqeen*) to the vertical dimension between earth and heavens, and related intelligence (*'aql*) or wisdom (*hikmah*) to the horizontal dimension between East and West. It is noteworthy to point out here that the difference between certainty (*yaqeen*) and wisdom (*hikmah*) is that certainty (*yaqeen*) applies to things that are beyond measure or computation, while wisdom (*hikmah*) is exactly about precision in measurement and computation. This is in order to give unto things their rightful balance so there is neither excess nor shortage.

The Wisdom (*Hikmah*) of Prophet Joseph (*Yusuf*)

The story of Joseph (*Yusuf*), peace be upon him, is another demonstration of the way God chooses His candidates to become builders to do His good works on earth. It was after going through many trials that Joseph was acknowledged as one in possession of knowledge (*'ilm*) and wisdom (*hikmah*) and who qualified to take on the charge of God's vicegerent (*khalifah*) to do God's good works and build God's community on earth.

In terms of his wisdom (*hikmah*), Joseph (*Yusuf*), peace be upon him, demonstrated it by interpreting the Pharaoh's dream of seven lean cows eating seven fat ones, and seven green corns and seven withered ones. Joseph applied the principle of the balance to explain this dream: there are seven east and seven west. The seven lean cows and seven withered corns represent the seven east; fire and dryness. The seven fat cows and seven green corns represent the seven west; water and abundance. Since the cycle always begins west, then the dream would mean seven years of rain and abundance of harvest, milk, meat and honey. Then another cycle begins of seven eastern years of drought and penury.

The conclusion then is to grow and harvest assiduously during the seven years of rain while consuming the basic minimum. Then the seven years of drought would come, consuming all the produce of the seven years of abundance, leaving only a little. Therefore, the person who consumes a lot in the time of ease will be deprived of everything in the time of dearth.

As for one who consumes little in the time of ease will still have a little left to survive on when adversity comes. When finally the cycle of 14 years arrives to completion, an era of absolute bliss and felicity will ensue wherein rain of mercy will pour down and people would be pressing wine. Wine is a symbol for the truth (*haqq*), meaning the truth of certainty (*haqq-al-yaqeen*).

The Rewards of Gratitude

The reward for gratitude is increase. This increase is not limited, however, to one area of your life. Rather, it covers every aspect of your life. God says:

"Your Lord solemnly declares: If you offered gratitude, I would give you increase."
[Surah Ibrahim (Abraham) 14:7]

The story of King Solomon (*Sulaiman*), offers us a wonderful example of someone who constantly offered gratitude to God and how God in return gave him back increase after increase (*mazeed*). The story begins with Solomon (*Sulaiman*) and his father David (*Dawud*) offering their gratitude (*shukr*) to God for the outstanding favours He gave them.

"We gave knowledge to David and Solomon. And they both said, "Praise be to Allah, Who has favoured us above many of His servants who believe."
[Surah An Naml (The Ant) 27:15]

In these words, David and Solomon expressed their gratitude to Allah for His favours that raised them in knowledge higher than many of God's servants who were also believers like them. Thus, when they offered gratitude to God for the knowledge He gave them, God in return increased them even further by granting them knowledge of the language of birds and expanding their kingdom at the hands of David's heir, Solomon. God says:

"And Solomon was David's heir. He said: 'O people! We have been taught the speech of birds, and we have been given of all things: this indeed is (God's) obvious favour.'"
[Surah An Naml (The Ant) 27:16]

In these words, Solomon publicly acknowledges God's favours upon him and his family. In this way, he is showing us the proper way of offering gratitude, namely, that it must be publicized. It is for this reason he said: "O people" in order to publicly acknowledge God's favours to all people regardless of their race, creed or colour. If God blesses your family, your race, or your country with His favours, these favours should be propagated among all people. The army of Solomon, peace be upon him, expanded to include humans, birds and jinns (invisible beings). God says:

"And before Solomon were marshaled his hosts of jinns [invisible beings] and humans and birds, all kept in ranks as they were ordered. When they came to the valley of ants, one of the ants said: 'O ants, get into your habitations lest Solomon and his hosts crush you without being aware. So he (Solomon) smiled, amused at its speech, and he said: 'O my Lord, so order me that I may be grateful for your favours which you have bestowed upon me and upon my parents and that I may work righteous works that will please thee. And admit me through your Mercy into the ranks of your righteous slaves."
[*Surah An Naml* (The Ant) 27:17-19]

In the previous narrative we see how each increase in gratitude leads to an increase in God's favours. Thus, when Solomon and his father David praised God for the knowledge He gave them, God increased them in knowledge by teaching them the speech of birds. In turn, when Solomon publicly thanked God for giving them the knowledge of the speech of birds, God further increased them in knowledge and taught Solomon the speech of ants. There is a vast difference between the speeches of these two creatures. The speech of birds is audible but not intelligible to many, while the speech of ants is neither audible to many and even less so understood, so this was a great increase in knowledge for Solomon and he profusely thanked God for the unique favour of understanding such a very fine speech such as that of the ants.

Through the story we see that Solomon experienced three major expansions, and that after each expansion he offered gratitude (*shukr*) to God. In the first major expansion, known as the vertical expansion, he came to know the speech of the birds and then offered thanks to God. Then he underwent a second major expansion known as the horizontal expansion and as a result he came to know the speech of the ants. The third expansion, called the extreme expansion or the greatest (*akbar*) expansion is also known as the expansion of the throne. It is called as such because this expansion stretches out to include the throne in its scope. The throne is the final station (*mustaqarr*). It is the station of those who are drawn most near to God (*muqarrabeen*). It is the third part of Solomon's story that relates the events, which are connected to the third expansion namely the throne expansion.

The pivot of the story is the throne of the Queen of Sheba (*Saba*), the queen herself and her people. On the other side are King Solomon and his people, in particular his two main advisors: the jinni (the invisible beings with invisible powers); and the man of knowledge of the scripture. In between the two sides stands the magnificent throne (*arsh*) as the ultimate prize. The person who will win the ultimate prize will be determined by the one who has the closest access (*wasilah*) to God.

I: The Hoopoe (*Hudhud*)

The originator of the story around the throne was none of the above-mentioned characters. It was a bird known as the hoopoe (*hudhud*). It was the hoopoe bird that discovered the kingdom of Sheba and their queen who had a magnificent throne. The hoopoe however noticed that regardless of all these remarkable favours God had bestowed upon this nation and their queen, they still thanklessly disregarded God, recognizing the sun as their supreme deity.

This account brought back by the hoopoe gives us the opportunity to recognize the personality and the character of the hoopoe in the larger context of the whole story as a visionary and a messenger. His role in the kingdom is to explore the unseen (*ghayb*) and report back to the king (*khalifah*) what vision he has from the unseen (*ghayb*), and there ends his role. If the king (*khalifah*) needs to send any message back into the unseen, then the hoopoe is in charge of taking this message back. God says:

"He (Solomon) reviewed the birds and then he said: 'How is it that I don't see the hoopoe (present) or was he among the absentees (those in the unseen). Surely I will punish him a severe punishment or I will slaughter him unless he brings me a clear proof'. He (hoopoe) delayed but a little while and he said: 'I have encompassed in knowledge what you have not encompassed and I have brought to you from Sheba a certain (yaqeen) news (naba-a). I have found their ruler was a woman and she was endowed with everything and had a magnificent throne. I found her and her people prostrating to the sun instead of God. Thus Satan caused them to see their deeds as good and therefore dissuaded them from the way that they may not find guidance. Why would they not prostrate to the One who brings forth what is hidden (even the size of an atom) in the heavens and the earth, and He knows what they do in secret or in public. Allah, there is no God but He, the Lord of the Most Magnificent Throne. He (Solomon) said: We will find out whether you are sincere or you were of those guilty of lying. Go with this letter of mine, deliver it to them and then leave them to see what will be their response."
[Surah An Naml (The Ant) 27:20-28]

There are a few words in these verses that help us further analyze the character and the role of the hoopoe in the story. Two words in particular stand out: certainty (*yaqeen*) and news (*naba-a*). This means that the hoopoe's role is only to bring the news of the unseen, in other words, to prophesize about the unseen (*ghayb*). Secondly, whatever news he brings from the unseen (*ghayb*) is certain; there is no doubt about it, thus he only prophesizes with certitude. In sum, we can call the hoopoe a prophet because he prophesizes. In the capacity of a prophet, the hoopoe counts as one of the four corners (*rukun*) or four pillars (*awtad*) of the kingdom of God. The other three pillars are represented by the *jinni*, the man with knowledge of the book, and the Queen of Sheba.

II: The *Jinni*

The *Jinni's* character here is trustworthiness (*sidq*) and he is called the trustworthy one (*siddiq*). This character signifies that he trusts what he hears, without hesitation, any certain (*yaqeen*) news (*naba-a*) that comes from the unseen. He says: "I hear and I believe;" this is the character of a trustworthy person (*siddiq*).

The *siddiq* are directed by their sense of hearing. As soon as they hear, they believe what they hear, and as soon as they believe what they hear, they find it. Also, the *siddiq* is granted the powers of giving life to one whose hearts are dead, but he cannot cause to die what is alive. The *siddiqs* are known as the people of remembrance (*ahl-al-dhikr*) with a living heart. Life and remembrance are inseparable, for only the living remember and it is only those who remember who are truly alive. For this, God says:

"Ask the people of remembrance (*ahl-al-dhikr*) when you know not." [*Surah Al Nahl* (The Bee) 16:43]

So when we forget, it is they we are supposed to ask because they have not forgotten:

"And We did not send before you any but men to whom We sent revelation, so ask the followers of the remembrance if you know not."
[*Surah Al Anbiyah* (The Prophets) 21:7]

"And We did not send before you any but men to whom We sent revelation—so ask the followers of the remembrance if you do not know."
[Surah An Nahl (The Bee) 16:43]

The people of remembrance are also described by God as the people of firm steps:

"Is it a wonder for mankind that We have inspired a man among them, saying: Warn mankind and bring unto those who believe the good tidings that they have a sure footing with their Lord. The disbelievers say: Lo! This is a mere wizard."
[Surah Yunus (Jonah) 10:2]

These are the people entrusted with the establishment of prayer (*salah*) and the support for the tranquility (*sakinah*), which is intertwined with prayer (*salah*). Wherever prayer (*salah*) is established, there will be tranquility (*sakinah*) and to establish prayer (*salah*) means to pray with a heart firmly established, neither leaning on one side or the other. It is such a prayer (*salah*) that draws the tranquility (*sakinah*), bringing tranquility (*sakinah*) into the heart. Since a *siddiq* is directed by hearing, the character of a *siddiq* is to be well-balanced because our balance comes through our hearing. Therefore, the siddiqs are the trustees of the wisdom (*hikmah*), also known as the balance (*mizan*). The *siddiqs* are the ones God entrusted to establish the balance (*mizan*).

The trust to maintain the balance was first presented to the heavens, the earth and the mountains, but they all declined. It was the human being who took it, thus, the trust became the responsibility of the *siddiqs* among the human beings:

"We did indeed offer the Trust to the heavens and the earth and the Mountains; but they refused to undertake it, being afraid thereof: but man undertook it; He was indeed unjust and ignorant."
[Surah Al Ahzab (The Confederates) 33:72]

III: Man with Knowledge of the Book

The third pillar of the kingdom is represented by the man with knowledge of the Book. Knowledge confers upon the person the ability to witness, for we only witness what we know:

"We bear witness only to what we know, and we could not well guard against the unseen!"
[*Surah Yusuf* (Joseph) 12:81]

A martyr is called a witness (*shahid*) because a person who gets killed in the way of God is raised to the rank of witnesses. For anyone to be admitted as a witness (*shahid*) by God he must exercise purification of the soul (*tazkiah-al-nafs*). When he has purified his soul of any rust or stain until it is shiny and smooth like a silver plate, he is then called the purified one (*zaki*). God then gives him knowledge and admits him into the ranks of the witnesses who stand for God and witness in uprightness, as well as stand in uprightness and witness for God:

"O you who believe! Stand out firmly for justice, as witnesses to Allah, even as against yourselves, or your parents, or your kin, and whether it be (against) rich or poor: for Allah can best protect both. Follow not the lusts (of your hearts), lest you swerve, and if you distort justice or decline to do justice, verily Allah is well-acquainted with all that you do."
[*Surah An Nisa* (The Women) 4:135]

"O you who believe! Stand out firmly for Allah, as witnesses to fair dealing, and let not the hatred of others to you make you swerve to wrong and depart from justice. Be just: that is next to piety (taqwa): and fear Allah. For Allah is well-acquainted with all that you do."
[*Surah Al Ma'idah* (The Table Spread) 5:8]

The witnesses (*shahids*) are associated with iron, since

iron is the instrument of cutting (*farq*) and uncovering (*kashf*). It means that the *Shahid* who is purified by Allah is endowed with the light to separate truth from falsehood (*furqan*). This *furqan* enables him to distinguish between falsehood and truth with unveiling (*kashf*) which then further enables him to uncover the veil (*hijab*) behind which things are hidden so that they see what they see with no veil in between.

The witness (*shahid*), unlike the trustworthy (*siddiq*) are directed by their sight (*baseerat*). God whetted their sight with His divine iron so that their gaze became as sharp as the sharpest weapon you could find, and when they direct their gaze at anything, it cuts through it right down to the core:

> "Today We have taken away (*kashf*) from you your veils and now your sight is sharp."
> [Surah Qaf (Qaf) 50:22]

The *shahid* are therefore the ones from whose sight God has taken away all veils. Their gaze can extend as far as the sunlight can go and beyond and anything that is within their gaze is within their reach in the blink of an eye.

With respect to the news that is certain from the unseen (*ghayb*), the *shahid* stand in uprightness and witness the commandment of God even if the commandment (*'amr*) goes against their own souls, or their parents, or their kinsmen. For this reason they are also known as the people of the commandment (*ulul-'amr*). They are the foremost in obeying God's commandment while testifying to God's Supreme authority over them (*Qahhar*). In return for their obedience to God's commandment, God has made obedience to them mandatory for others:

> "O you who believe, obey Allah, obey the Messenger and the people of the commandment among you."
> [Surah An Nisa (The Women) 4:59]

The similitude of a *shahid's* obedience to God's commandment is the similitude of a dead person in the hands of the one who is washing him as he turns him on his sides right or left. Similarly with a sign from their eyes, anything would respond obediently to a witness. As God has given the *siddiq* power over life, so has He given the *shahid* power over death. Death belongs to the past, hence it relates to the question of God's judgement (*qada*). Life belongs to the future or the new, hence it relates to the question of providence (*qadar*).

In order for careful dispensation of God's bounties, so that there is neither excess nor shortage, for both are life threatening, the *siddiq* is given the wisdom to maintain the proper measure of things so that life is not jeopardized in the time to come. The *siddiq* therefore is one who saves lives. He realizes that in order to live, one must be in harmony with the laws of contraction and expansion (*'adl* and *'afu*) that regulate life. To disregard those laws is to expose one's soul to peril.

The *shahid*, on the other hand, is well acquainted with the nature of God's judgement called (*qada*) and he knows that when God pronounces His commandment (*qada*), all that is required from him is to witness, watch, and testify to its truthfulness:

"And Our Command is but a single (Act), like the twinkling of an eye."
[*Surah Al Qamar* (The Moon) 54:50]

He is not permitted to do anything except watch what God does. In order for him to be able to do this, he must incorporate acceptance of death into his heart. It is that longing for death that brings the stillness and tranquility (*sukoon*) that he needs to be able to witness without interfering and without interrupting the procedure of God's action.

Another function of the *shahid* in the kingdom of God is to judge between people in matters of dispute. This role is assigned to them by virtue of the *furqan* (the light to distinguish between truth and falsehood). Certainly, disputes arise between people only when the truth in the matter disputed is not obvious. Such a matter is known as *"mutashabih"* - something that is unclear and mixed up. God therefore has picked from among the community of believers a number of people, designating them as witnesses (*shuhadaa*) and giving them the authority to judge between people in matters of dispute to pronounce a verdict. God has therefore enjoined the believers to accept the judgment and obey the orders of the *shuhadaa*.

"If you have received a blow, the (disbelieving) people have received a blow the like thereof. These are (only) the vicissitudes which We cause to follow one another for mankind, to the end that Allah may know those who believe and may choose witnesses (shuhadaa) from among you; and Allah loves not wrong-doers."
[Surah Al Imran (The Family of Imran) 3:140]

As well, the *shahid* are those who are given the task of conducting *'amr-bil-ma'roof wal nahyu 'anil munkar'* (to exhort people to do what is right and prohibit them from what is wrong), in other words, to enforce God's commandment. This task is known as reform (*islaah*). This reform in essence means to exhort people to uprightness (*qist*) and therefore the *shahids* are also called the upright ones (*muqsiteen*):

"As to those who deny the Signs of Allah and in defiance of right slay the prophets, and slay those who teach just dealing with mankind (ya'muroona bil-qisti), announce to them a grievous penalty."
[Surah Al Imran (The Family of Imran) 3:21]

The *shahids* or upright ones (*muqsiteen*) are often mentioned in conjunction with the Prophets, since their tasks are complementary. The Prophets are given the task to safeguard their trust (*amanah*), and to render their trust in good faith (*sidq*). However, the upright ones are charged with the task of commanding people to stand for God in uprightness and to render their witnessing.

"And those who respect their trusts and covenants; and those who stand firm in their testimonies (shuhadaa); and those who guard (the sacredness) of their worship; such will be the honoured ones in the Gardens (of Bliss)."
[Surah Al Ma'arij (The Ladder Steps) 70:32-35]

On the Day of Judgment, the book is brought forth and the prophets and the *shahids* are brought forward:

"And the Earth will shine with the Glory of her Lord: the Record (of Deeds) will be placed (open); the prophets and the witnesses will be brought forward and a just decision pronounced between them; and they will not be wronged (in the least)."
[Surah Az Zumar (The Crowds) 39:69]

The prophets are then requested to deliver their trusts and the *shahids* are also requested to deliver their witnessings.

"That (Allah) may question the (custodians) of Truth concerning the Truth they (were charged with): And He has prepared for the Unbelievers a grievous Penalty."
[Surah Al Ahzab (The Confederates) 33:8]

IV: Queen of Sheba

The fourth character in the story of Solomon is the Queen of Sheba. In the kingdom of God, she represents the person who abandons her land, possessions, kingdom, throne, people and migrates to God and His Messenger ﷺ. This person is known as *"muhajir"* (migrant to God and His Messenger) and comes from the word *"hijra"* (migration). He is also known as *"ghareeb"* (stranger). As a result, God will admit such a person into His kingdom and compensate him for everything he had forsaken for the sake of God. He will give him people better than his people, possession better than his possession, kingdom better than his kingdom, throne better than his throne. This was what happened for the Queen of Sheba. When she abandoned her kingdom and her throne and came to God in submission to Him, God brought her throne before her arrival and transformed that throne into something better and greater than it was before her submission (*Islam*).

> *"He said: O chiefs! Which of you will bring me her throne before they come unto me, in submission? Said an 'Ifrit, of the Jinns: "I will bring it to thee before thou rise from thy place: indeed I have full strength for the purpose, and may be trusted." Said one who had knowledge of the Book: "I will bring it to thee within the twinkling of an eye!" Then when (Solomon) saw it placed firmly before him, he said: "This is by the Grace of my Lord - to test me whether I am grateful or ungrateful! And if any is grateful, truly his gratitude is (a gain) for his own soul; but if any is ungrateful, truly my Lord is free of all needs, Supreme in Honour!" He said: "Transform her throne out of all recognition by her: let us see whether she is guided (to the Truth) or is one of those who receive no guidance." So, when she came, it was said (unto her): "Is thy throne like this?" She said: "(It is) as though it were the very one." And (Solomon said): "We were given the knowledge before her and we had submitted (to Allah)."*
> [*Surah An Naml* (The Ant) 27:38-42]

Similarly, any person who abandons his home and migrates to God while in submission (*Islam*), God will reserve a mighty throne for him around His throne and admit him to the ranks of his servants who are drawn near unto Him. However, it must be noted that *Islam* (submission) is presented as a condition to earn the great prize of a magnificent throne beside God. There are many ways in which people come to God, however, only those who come in unconditional submission to the will of the God will earn the throne as a prize.

Islam: Unconditional Submission

The submission that is accepted by God as the true way is the unconditional submission. It means the unconditional acceptance of God's Judgment (*qadaa*), God's providence (*qadar*), God's invitation (*dawah*), and the unconditional compliance with God's orders (*ta'at*). Thus, there are a total of four submissions, which are evident in the story of Solomon in *Surah An Naml* (27:31,38,42,44):

I. *"Be not arrogant against me, but come to me in submission (to the true Religion)."*
[*Surah An Naml* (The Ant) (27:31)

II. *" He said: O chiefs! Which of you will bring me her throne before they come unto me, in submission?"*
[*Surah An Naml* (The Ant) 27:38]

III. *"So, when she came, it was said (unto her): "Is thy throne like this?" She said: "(It is) as though it were the very one." And (Solomon said): "We were given the knowledge before her and we were in submission (to Allah)."*
[*Surah An Naml* (The Ant) 27:42]

IV. *She was asked to enter the lofty Palace: but when she saw it, she thought it was a wave of water, and she (tucked up her skirts), uncovering her legs. He said: "This is but a palace paved smooth with slabs of glass." She said: "O my Lord! I have indeed wronged my soul: I do (now) submit (Tasleem), with Solomon, to the Lord of the Worlds."* [*Surah An Naml* (The Ant) 27:44]

If these four submissions constitute the four corners of the kingdom of God, we will assume that there is a central pillar which is one that combines in it alone the sum of all the other submissions, thus a one to four ratio (1:4). The central character in the story, King Solomon, occupies this central position.

This signifies that he made four unconditional submissions to God, and after each submission God granted him a favour. After the first submission, he was granted prophethood (symbolized by the hoopoe); after the second submission, he was given sincerity (*siddiq*—symbolized by the jinni); after the third submission, he was given witnessing (*shahid*—symbolized by the man with knowledge of the Book); and after the fourth submission, he was granted righteousness (*salih*—symbolized by the Queen of Sheba and her migration to God).

These four submissions add up to the fifth which is all in one, the absolute submission upon which God appointed King Solomon as Messenger (*rasuul*) or God's Vicegerent (*khalifah*) or Pole (*qutb*). This position puts him directly in line with the face of God and he is therefore called "*wajeeh*" (People of the Face). They are immediately under the direct radiance of God's face called *Ridwan*, which signifies that God is pleased with them and they are pleased with God.

"Their reward is with Allah: Gardens of Eternity, beneath which rivers flow; they will dwell therein for ever; Allah well pleased with them, and they with Him: all this for such as fear their Lord and Cherisher."
[*Surah Al Bayyinah* (The Pledge) 98:8]

"All who obey Allah and the Messenger are in the company of those on whom is the Grace of Allah - of the prophets (who teach), the sincere (lovers of Truth), the witnesses (who testify), and the righteous (who do good): Ah! What a beautiful fellowship!"
[*Surah An Nisa* (The Women) 4:69]

Witness (Shaheed)		**Prophet (Nabiyyi)**
	Qutb (Rasool)	
Righteous (Salih)		**Sincere Ones (Siddiq)**

The superiority of one position above all the others is

determined by the degree of nearness to the throne (in reality the Throne of God). If we analyze the story well, we will notice that all four positions represent the four corners of the Islamic kingdom. Each of them is associated with some time designation. As for the hoopoe bird, it delayed a little while; as for the sincere (*siddiq*), his time designation was "before you rise from your seat." As for the witness (*shahid*), his time designation was "before you blink your eye."

The only position with no time designation is the central position occupied by Solomon himself that is what he attained after reaching the station of the Righteous (*salih*) as well. It is the position of absolute presence, which does not involve any movement or action since every movement or action must involve some sort of relationship to time and space.

Even a movement as fast as the wink of an eye, like the case of the man with knowledge of the book, or the period of time that lapses as one rises from sitting to standing, or as slow as travelling from kingdom on earth to another, as is the case of the Queen of Sheba—all these have a relationship to time and space. And the time period with regards to the hoopoe bird should be placed between the speed of rising up and the speed of winking an eye. It is the speed of the spirit during sleep.

As we notice, all these four positions entail some sort of effort as simple as it may be, and requires some sort of time to accomplish it, as brief as that may be, except the fifth position which combines the qualities of all the other four positions into a unique quality which is absolute presence in the permanent station (*mustaqarr*).

The Angel, the Jinn, the Human (Children of Adam)

God's kingdom comprises three categories of creatures: 1) the angel made of cool light (*nur*) 2) the jinn made out of smokeless fire (*naar*) and 3) the human being (Adam) made out of dust (*teen*). The form of the human being is the most accomplished among all three categories of creatures. While each is made out of a particular substance, water is a common source for all three:

> *"For every living thing is made out of water."*
> [Surah Al Anbiyah (The Prophets) 21:30]

Each of the three stands out for one distinguished quality. The angel's outstanding quality is vision (*ru'ya*) and certainty (*yaqeen*). The outstanding quality of the jinn is hearing (*sama'*) with wisdom and balance. The outstanding quality of the human being (Adam's children) is seeing (*baseera*) with knowledge (*'ilm*) and witnessing (*shahada*). The human being, who was the last created, has the most comprehensive form and has incorporated within himself the forms of jinns and angels. Therefore, when a human being wishes to enter into the realm of angels or jinns, he is able to do so because of his nature, which includes the essence of the angels and jinns. On the other hand, however, if an angel or jinn wishes to enter the realm of human beings, they must assume human forms even though this may not always be easy for them. This is because the lesser should emulate the better and not the reverse. The angel Gabriel (*Jibril*) often used to come to the Prophet Muhammad ﷺ in the form of a human as in the famous prophetic tradition (*hadith*) of Umar when Jibril came to ask the Prophet Muhammad ﷺ about Islam, Iman and Ihsan.

In the story of Abraham (*Ibrahim*) and Lot (*Lut*), peace be upon them, we also find in the Qur'an that angels came to them in the form of humans:

"There came Our messengers to Abraham with glad tidings. They said, "Peace!" He answered, "Peace!" and hastened to entertain them with a roasted calf. But when he saw their hands went not towards the (meal), he felt some mistrust of them, and conceived a fear of them. They said: "Fear not: We have been sent against the people of Lut." And his wife, standing by laughed when We gave her good tidings (of the birth) of Isaac, and, after Isaac, of

Jacob. She said: "Alas for me! shall I bear a child, seeing I am an old woman, and my husband here is an old man? That would indeed be a wonderful thing!" They said: "Do you wonder at Allah's decree? The grace of Allah and His blessings on you, O you people of the house! for He is indeed worthy of all praise, full of all glory!" When fear had passed from (the mind of) Abraham and the glad tidings had reached him, he began to plead with us for Lut's people. For Abraham was, without doubt, forbearing (of faults), compassionate, and given to look to Allah. O Abraham! Seek not this. The decree of your Lord has gone forth: for them there comes a penalty that cannot be turned back! When Our messengers came to Lot, he was grieved on their account and felt himself powerless (to protect) them. He said: "This is a distressful day." And his people came rushing towards him, and they had been long in the habit of practising abominations. He said: "O my people! Here are my daughters: they are purer for you (if you marry)! Now fear Allah, and cover me not with shame about my guests! Is there not among you a single right-minded man?" They said: "Well do you know we have no need of your daughters: indeed you know quite well what we want!" He said: "Would that I had power to suppress you or that I could betake myself to some powerful support." (The Messengers) said: "O Lot! We are Messengers from your Lord! By no means shall they reach you! Now travel with your family while yet a part of the night remains, and let not any of you look back: but your wife (will remain behind): To her will happen what happens to the people. Morning is their time appointed: Is not the morning nigh?"
[Surah Hud (Hud) 11:69-91]

"Tell them about the guests of Abraham. When they entered his presence and said, "Peace!" He said, "We feel afraid of you!" They said: "Fear not! We give you glad tidings of a son endowed with knowledge." He said: "Do you give me glad tidings that old age has seized me? Of what, then, is your good news?" They said: "We give you glad tidings in truth: be not then in despair!" He said: "And who despairs of the mercy of his Lord, but such as go astray?" Abraham said: "What then is the business on which you (have come), O you messengers (of Allah)?" They said: "We have

been sent to a people (deep) in sin, (all) save the family of Lot. Them we shall deliver every one, except his wife who, We have ascertained, will be among those who will be left behind." And when the messengers came unto the family of Lot, He said: "Ye appear to be uncommon folk." They said: "Yea, we have come to thee to accomplish that of which they doubt. "We have brought to you that which is inevitably due, and assuredly we tell the truth. "Then travel by night with thy household, when a portion of the night (yet remains), and do thou bring up the rear: let no one amongst you look back, but pass on whither you are ordered." And We made known this decree to him, that the last remnants of those (sinners) should be cut off by the morning." [Surah Al-Hijr (The Rocky Tract) 15:51-66]

**When Our Messengers came to Abraham with the good news, they said: "We are indeed going to destroy the people of this township: for truly they are (addicted to) crime." He said: "But there is Lot there." They said: "Well do we know who is there: we will certainly save him and his following, except his wife: she is of those who are left behind!" And when Our Messengers came to Lot, he was grieved on their account, and felt himself powerless (to protect) them: but they said: "Fear not, nor grieve: we are (here) to save thee and thy following, except thy wife: she is of those who are left behind. "For we are going to bring down on the people of this township a Punishment from heaven, because they have been wickedly rebellious."
[Surah Al Ankabut (The Spider) 29:31-34]**

"Has the story reached thee, of the honoured guests of Abraham? Behold, they entered his presence, and said: "Peace!" He said, "Peace!" (and thought, 'These seem unusual people.") Then he turned quickly to his household, brought out a fatted calf, and placed it before them saying, "Will you not eat?" (When they did not eat), He conceived a fear of them. They said, "Fear not," and they gave him glad tidings of a son endowed with knowledge. But his wife came forward (laughing) aloud: she smote her forehead and said: "A barren old woman!" They said, "Even so has thy Lord spoken: and He is full of Wisdom and Knowledge." (Abraham)

said: "And what, O ye Messengers, is your errand (now)?" They said, "We have been sent to a people (deep) in sin to bring on, on them, (a shower of) stones of clay (brimstone), marked as from thy Lord for those who trespass beyond bounds." Then We evacuated those of the Believers who were there, but We found there but one house of those surrendered (to Allah). And We left there a Sign for such as fear the Grievous Penalty."
[Surah Adh Dhariyat (The Winds That Scatter) 51:24-37]

In addition to having access to the realms of angels or jinns without needing to abandon human form, the human being also has access to the aptitudes special to the angels like the power of envisioning with certainty, or the aptitudes special to the jinns like wisdom and balance.

Furthermore, the human being has the unique qualities of knowledge (*'ilm*), which is also called perception (*baseera*) or distinction (*furqan*), which enables him to distinguish and judge between things and be able to determine their degree of superiority.

Hence, the human being can fulfill the functions of both a witness and a judge by virtue of the perception (*baseera*) he has been given by God. He is also the only one among the three who has been given the mandate to command (*ulul-'amr*). It is therefore narrated in the prophetic tradition (*hadith*) that God created Adam in His image, which means that God gave Adam His quality to command. However, this quality of commandment only applies to those humans who are truly Adamic, meaning that they are endowed with knowledge (*'ilm*), which is the distinctive mark of human beings as children of Adam. There are human beings who rank among the angels. They are the visionaries among the humans who capture visions from the unseen (*ghayb*) and are known in the prophetic tradition (*hadith*) as inspired visionaries (*muhaddathoon*), those who are instructed in their sleep. Umar, companion of the Prophet ﷺ was identified by the Prophet ﷺ as an inspired visionary (*muhaddath*).

There are also human beings who rank among the jinns. They are the interpreters who translate the vision in a well-balanced manner into its true proportions. In other words, when a vision is presented to them by the *muhaddath,* they look for its pair and when they find the pair, they place each on one side of the scale and weigh them until the two become justly equal. In this manner, the vision is interpreted accurately and therefore comes to pass. These interpreters are known as the *siddiqs* (the sincere ones) or the *hakeems* (the wise ones). Their wisdom consists in knowing that everything has a pair and knowing how to find the right pair and thus fulfill the balance. They are also known as people of remembrance (*ahl-al-dhikr*) who always remember God as One (unity) and therefore do not discriminate or differentiate. They see all pairs as one and equal.

> "And of every thing We have created pairs: That you may remember God (as one)."
> [*Surah Adh Dhariyat* (The Winds That Scatter) 51:49]

The *siddiq* must give measure for measure and come up with double measure of mercy (*rahmah*).

> "O you that believe! Fear Allah, and believe in His Messenger, and He will bestow on you a double portion of His Mercy: He will provide for you a Light by which you shall walk (straight in your path), and He will forgive you (your past): for Allah is Oft-Forgiving, Most Merciful."
> [*Surah Al Hadid* (The Iron) 57:28]

A measure of justice (*'adl*) should be weighed against a measure of charity (*'afu*), then the balance is fulfilled. Justice should not measure against justice nor charity against charity. That is transgressing the balance on the one hand and cheating it on the other hand.

Justice is a measure of mercy and charity is another measure of mercy. And full measure of mercy will only be attained if both of these measures are weighed together. When realized, mercy brings unity and remembrance of God.

In terms of proportion, a little justice is equal to an abundance of charity. This ratio of little (*qalil*) to abundant (*kathir*) cannot be reversed or else the balance will not be fulfilled. Little charity against abundant justice will constitute cheating the balance (shortcoming). Conversely, abundant charity without even little justice constitutes transgression.

> *"Whatever misfortune happens to you is because of the things your hands have wrought, and for many (of them) He grants forgiveness." "Or He can cause them to perish because of the (evil) which (the men) have earned; but much does He forgive."*
> [Surah Ash Shuraa (The Consultation) 42:30,34]

Thus, God exercises little justice and pardons a great deal:

> *"The sun must not overtake the moon nor must the night advance the day."*
> [Surah Ya Seen (Ya Seen) 36:40]

Through this verse we see that the sun represents pardon (*'afu*), which is abundant, and the moon represents justice (*'adl*). Therefore the sun, which has abundant light, must not overtake the moon, which has but little light. Conversely the night, which has little light (moon), must not try to overtake the day, which has abundant light (sun). The energy constituents of the daylight are known as '*kunnas*' and the energy constituents of the night are called '*khunnas*'. The *kunnas* are lighter, swifter and faster than the *khunnas*. Therefore, day is faster than night and night would be indicted for arrogance if it tries to lead the day.

> *"So verily I call to witness the planets that recede (khunnas), the stars which rise and set (kunnas), and the Night as it dissipates; and the Dawn as it breathes away the darkness."*
> [Surah At Takwir (The Covering Up) 81:15-18]

By observing the proper order, the right ratio, logistics, sequence and appropriate configuration, we can keep everything in our universe in balance, order and harmony.

The Rule of Joseph (Yusuf)

Knowing that against every abundance of charity (*'afu*), there should be a corresponding little of justice (*'adl*), it is this rule of little against most that prophet Joseph, peace be upon him, applied in order to interpret the vision of the King of Egypt. Therefore, the seven fat cows and the seven green corn tassels signify abundance; an abundance of charity (*'afu*). That abundance must be measured against a corresponding little justice—seven lean cows and seven withered corns—in order to fulfill the balance and keep harmony and peace in the land. His interpretation as a sincere one (*siddiq*) came thus:

"You must cultivate assiduously for seven years and whatever crop you harvest in those seven years of rain, you must keep the most and eat little."
[*Surah Yusuf* (Joseph) 12:47]

In the next period of seven years, drought and famine will strike, consuming the most of what you kept and sparing little. Thus, the balance is fulfilled and the next period—the third—mercy will prevail indefinitely.

"The king (of Egypt) said: I do see (in a vision) seven fat cows, whom seven lean ones devour, and seven green ears of corn, and seven (others) withered. O ye chiefs! Expound to me my vision if it be that ye can interpret visions. They said: A confused medley of dreams: and we are not skilled in the interpretation of dreams. But the man who had been released, one of the two (who had been in prison) and who now bethought him after (so long) a space of time, said: I will tell you the truth of its interpretation: send ye me (therefore). O Joseph! (he said), O man of sincerity! Expound to us (the dream) of seven fat cows whom seven lean ones devour, and of seven green ears of corn and (seven) others withered: that I

may return to the people, and that they may understand. (Joseph) said: For seven years you shall diligently sow as is your wont: and the harvests that you reap, you shall leave them in the ear, except a little, of which you shall eat. Then will come after that (period) seven dreadful (years), which will devour what you shall have laid by in advance for them, (all) except a little which you shall have (specially) guarded. Then will come after that a year in which the people will have abundant water, and in which they will press (wine and oil)." [Surah Yusuf (Joseph) 12:43-49]

The Sun, the Moon, the Star

In computation and balance, the sun represents the most (*kathir*) because it is an expansive state (*bast*) while the moon represents the little (*khaleel*) because it is a contractive state (*qabd*). The one that is in expansive state is enjoying God's pardon and release ('*afu*), and the other, which is in contractive state, is under God's justice ('*adl*). In order to fulfill the balance and maintain harmony, the expansive state must not override the contractive one, nor should the contractive state force itself to go ahead of the expansive one. That would lead to both transgression and regression.

It must be borne in mind that people must not overlook the least in favour of the most, nor should they attempt to raise the least above the most. They must all be given due consideration and be placed in the appropriate order. The sun and the moon are the archetypal pair in our universe after which all pairs are modeled.

If we were to remove the moon from our universe because of the littleness of its light and size and just keep the sun, the immediate consequence of that would throw our universe into chaos. In fact, it would render destruction because the moon stands as a veil between the sun and us so that if the moon is no longer there, the sunlight will increasingly encroach on our earth and dry it up.

Secondly, life on earth whether it is plant or animal (flora or fauna), grows and thrives as a result of the blend between the sunlight at day and moonlight at night. If one of the two is missing, that will certainly affect life on earth as we see in the story of Joseph (*Yusuf*) with seven fat cows eaten up by seven lean ones and seven green corns and seven withered ones.

Prophet Joseph (*Yusuf*), peace be upon him, was able to strike the right balance by weighing the little against the most, the moon against the sun. God, in His infinite wisdom, has created everything in pairs and given one in each pair solar and lunar characteristics.

"(Allah) Most Gracious! It is He Who has taught the Qur'an. He has created man. He has taught him speech (and intelligence). The sun and the moon follow courses (exactly) computed. The stars and the trees prostrate. And the Firmament He has raised high, and He has set up the Balance (of Justice) in order that you may not transgress (due) balance. So establish weight with justice and fall not short in the balance. It is He Who has spread out the earth for (His) creatures. Therein is fruit and date-palms, producing spathes (enclosing dates); also corn, with (its) leaves and stalk for fodder, and sweet-smelling plants."
[*Surah Ar Rahman* (The Most Gracious) 55:1-12]

Out of the relationship between the two comes mercy, which is a reminder of God's Oneness (*Wahdaniyyah*).

"Among His Signs is this, that He created you from dust; and then - behold, you are men spread and multiplied (far and wide)!"
[*Surah Ar Rum* (The Romans) 30:20]

There are those for whom God has expanded their provision, and others whose provision God has constricted.

"See they not that Allah enlarges the provision and restricts it, to whomsoever He pleases? Verily in that are Signs for those who believe."
[*Surah Ar Rum* (The Romans) 30:37]

"Know they not that Allah enlarges the provision or restricts it, for any He pleases? Verily, in this are Signs for those who believe!"
[*Surah Az Zumar* (The Crowds) 39:52]

Therefore, in order to generate mercy and love amongst us, the rich (in expansion) must give a little of their riches to the poor to fulfill the balance. That little given to the poor fulfills the needs of the poor, allowing the rich to keep the most. When the reign of the moon comes adversity will consume the most kept by the rich and spare a little in the amount of what they had given away to the poor.

The sun and the moon alternate directly influencing you. When the sun is nearest to you and the moon is furthest, in this condition you are experiencing an expansion from God. When this occurs, however, do not ignore the moon completely but give it its share of recognition. Then, in the next round, the moon will be near to you and the sun will be farther. In this case do not try to overlook the moon because of its littleness and long for the sun to come back. Rather, you should maintain *tasleem* —unconditional surrender to God—whether it is the sun's turn or the moon's turn to be near to you. This way, if it is the moon's turn, the contraction will not be hard for you and if it is the sun's turn, the expansion will not be overwhelming for you. In this manner, your contraction and your expansion will be well-balanced as it is demonstrated by the rule of Prophet Joseph (*Yusuf*), peace be upon him.

"Verily thy Lord provides sustenance in abundance for whom He pleases, and He provides in a just measure. For He knows and regards all His servants."
[*Surah Al Isra* (The Night Journey) 17:30]

As for the alternation of day and night, the same rule applies with regards to the manner in which we spend the day and the night. If the night is a time of stillness and the day is a time of movement, the rule teaches us then to be still most of the night and spend a little part of it in motion and to spend most of the day in motion but spend a little part of it in stillness. This rule will help you overcome the tendency to live in extremes. Rather, your day and your night will be well-balanced.

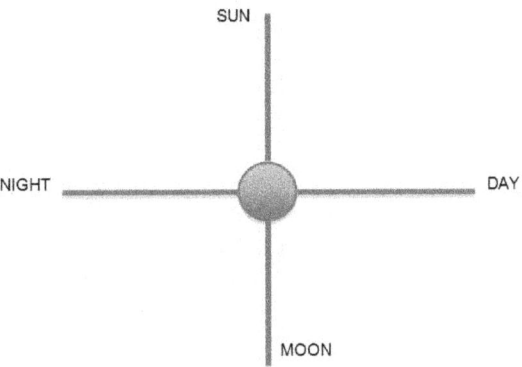

The sun, the moon, the day and the night are the essential four principal factors set up by God to maintain order and harmony in the world. The four principles that they represent are applicable at all times in all places, known and unknown to humankind. The rule reigns in the world of the smallest creatures that crawl on the earth as much as the vast and lofty galaxies in the remote space. God thus releases His commandment to the sun, the moon, the day and the night saying that:

> "The sun is not permitted to overtake the moon, the night must not outrun the day, but all must keep to their orbits that they are assigned." [Surah Ya Seen (Ya Seen) 36:40]

This means that the sun with the most light must not expand extremely to the point of overshadowing the moon with the least light. That would be unjust, for that little light of the moon, as little as it is, stands as a pair to the sun's light, as abundant as it is. On the other hand, the night with its slow constituents called *khunnas* must not exert itself to outrun the day with its weightless and fast constituents called *kunnas*.

In terms of how this ordinance applies to us, God has set the night causing its constituents to be slow so that we can find stillness in it. But this stillness must not be pushed to the extreme so in order to avoid that extremeness, it is necessary to perform some wakeful moments in it. These wakeful moments should be little compared to the periods of stillness and rest.

On the contrary, the day is a time of wakefulness and movement. As a consequence, He has caused its constituents to be weightless and fast to facilitate movement with wakefulness for us. However, these long moments of wakefulness and movement must be punctuated with brief moments of sleep and stillness to avoid the extreme condition of wakefulness and movement.

By applying this principle you can avoid extreme stillness that turns into sluggishness and extreme motion that turns into feverish hysteria. The heart in the end is adjusted into a perfect balance. Your rest and your work, your motion and your stillness are all finely disposed. Fatigue does not overwhelm you on one hand and neither do you get bogged down in inertia. So your night must not outstrip your day, nor should your day lag behind your night, meaning that you should not allow your wakefulness and action to exceed your sleep and rest at night while your rest and sleep should not exceed your wakefulness and action during the day. If either of these situations occurs, then you have upset the balance, and when the balance is upset, no mercy or peace can come.

"A Sign unto them is the night. We strip it of the day, and lo! they are in darkness. And the sun runs his course for a period determined for him: that is the decree of (Him), the Exalted in Might, the All-Knowing. And the Moon, We have measured for her mansions (to traverse) till she returns like the old (and withered)

lower part of a date-stalk. It is not permitted to the Sun to overtake the Moon, nor can the Night outstrip the Day: all must keep to their orbits that they are assigned."
[Surah Ya Seen (Ya Seen) 36:37-40]

The calm, still energy that is released by the night constituents is known as tranquility (*sakinah*) and the energy released by the day constituents is known as sight (*baseera*).

When these energies mix proportionately, then your stillness and your motion become well-balanced. Your rest is fulfilling and your action is excellent:

"Say: Have you thought, if Allah made night perpetual over you till the Day of Resurrection, who is a god beside Allah who could bring you light? Will you not then hear? Say: Have you thought, if Allah made day perpetual over you till the Day of Resurrection, who is a god beside Allah who could bring you night wherein you rest (taskunoon)? Will you not then see (tabsiroon)? It is out of His Mercy that He has made for you Night and Day, that you may rest therein, and that you may seek of his Grace - and in order that you may be grateful (tashkuroon)."
[Surah Al Qasas (The Narrations) 28:71-73]

"Have they not seen how We have appointed the night that they may rest (liyaskunoo) therein, and the day sight-giving (mubsiran)? Lo! Therein verily are portents for a people who believe."
[Surah An Naml (The Ant) 27:86]

As for the sun and the moon, they represent another set of principles different from that of the day and the night, but in complementary relationship. The energies of day and night, called wakefulness and tranquility (*baseerah* and *sakinah*) are concerned with motion and stillness and how to regulate the two. As for the sun and moon, it is about two types of energies in which one is ascending and the other is descending. The ascending energy is solar and the descending energy is lunar.

The solar energy is called *diyaa* and the lunar energy is called *nur*. The solar energy (*diyaa*) has levitational power while the lunar energy has lowering power. As a consequence, extreme exposure to the solar energy (*diyaa*) will result in extreme elevation internally and externally producing some extreme behaviour like arrogance, pride and self-righteousness. In short, extreme uprising produces an extreme condition called transgression (*tughyan*). On the other hand, extreme exposure to the lunar energy (*nur*) will result in extreme lowering internally and externally, which in turn produces some extreme behaviours like self-debasement, low self-esteem, lack of courage, excessive shyness, etc. In sum, extreme lowering results in an extreme condition called regression (*dhulm*).

Therefore, in order to reach the just middle between high and low, so that the *diyaa* (solar energy) does not pull you too high and the *nur* (lunar energy) does not pull you too low, you must apply the rule of Joseph (*Yusuf*), peace be upon him, as a discipline upon yourself. This means that when you are expanded and elevated, you are being exposed to the solar energy (*diyaa*). Therefore, do not get carried away and be overwhelmed by this feeling of expansiveness. Allow this *bast* to be counterbalanced by a measure of *qabd* (contraction). In other words, use a little portion of this euphoric solar energy and save most of it. In turn, when you begin to feel contracted and pulled down, it means you are being exposed to the lunar energy (*nur*). This contraction by lunar energy can become extreme and therefore painful unless counterbalanced by the abundant solar energy that was saved up earlier. After the abundant solar energy sets off this extreme lunar contraction, a little still remains of the solar energy and a little remains of the lunar energy. With the combination of these two, the just middle is attained which is neither too high nor too low.

In conclusion, the just middle (*wusta*) is reached twice. Once when the day energy (*baseera*) and night energy (*sakinah*) are equally balanced, then the method of that person along the path is neither too fast nor too slow. If it is too fast, it will bypass the mark and if it is too slow, it will fall short of the mark. The just middle (*wusta*), is reached a second time when the solar energy (*diyaa*) and the lunar energy (*nur*) are equally balanced so that a person can reach the target of the just middle without aiming too high because of excessive exposure to solar energy or aiming too low because of excessive exposure to lunar energy.

> "So glory be to Allah when you enter the night and when you enter the morning. Unto Him be praise in the heavens and the earth! And at the sun's decline and in the noonday."
> [*Surah Ar Rum* (The Romans) 30:17-18]

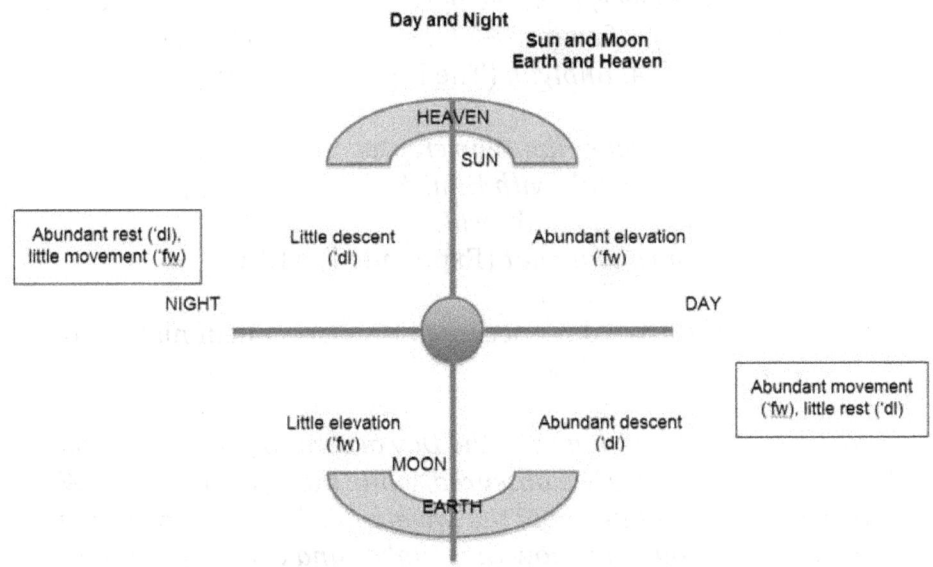

> "And of His signs is your sleep by night, and by day your seeking of His bounty. Lo! Herein indeed are signs for folk who heed."
> [*Surah Ar Rum* (The Romans) 30:23]

Six Days of Creation

> "Your Guardian-Lord is Allah, Who created the heavens and the earth in six days, and is firmly established on the throne (of authority): He draws the night as a veil over the day, each seeking

the other in rapid succession: He created the sun, the moon, and the stars, (all) governed by laws under His command. Is it not His to create and to govern? Blessed be Allah, the Cherisher and Sustainer of the worlds!"
[*Surah Al A'raf* (The Heights) 7:54]

Thus, the six days of creation are distributed in pairs of two:

1. In the first two days occurred the partition of the earth and the heavens:

"Have not those who disbelieve known that the heavens and the earth were of one piece, then We parted them, and we made every living thing of water? Will they not then believe?"
[*Surah Al Anbiyah* (The Prophets) 21:30]

"Say: Is it that you deny Him Who created the earth in two Days? And do you join equals with Him? He is the Lord of (all) the Worlds."
[*Surah Fussilat* (Expounded) 41:9]

2. In the next two days occurred the partition of night and day:

"We have made the Night and the Day as two (of Our) Signs: the Sign of the Night have We obscured, while the Sign of the Day We have made to enlighten you; that ye may seek bounty from your Lord, and that you may know the number and count of the years: all things have We explained in detail."
[*Surah Al Isra* (The Night Journey) 17:12]

3. In the last two days occurred the partition of the sun and the moon:

"It is He Who made the sun to be a shining glory and the moon to be a light (of beauty), and measured out stages for her; that ye might know the number of years and the count (of time). No wise did Allah create this but in truth and righteousness. (Thus) does

He explain His Signs in detail, for those who understand."
[Surah Yunus (Jonah) 10:5]

Each of these six days (i.e. dimensions) constitutes a specific type of energy. The seventh day, or the one dimension, constitutes the sum of all six dimensions, therefore six energies. When the seventh or one dimension is reached, then the person becomes aligned with the throne and his face aligned with the light of God's Face (*Ridwan*).

"But whoso cometh unto Him a believer, having done good works, for such are the high station."
[Surah TaHa (TaHa) 20:75]

"(All) faces shall be humbled before (Him) - the Living, the Self-Subsisting, Eternal: hopeless indeed will be the man that carries iniquity (on his back). But he who works deeds of righteousness, and has faith, will have no fear of harm nor of any curtailment (of what is his due)."
[Surah TaHa (TaHa) 20:111-112]

"So set thou thy face steadily and truly to the Faith: (establish) Allah's handiwork according to the pattern on which He has made mankind: no change (let there be) in the work (wrought) by Allah: that is the standard Religion: but most among mankind understand not."
[Surah Ar Rum (The Romans) 30:30]

At this point the soul is enthroned on its own throne beside the throne of God. The soul has found its final station (*mustaqarr*).

"It is He Who has produced you from a single soul: here is a final place of sojourn (mustaqarr) and a temporary place of departure (mustawda): We detail Our signs for people who understand."
[Surah Al An'am (The Cattle) 6: 98]

"So also did We show Abraham the power and the laws of the

heavens and the earth, that he might (with understanding) have certitude. When the night covered him over, He saw a star: He said: "This is my Lord." But when it set, He said: "I love not those that set." When he saw the moon rising in splendour, he said: "This is my Lord." But when the moon set, He said: "Unless my Lord guide me, I shall surely be among those who go astray." When he saw the sun rising in splendour, he said: "This is my Lord; this is the greatest (of all)." But when the sun set, he said: "O my people! I am indeed free from your (guilt) of giving partners to Allah. For me, I have set my face, firmly and truly, towards Him Who created the heavens and the earth, and never shall I give partners to Allah."
[*Surah Al An'am* (The Cattle) 6:75-79]

The soul in its final station is called a well-stationed soul (*nafs mutmainnah*) because after going through so many temporary stations it is finally settled in its final station. It is then called "*radiyah*"—a soul that is pleased with its Creator, and also called "*mardiyyah*"—a soul that is well-pleasing to its Creator:

"To the righteous soul will be said: "O soul (alnafsu almutmainnah), in (complete) rest and satisfaction! Come back thou to thy Lord, well pleased (radiyah), and well-pleasing unto Him (mardiyyah)!"
[*Surah Al Fajr* (The Break of Dawn) 89:27-28]

The purpose of creating the earth, the heavens and what lies between them in gradual stages was to allow the human being to come to witness how God performs the miracle of the creation of the world (witness) and eventually find the just balance in his heart that would allow his heart neither to waver nor to transgress:

"(His) sight never swerved, nor did it go wrong! For truly did he (Muhammad) see, of the Signs of his Lord, the Greatest!"
[*Surah An Najm* (The Star) 53:17]

This is the ultimate achievement for a human being.

The One Day

The seventh day or the "One Day" is the day of the throne, the single and unique day that extends from the beginning to the ending. Once a person reaches this day, all his views and perceptions change. The simple reason being that he sees everything from the point of view of this absolute unity. Until then, he used to perceive God from the standpoint of the world, and now he perceives the world from the standpoint of God. Through the One, he sees the plural, whereas before he used to see the One through the plural.

The difference in outcome between the two modalities of perception is immense. When you perceive the plural through the One, the many-ness of the plural does not affect the integrity of yourself. But if you perceived the One through the plural, your view of the One is distorted and fragmented. In the first instance, you are looking at the creation through the eyes of the Creator. In the second, you are looking at the Creator through the eyes of the creation. While the gaze of the Creator encompasses the creation, the gaze of the creation does not encompass the Creator.

As long as the person remains in the six days, his views of the Creator and even of the creation will remain fragmented and distorted. Duality in this case is unavoidable. So in order for a person to truly see, you must see with God and in order to see with Him, you must be with Him. And in order to be with Him, you must enter the time zone of the throne (*arsh*) which is the One Day. Then you can see the Creator and the creation through the eyes of the Creator.

In *Surah TaHa*, God relates to us the story of two groups of people when they were questioned how long they remained in the world. One said, "ten days." The other said "one day." God says that: "The one who said, 'It was one day' has the most upright way."

"The Day when the Trumpet will be sounded: that Day, We shall gather the sinful, bleary-eyed (with terror). In whispers will they consult each other: "You tarried not longer than ten (days). We know best what they will say, when their leader most eminent in conduct will say: "You tarried not longer than a day!"
[*Surah TaHa* (TaHa) 20:102-104]

Therefore, the person who sees all time as one, all places as one, and all people as one is the person who has the best way. However, this all-encompassing vision of time, people and space is not achievable except by someone who has reached up to the one day and from this viewpoint he looks at everything else. There have been attempts made by several individuals to create a universal religion in order to unite the world into one nation, but their point of departure has always been from the plural to the unity. Consequently, their efforts have met with failure. Such efforts of unification would only meet with success if the approach is from the viewpoint of oneness towards plurality. Indeed, humanity was at one time one nation and it can return back to being one nation again if the right principles are applied.

"Mankind was one nation, and Allah sent (unto them) prophets as bearers of good tidings and as warners, and revealed therewith the Scripture with the truth that it might judge between mankind concerning that wherein they differed. And only those unto whom (the Scripture) was given differed concerning it, after clear proofs had come unto them, through selfish contumacy. And Allah by His Will guided those who believe unto the truth of that concerning which they differed. Allah guides whom He will unto a straight path."
[*Surah Al Baqarah* (The Cow) 2:213]

Conclusion

In conclusion we come to realize that the ultimate reward for gratitude is to have the pleasure of God (*Ridwan*).

But gratitude (*shukr*) itself as a way consists of two things:

1. By means of gratitude for God's mercy comes mercy from God, which leads to another mercy and then another until one attains to God's pleasure (*Ridwan*).

2. By means of gratitude for knowledge from God, which leads to another knowledge which in turn leads to another knowledge and then another until one attains to God's pleasure. Hence God makes the following promise to Prophet Muhammad:

> "*Your Lord shall indeed give you until you are pleased.*"
> [*Surah Ad Duha* (The Daylight) 93:5]

This means the Lord shall give and give and give to you until attaining God's pleasure pleases you. In the verse what is given is not mentioned but from other verses we learn that the gift here means either God's mercy or his knowledge or both of them. Therefore God had promised the Prophet Muhammad that he would attain to God's pleasure. Secondly He instructed him in the way to attain this objective. He said:

> "*Glorify the praises of your Lord before the rising of the sun and before its setting and in parts of the night glorify and in parts of the day so that you will be pleased.*"
> [*Surah TaHa* (TaHa) 20:130]

God has therefore instructed him to remember Him (*dhikr*) during the day and during the night and to follow remembrance with gratitude:

> "*And it is He Who made the Night and the Day to follow each other: for such have the will to celebrate His praises or to show their gratitude.*"
> [*Surah Al Furqan* (The Criterion) 25:62]

In the end when God's pleasure (*Ridwan*) is obtained that pleasure reflects back on us: as we are pleased with God we are also pleased with ourselves because God is pleased with us. It is obligatory upon us to be pleased with whatever God is pleased with, including ourselves. This pleasure with ourselves as a result of God's pleasure with us translate into reality in three forms:

1. That God grants us a place of dwelling, which pleases Him and pleases us. This includes a family that we are pleased with, a home that we are pleased with, and company that we are pleased with. Allah says:

> "Did He not find thee an orphan and give thee shelter (and care)?"
> [Surah Ad Duha (The Daylight) 93:6]

2. That God grants you a point of direction (*Qiblah*), which pleases you. This point of direction constitutes the direction towards which God instructs you to turn your face to, in order to find His pleasure.
God says:

> "He found you bewildered but then He (God) guided you... to the right direction."
> [Surah Ad Duha (The Daylight) 93:7]

We find a similar concept in another chapter of Qur'an:

> "We (God) see you (Muhammad) turn your face here and there in the heaven, But We indeed shall turn your face towards a point of direction (Qiblah) which you please."
> [Surah Al Baqarah (The Cow) 2:144]

3. That God grants you a word, which pleases you. This is the word of fulfilment and satisfaction called word of *taqwa*. God says:

> "He (God) found you (Muhammad) impoverished but then He (God) enriched you to satisfaction."
> [Surah Ad Duha (The Daylight) 93:8]

It must be noted that none can fulfill the soul except *taqwa*, the fulfilling word from God. *Taqwa* in turn is a means of gratitude. Keep *taqwa* and you will attain to gratitude; gratitude in turn leads to pleasure (*Ridwan*). God says:

"Allah had helped you at Badr, when ye were a contemptible little force; then fear Allah; thus May ye show your gratitude."
[*Surah Al Imran* (The Family of Imran) 3:123]

Also Allah says:

"...If you offer gratitude God will receive it with pleasure from you..." [*Surah Az Zumar* (The Crowds) 39:7]

In the end that pleasure translates into the word of pleasure. God says:

"On that day no one's intercession will be of any use except such one as received permission from the All Merciful and with by His (God's) pleasure he speaks."
[*Surah TaHa* (TaHa) 20:109]

Once these three forms of pleasure are achieved by someone he is considered to have achieved the greatest pleasure (*Ridwan Akbar*); namely:

1) pleasure with place of abode (*maskan*)
2) pleasure with point of direction (*qiblah*)
3) pleasure with the word (*qawl*)

These three stand instead of pleasure with kinsfolk, with home, with commerce. God says:

"Say (O Muhammad) if your parents, your brethren, your spouses, your clan and wealth which you earn and commerce which you are concerned to lose and dwellings which you please are dearer to you than Allah and His messenger and struggling in His way, then wait therefore until God brings all His judgment. For God

guides not those who transgress against His commandment."
[Surah At Tawbah (The Repentance) 9:24]

In case of the Prophet Muhammad ﷺ these three were represented by the city of Madinah, which God chose for him to be his place of dwelling with his family (*ahlal bayt*) and his companions (*sahabah*). God is pleased with Madinah and so was the Prophet ﷺ. The second one was the Holy sanctuary of *Ka'ba* (*Al Masjid Al Haram*), which God was pleased to appoint as his point of direction (*qiblah*) so that he is pleased.

"We see the turning of thy face (for guidance to the heavens: now shall We turn thee to a Qibla that shall please thee. Turn then Thy face in the direction of the sacred Mosque: Wherever ye are, turn your faces in that direction. The people of the Book know well that that is the truth from their Lord. Nor is Allah unmindful of what they do."
[Surah Al Baqarah (The Cow) 2:144]

The third is Qur'an, which constitutes the good word and the word of fulfillment, which God chose as a speech for him: they are guided to the good word.

"Say O Muhammad ﷺ I was only instructed to worship the Lord of this city (Mecca) who has consecrated it and to Him everything belongs and was instructed as well to be of those who are submitted to God and (am also instructed to) read the Qur'an."
[Surah An Naml (The Ant) 27:91-92]

Counter-Spinning The Solar System

Our cosmic system, including the solar system, the earth, the seven firmaments, the stars and the moon and the various planets, was set in motion in the direction of its final station.

"Then turned He to the heaven when it was smoke, and said unto it and unto the earth: Come both of you, willingly or unwillingly. They said: We come, obedient. So He completed them as seven firmaments in two Days, and He assigned to each heaven its duty and command. And We adorned the lower heaven with lamps, and (provided it) with guard. Such is the Decree of (Him) the Exalted in Might, Full of Knowledge."
[*Surah Fussilat* (Expounded) 41:11-12]

This spinning of the cosmic wheel began with the completion of the sixth dimension (six days of creation), and its final destination is the throne (*arsh*) of God. This synchronized movement of the cosmos is, at the same time both the cause of birth and decay, death and regeneration, rise and fall, proliferation of species, diversity of forms and colours:

"He brings forth the living from the dead and brings forth the dead from the living and gives life to the earth after its death, and thus shall you be brought forth. And of His signs is this: He created you of dust, and behold you are human beings, ranging widely!"
[*Surah Ar Rum* (The Romans) 30:19-20]

"It is Allah Who has created you: further, He has provided for your sustenance; then He will cause you to die; and again He will give you life."
[*Surah Ar Rum* (The Romans) 30:40]

"And among His Signs is the creation of the heavens and the earth, and the variations in your languages and your colours: verily in that are Signs for those who know."
[*Surah Ar Rum* (The Romans) 30:22]

"If Allah had so willed, He could have made them a single people; but He admits whom He will to His Mercy; and the wrong-doers will have no protector nor helper."
[Surah Ash Shuraa (The Consultation) 42:8]

"(He is) the Creator of the heavens and the earth: He has made for you pairs from among yourselves, and pairs among cattle: by this means does He multiply you: there is nothing whatever like unto Him, and He is the One that hears and sees (all things). To Him belong the keys of the heavens and the earth: He enlarges and restricts the Sustenance to whom He will: for He knows full well all things."
[Surah Ash Shuraa (The Consultation) 42:11-12]

"And among His Signs is the creation of the heavens and the earth, and the living creatures that He has scattered through them: and He has power to gather them together when He wills."
[Surah Ash Shuraa (The Consultation) 42:29]

"To Allah belongs the dominion of the heavens and the earth. He creates what He wills (and plans). He bestows (children) male or female according to His Will (and Plan), or He bestows both males and females, and He leaves barren whom He will: for He is full of Knowledge and Power."
[Surah Ash Shuraa (The Consultation) 42:49-50]

With regards to the formation of the earth and the heavens, they were, as told by God in the Qur'an, a single piece of mass. Thereafter, they were partitioned into two with the earth below and the heavens above:

"Have not those who disbelieve know that the heavens and the earth were of one piece, then We parted them, and we made every living thing of water? Will they not then believe?"
[Surah Al Anbiyah (The Prophets) 21:30]

> *"And We have made the heavens as a canopy well guarded: yet do they turn away from the Signs which these things (point to)!"*
> [*Surah Al Anbiyah* (The Prophets) 21:32]

We are also told in *Surah Fussilat* (41:11-12) that the heavens (firmament) were at one time in the form of smoke and then it was divided into seven layers called the seven heavens. We may conclude from this that the earth might have been in a smoky state since it formed a single body of mass with the heaven before the partition and that after he partition, the earth was soaked in water and cooled off to some degree while the heavens (firmament) retained their smokiness.

Whenever we think of smoke or we see smoke, we always assume with justice that it is but an effect and that there is a cause behind it, which is fire. We therefore suppose that the smoke, which once constituted the simple mass of earth and heaven, came out of fire that seems invisible to us.

The distinction between the fire and the smoke (that came out of the fire) is that one is a smokeless fire and the other is a smoky fire. The smokeless fire is by far the more intense fire. The fires as we know it on the earth, and other forms of energy, belong to the smoky type. The sun's brilliance makes a good example of the smokeless fire.

It is narrated in a hadith that the Prophet Muhammad ﷺ said once, upon looking at the sun:

> *"O God's blazing fire, had it not been restrained by God's order, it would have burnt down everything on the earth."*

It is therefore God's mercy and grace to the earth, and those inhabiting it, that they are protected from the dual onslaught of the smoke that fill the space and firmament as well as the smokeless fire, which extends beyond the smoke. However, the heavens are like the cover of a sizzling cauldron rattling under the pressure of vapor trying to escape out of the cauldron. The heavens are bulging under the extreme heat that is rapidly building within them, forcing them to expand continuously.

> "And the heaven, We raised it high with power."
> [*Surah Adh Dhariyat* (The Winds That Scatter) 51:47]

At one point however, the heavens will reach the utmost limit of their expansion and consequently the smoke, finding no more room to expand, will force the heavens open. At such a time, everything on earth, including humans, animals and birds will assemble together in awe as they see the smoke descending upon the earth suffocating everything except those who have remained steadfast in remembrance (*dhikr*) and gratitude (*shukr*).

> "Therefore keep waiting for the day when the heaven shall bring an evident smoke that will envelop the people. This will be a painful torment."
> [*Surah Ad Dukhan* (The Smoke) 44:10-11]

> "A day when the heaven with the clouds will be rent asunder and the angels will be sent down, a grand descent."
> [*Surah Al Furqan* (The Criterion) 25:25]

> "Lo! Those who kept their duty will be in a place secured amid gardens and water-springs, They shall wear fine and thick silk, (sitting) face to face; even so (it will be). And We shall wed them unto fair ones with wide, lovely eyes. There they can call for every kind of fruit in peace and security; nor will they there taste Death, except the first death; and He will preserve them from the Penalty of the Blazing Fire, a grace from your Lord; this is the great achievement."
> [*Surah Ad Dukhan* (The Smoke) 44: 51-57]

Finding a Way Out of the Heavens and the Earth

If the domain of light lies beyond the heavens and earth, how then can we reach that light considering there are so many obstacles? How can we take up God's challenge to brave all these hurdles and transcend beyond the confines of the heavens and earth? What about this blinding smoke that is everywhere in the space within the earth, the heavens, and what about the consuming fire that burns everything that comes an inch closer? Considering all these, God the Almighty challenges us:

"O company of jinn and men, if you have power to penetrate (all) regions of the heavens and the earth, then penetrate (them)! You will never penetrate them save with (Our) authority. Which is it of the favours of your Lord that you deny? On you will be sent (if you attempt to pass without authority) a flame of fire (to burn) and a smoke (to choke): so you will not succeed."
[Surah Ar Rahman (The Most Gracious) 55:33-35]

As the verse indicates, if you try to break through the confines of the heavens and the earth, smoke will choke you and fire would consume you except if you have the authorization. What is the authorization that permits you to transcend beyond the confines of the earth and heavens unharmed? It is a sound heart.

"But only he (will prosper) that comes to Allah with a sound heart."
[Surah Ash Shu'ara (The Poets) 26:89]

"Behold! He (Ibrahim) approached his Lord with a sound heart."
[Surah As Saffat (Those Ranged in Ranks) 37:84]

A sound heart means a heart that stands detached from everything in the heavens and the earth, and thus stands absolutely unrelated to anything in the entire cosmic order. The truth of this statement lies in a principle of wisdom (*hikmah*) that in order for you to exit out of a cycle, you must move counter to the cycle.

In order to disengage yourself from a current, you must go against the flow of the current. Similarly, if you wish to transcend the confines of the heavens and earth, you have to spin counter to the cosmic system that governs them.

In order for you to counter-spin the cosmic spin, you must first disengage yourself from that system. When you disengage yourself and are free from the cosmic system, then will get you the opportunity to watch and observe the cosmic order and then understand how it proceeds. This gives you the vantage position of a witness rather than a participant. However, as long as you are a participant, you cannot witness, and if you cannot witness, certainly you cannot move counter to a system in which you are a participant.

Clockwise and Anti-Clockwise

Everything that is a participant of the cosmic order, including the sun and its system, all move clockwise. Conversely, the one who attempts to transcend that order must move anti-clockwise. However, for a single being to move counterclockwise against such a powerful system is not easy. Therefore, before launching a counterclockwise movement against the cosmic system and it's powerful machine, certain preliminary steps must be taken.

I: Stillness (*Sukoon*)

The first measure you must take before spinning counter clockwise is to find stillness of the heart. In order for you to make a counter move against a movement you do not start by engagement in another type of movement. Rather, you must bring yourself to a stand still and take an absolute break from all forms of outer and inner movement. Once you have brought yourself and your heart to a complete stillness, then you can initiate a movement voluntarily. Then, and only then, your move will be counterclockwise. This act of retreat into complete stillness is known as repentance (*tawbah*). It means to return to the pre-time, pre-space era before the coming of the six dimensions into being. That is called the beginning.

> *"See they not how Allah originates creation, then repeats it: truly that is easy for Allah. Say: Travel in the earth and see how Allah did originate creation; so will Allah produce a later creation: for Allah has power over all things."*
> [*Surah Al Ankabut* [The Spider] 29:19-20]

Once you have seen the beginning, you have become a witness. In stillness, you observe everything, while everything moves around you. This is exemplified in the stories of Joseph (*Yusuf*), peace be upon him, when he witnessed the sun, the moon and the stars bowing down to him.

The correlating story in the Bible is the sheaves of Joseph's brothers that were circumambulating him. Similarly we have the story of Abraham (*Ibrahim*), peace be upon him, who saw the sun, the moon and the stars rising and setting. He witnessed them because he was still, while they were in movement.

> *"And thus did We show Ibrahim the kingdom of the heavens and the earth and that he might be of those who are sure. When the night grew dark upon him he beheld a star. He said: 'This is my Lord.' But when it set, he said: 'I love not things that set.' And when he saw the moon uprising, he exclaimed: 'This is my Lord.' But when it set, he said: 'Unless my Lord guides me, I surely shall become one of the folk who are astray.' And when he saw the sun rising in splendour, he cried: 'This is my Lord! This is greater!' And when it set he exclaimed: 'O my people! Lo! I am free from all that you associate (with Him). For me, I have set my face, firmly and truly, towards Him Who created the heavens and the earth, and never shall I give partners to Allah'"*
> [*Surah Al An'am* (The Cattle) 6:75-79]

As for Moses, peace be upon him, when he saw the fire, his heart had come to stillness. Only then was it possible for him to see through the smoke that fills the space, the heavens and earth and espy the fire that is beyond the smoke. Beyond the fire is the Kingdom of God. Again, like Joseph and Abraham, Moses too, peace be upon them all, was also in the position of repentance (*tawbah*).

> *"When Moses said to his family: 'Surely I see fire; I will bring to you from it some news, or I will bring to you therefrom a burning firebrand so that you may warm yourselves.' But when he reached it, he was called, saying: 'Blessed is whosoever is in the fire and whosoever is round about it! And Glorified be Allah, the Lord of the Worlds!'"*
> [*Surah An Naml* (The Ant) 27:7-8]

> *"And has the story of Moses come to you? When he saw a fire and said unto his folk: 'Lo! Wait! I see a fire afar off. Peradventure I may bring you a brand therefrom or may find guidance at the fire.'"*
> [*Surah TaHa* [TaHa] 20:9-10]

> *"Now when Moses had fulfilled the term, and was travelling with his family, he perceived a fire in the direction of Mount Tur. He said to his family: 'Tarry ye; I perceive a fire; I hope to bring you from there some information, or a burning firebrand, that ye may warm yourselves.' And when he reached it, he was called from the right side of the valley in the blessed field, from the tree: 'O Moses! Lo! I, even I, am Allah, the Lord of the Worlds.'"*
> [*Surah Al Qasas* (The Narrations) 28:29-30]

In the story of Prophet Muhammad ﷺ, the stage of *tawbah* corresponds to the period he used to spend in the cave of Hira until the angel Gabriel (*Jibril*) appeared before him and asked him to read three times. Each time he read corresponded to each of the three forms of darkness. Reading Qur'an was the means by which he was able to transcend the three darknesses and reach the light. These darknesses are namely the darkness of the land, the sea and the boundary, or in other words, the darkness of the earth, the heavens and the space in between them.

II: Counterclockwise Movement

The second step involves the actual counter-spinning in a motion that is gentle and graceful. A motion can truly be gentle and graceful if it is counterclockwise. For then, it is performed under no impulse, constraint or compulsion.

"And the servants of (Allah) Most Gracious are those who walk on the earth in humility, and when the ignorant address them, they say, "Peace!"
[Surah Al Furqan (The Criterion) 25:63]

When this counterspin is underway you experience first hand the presence of stars, moon and sun. In fact, the sun can glare at you without causing you any harm because it has no claim or authority over you. This is exemplified in the youth of cave (*kahf*) who were positioned anti-clockwise to the sun at rising and setting and hence were unduly affected by the sunlight or by the moisture of the cave for more than three hundred years.

"And you might see the sun when it rose, decline from their cave towards the right hand, and when it set, leave them behind on the left while they were in a wide space thereof. This is of the signs of Allah; whomsoever Allah guides, he is the rightly guided one, and whomsoever He causes to err, you shall not find for him any friend to lead (him) aright. And you might think them awake while they were asleep and We turned them about to the right and to the left, while their dog (lay) outstretching its paws at the entrance; if you looked at them you would certainly turn back from them in flight, and you would certainly be filled with awe because of them."
[Surah Al Kahf (The Cave) 18:17-18]

Furthermore, God gives us a clue as to why they were unaffected by the factors of both time and space that cause aging and degeneration after generation and growth. That clue is the statement, "We placed a seal on their ears for years in the cave and then we resurrected them."

"Then We draw (a veil) over their ears, for a number of years, in the Cave, (so that they heard not)."
[*Surah Al Kahf* (The Cave) 18:11]

In other words, during all this period they spent in the cave, they were deprived of hearing even though they were able to witness in their sleeping state. The fact that they were deprived of hearing meant that they existed beyond the domain of worldly life and, by extension, its characteristics of growth and decay. Since they existed beyond the domain of worldly life, it meant that they stopped growing but also stopped degenerating since the domain of worldly life operates in pairs. If something grows at one time, it will degenerate at another time. If it increases at one point, it will decrease at another point. This is the truth about the life of this world and there is no exception to that for whatever lives within its parameters.

We have an example of this in the story of Prophet Joseph (*Yusuf*), peace be upon him, whereby the King of Egypt dreamt of seven fat cows being eaten up by seven lean cows, and seven green tassels of corn and seven withered ones. Prophet Joseph interpreted the dream in view of the dual nature of things in this worldly life. Fat cows indicate growth and lean cows indicate decay. Green tassels indicate abundance and withered tassels indicate scarcity. He concluded therefore that there would come seven years of rain and abundance of harvest followed by another seven years of drought and shortage of sustenance. He then recommended that the people of Egypt should exert themselves in hard work during the years of rain and abundance, and then store up all their crop except for a little to eat. When the years of drought finally come in its turn, they could live on what they had saved during the years of abundance, always with moderation, and a little would still remain. The fifteenth year would introduce a lasting period of prosperity and abundance. Prophet Joseph was able to interpret the dream correctly on the basis of the infallible law of growth and decay, which govern this world.

Therefore, in order for someone to escape the implacable dualistic law of this worldly existence, he has to counter its movement, alter its configuration and reverse the sequence of its structure. Such was the lesson to be learned from the story of the Youth of the Cave. When God the Almighty willed to pull them out of the cycle of this worldly life, He altered the configuration of their hearing and seeing. He simply changed the order between hearing and seeing by shutting out the hearing and letting the sight prevail to the point that their sight became absolute with no interference from the hearing. God let them be in this state until they reached certainty (*yaqeen*), and then He allowed their hearing to come back into action, but already the order of sight-hearing was established in place of hearing-sight. Thus, they see first before they hear, and what they hear did not affect the certainty of what they saw. Unlike those who have not attained this state, they hear before they see and what they hear influences what they see. In the former case, sight is the witness and judge over the hearing. In the latter case, hearing is the judge that determines the outcome of decisions. This change of position between hearing and seeing takes place during sleep or at death. During sleep, God shuts off the hearing and then the sight operates freely resulting in visions and dreams. If not, at death God removes the veil of the eyes and shuts the hearing down. When the soul finally leaves the body, the hearing would then return, which explains the prophetic tradition (*hadith*) that the dead hear the footsteps of those who came to bury them as they leave.

"(And unto the evil-doer it is said): You were in heedlessness of this. Now We have removed from you your veils, and piercing is your sight this day!"
[*Surah Qaf* (Qaf) 50:22]

> *"Say: Allah knows best how long they remained; to Him are (known) the unseen things of the heavens and the earth; how clear His sight and how clear His hearing! There is none to be a guardian for them besides Him, and He does not make any one His associate in His Judgment."*
> [Surah Al Kahf (The Cave) 18:26]

Then hearing comes first before seeing:

> *"How clearly shall they hear and how clearly shall they see on the day when they come to Us; but the unjust this day are in manifest error."*
> [Surah Maryam (Mary) 19:38]

The reason for putting hearing before seeing is that the verse from *Surah Al Kahf* refers to certainty (*yaqeen*), while this verse from *Surah Maryam* refers to faith (*iman*).

If God therefore wishes to raise someone to the station of certainty (*yaqeen*), He does so either through dead in his waking or in his sleep. He will lift his soul up to Him and closes down his hearing, so that only his faculty of seeing remains in operation. God will show him or her all that He wishes to show him and then allow the hearing to come back into function. From this point onwards precedence of seeing will take place first unlike before when hearing came first. This person is considered to have attained certainty while he still exists in the world, before dying-- for everyone at death reaches certainty. This process of introducing a person into the level of certainty is mentioned in the following verses:

> *"Allah takes the souls at the time of their death, and those that die not during their sleep; then He withholds those on whom He has passed the decree of death and sends the others back till an appointed term; most surely there are signs in this for a people who reflect."*
> [Surah Az Zumar (The Crowds) 39:42]

"Have you not considered (the work of) your Lord, how He extends the shadow? And if He had willed He would certainly have made it stationary; then We have made the sun lower down on it. Then We draw it in towards Ourselves, a contraction by easy stages."
[*Surah Al Furqan* (The Criterion) 25:45-46]

Conflict Between Seeing and Hearing

There is continuous conflict between the hearing and the seeing, with each struggling to take the lead. If the seeing takes the lead, the person is proceeding with certainty (*yaqeen*), also known as inner sight (*baseera*). On the other hand, if the hearing takes the lead, the person is proceeding with faith (*iman*). The fundamental difference between the two procedures is that seeing originates internally from the heart and then ascends into the eyes so that what is seen internally is projected externally. In this procedure, it is not the physical eyes that see but the heart.

"Do they not travel through the land, so that their hearts (and minds) may thus learn wisdom and their ears may thus learn to hear? Truly it is not their eyes that are blind, but their hearts which are in their breasts."
[*Surah Al Hajj* (The Pilgrimage) 22:46]

Therefore, seeing is attributed to the heart (*qalb*), and not the eyes because it originates from the heart and the eyes only reflect it outwardly so that what is seen is perceived internally is also perceived externally.

As for the hearing, it moves in the opposite direction - from outside to inside and what exists outside is always dual while what exists from inside (heart) is always unique and singular. Therefore when hearing receives a communication with its dualistic nature, there is a momentary hesitation and indetermination as it tries to analyze the message. Whereas the certainty in the heart well up to the eyes and the eyes will look at the communication and with certainty settle the issue, bringing peace and tranquility to the soul and the heart.

> *"Allah has revealed (from time to time, the most beautiful message in the form of a book ; with itself, (yet) repeating (its teaching in twains): the skins of those who fear their Lord tremble thereat; then their skin and their hearts do soften to the remembrance of Allah's praises. Such is the guidance of Allah: He guides therewith whom He pleases but such as Allah leaves to stray, can have none to guide"*
> [Surah Az Zumar (The Crowds) 39:23]

In the event where there is no previous certainty in the heart, which projects itself through the eyes, a person will always be unsettled because hearing alone cannot guarantee consistent tranquility for the heart and soul.

Physiological Positions of the Eyes and the Ears

By observing the respective positions of the eyes and the ears in the head, we see that the eyes are ahead and the ears are behind them. We also notice that the ears are on the sides of the head while the eyes are directly in the front and centre of the head. The conclusion from this is that God placed the eyes in front of the ears because they are supposed to take the lead. In terms of the movement of the heart, hearing moves the heart backward, while sight helps the heart move forward. Secondly, since the ears are on the sides of the head located apart from one another, we can conclude that this indicates their dualistic nature, which may cause the listener to waver for a moment before rightly adjusting his balance. This is unlike the eyes, which are close beside one another and are separated only by a thin boundary, the nose. In fact, we see that the pre-eminence of the eyes indicated in some verses:

> *"We ordained therein for them: Life for life, eye for eye, nose or nose, ear for ear, tooth for tooth, and wounds equal for equal. But*

if anyone remits the retaliation by way of charity, it is an act of atonement for himself. And if any fail to judge by (the light of) what Allah hath revealed, they are (no better than) wrong-doers."
[Surah Al Ma'idah (The Table Spread) 5:45]

In conclusion, even the physiognomy of the human corroborates the assumption that the eyes must lead the ears and that sight comes before hearing and that what you know must determine the outcome of your decision, not what you hear. If what you hear is ratified by what you know (i.e. what you see with your heart), then all is fine. If what you hear is contradicted by what you see with your heart (knowledge), then throw away what you hear and go on what you know (i.e. what you see with your heart). The role of hearing therefore is to confirm and bear truth to the information provided by seeing which is called (*tasdeeq*). The sight informs with certainty what the ears hear and obey.

"Most surely there is a reminder in this for him who has a heart or he gives ear and is a witness."
[Surah Qaf (Qaf) 50:37]

The Reordering of Seeing and Hearing

The story of the youth of the cave offers us a remarkable example of the striking contrast between the conduct of a person before and after the reordering of the sequence of his consciousness, from hearing first and then seeing, to seeing first and then hearing. The conduct of a person changes completely due to the order between sight and hearing.

"Or dost thou reflect that the Companions of the Cave and of the Inscription were wonders among Our Sign? Behold, the youths betook themselves to the Cave: they said, "Our Lord! bestow on us Mercy from Thyself, and dispose of our affair for us in the right way!" Then We draw (a veil) over their ears, for a number of years, in the Cave, (so that they heard not). Then We roused them, in order to test which of the two parties was best at calculating

the term of years they had tarried! We relate to thee their story in truth: they were youths who believed in their Lord, and We advanced them in guidance: We gave strength to their hearts: Behold, they stood up and said: "Our Lord is the Lord of the heavens and of the earth: never shall we call upon any god other than Him: if we did, we should indeed have uttered an enormity! "These our people have taken for worship gods other than Him: why do they not bring forward an authority clear (and convincing) for what they do? Who doth more wrong than such as invent a falsehood against God? "When ye turn away from them and the things they worship other than God, betake yourselves to the Cave: Your Lord will shower His mercies on you and disposes of your affair towards comfort and ease." Thou wouldst have seen the sun, when it rose, declining to the right from their Cave, and when it set, turning away from them to the left, while they lay in the open space in the midst of the Cave. Such are among the Signs of God: He whom God guides is rightly guided; but he whom God leaves to stray, for him wilt thou find no protector to lead him to the Right Way. Thou wouldst have deemed them awake, whilst they were asleep, and We turned them on their right and on their left sides: their dog stretching forth his two fore-legs on the threshold: if thou hadst come up on to them, thou wouldst have certainly turned back from them in flight, and wouldst certainly have been filled with terror of them. Such (being their state), we raised them up (from sleep), that they might question each other. Said one of them, "How long have ye stayed (here)?" They said, "We have stayed (perhaps) a day, or part of a day." (At length) they (all) said, "God (alone) knows best how long ye have stayed here.... Now send ye then one of you with this money of yours to the town: let him find out which is the best food (to be had) and bring some to you, that (ye may) satisfy your hunger therewith: And let him behave with care and courtesy, and let him not inform any one about you. "For if they should come upon you, they would stone you or force you to return to their cult, and in that case ye would never attain prosperity."*
[Surah Al Kahf [The Cave] 18:9-20]

In the story we notice that during the 300 years they

were guided by their sight, their hearing was put on hold and they never once felt any concern or urge of any kind. This was due to the fact that during this period they were completely rapt in their visions. There was no outside interference coming through the hearing, which usually draws a person's attention and from thence arise needs like eating or drinking or concerns like safety.

On the contrary, we notice that immediately after they were woken up by the removal of the obstruction from their hearing, they began to express their concerns and urges. These concerns are in the following categories:

1. Concern about time: Immediately after they were woken up they stared to wonder how long they had stayed in the cave.

2. Concern about sustenance: After they were woken up, they began to feel hungry and hence were concerned about finding the most suitable kind of food.

3. Concern about safety: They expressed concern regarding their safety and they instructed the one assigned to get them food to be very cautious to avoid raising any suspicions for fear of being forced back into the religion of their people, or worse yet, getting stoned to death.

These three concerns are representative of the majority of concerns that people have in this worldly life. People are concerned about their sustenance (*rizq*). The concern about one's sustenance (*rizq*) is related to both the first and the last concern. The concern for sustenance is related to the concern over time as far as the amount of sustenance that we have is concerned. When we have less we are worried about it finishing and when we have more we are worried about it getting reduced. Therefore, both anxiety about time and concern over money are primarily a result of a preoccupation with numbers. As for the third concern, which is safety, it converges with sustenance on the common point about security and safety.

People attach their security to the amount of money they have. If they have more, they feel safe. If they have less, they feel unsafe. Another point worth mentioning is the youth's concern about the quality of the food. They didn't want just any food that might be available, but they went out of their way to be selective about what they ate. This concern raised here by the youth of the cave, after their waking to this worldly life, bear striking resemblance with those raised by the people of Moses (*Musa*), peace be upon him. When he told them that God commanded them to slaughter a cow, they began to raise all these concerns about three things in particular: 1) The age of the cow, which is about numbers and time (quantity) 2) The colour of the cow, which is about quality and 3) The function of the cow.

And when Moses said unto his people:

> *"Lo! Allah commands you that you sacrifice a cow, they said: Do you make game of us? He answered: Allah forbid that I should be among the foolish! They said: Pray for us unto your Lord that He make clear to us what (cow) she is. (Moses) answered: Lo! He says, verily she is a cow neither with calf nor immature; (she is) between the two conditions; so do that which you are commanded. They said: Pray for us unto your Lord that He make clear to us of what colour she is. (Moses) answered: Lo! He says: Verily she is a yellow cow. Bright is her colour, gladdening beholders. They said: Pray for us unto your Lord that He make clear to us what (cow) she is. Lo! Cows are much alike to us; and Lo! If Allah wills, we may be led aright. (Moses) answered: Lo! He says: Verily she is a cow unyoked; she ploughs not the soil nor waters the fields; sound and without blemish. They said: Now you have brought the truth. So they sacrificed her, though they almost did not."*
> [Surah Al Baqarah (The Cow) 2:67-71]

All of these three concerns are reflective of the dualistic nature of the life of this world between less and more in quantity, between poor and rich in quality, and the division of labour between genders (instrumentality). All these concerns fall away from our consciousness once we revert to our first creation whereby the seeing comes before hearing, in order that we attain certainty (*yaqeen*). Just by virtue of the position of the eyes within the face, which are means of seeing, they look from inside out. This takes man's focus away from his person and projects it upon what lies ahead of him. This inside-out process helps the individual to transcend the boundaries of the self, which eventually helps him transcend the boundaries of the earth and heavens, which are larger forms of his self. In this manner, he goes on transcending boundary after boundary until his sight connects with the Divine Manifestation.

On the contrary, hearing is an energy that moves from outside-in, drawing our attention back unto ourselves. When our focus is drawn towards our self, it increases our awareness with regards to our self and this awareness of our self will raise concerns about its welfare. Then we fall into the cycle of duality, for it then becomes you and the others. In his definition of excellence, the Prophet Muhammad ﷺ said:

Worship your God as though you see Him.
If you don't see Him, know that He sees you.

The latter reflects the second case whereby the hearing is outside-in and you know God sees you albeit you do not see Him. When seeing is truly inside-out, it is you who sees God and you worship Him as though you see Him.

Certainty (*Yaqeen*) and the Stage After

If certainty (*yaqeen*) means to be able to see inside-out after the reordering of hearing-seeing to seeing-hearing, what comes next after attaining certainty (*yaqeen*)? Certainty (*yaqeen*) is not an end in itself. Rather, it is a means towards a greater goal, which is known as worship (*'ibadah*) or righteous deed, for every righteous deed is a form of worship. Every worship or righteous deed (*islah*) is made up of two things: remembrance (*dhikr*) and gratitude (*shukr*). If you remember as though you see God and you offer gratitude as though you see God, then you are considered to belong to the upper rank of those who worship as though they see Him. On the contrary, if you remember God or offer Him gratitude knowing that God sees you, then you belong to the lower rank of the worshippers. If however, you do not belong to either one of these two ranks, then you are surely among the losers.

"If only you could see when the guilty ones will bend low their heads before their Lord, (saying:) "Our Lord! We have seen and we have heard: Now then send us back (to the world): we will work righteousness: for we do indeed (now) believe."
[Surah As Sajdah (The Prostration) 32:12]

The Three Categories of Certainty (*Yaqeen*)

Certainty (*yaqeen*) has three categories: The taste of certainty (*haqq-al-yaqeen*), the essence of certainty (*'ilm-ul-yaqeen*) and the ornament of certainty (*'ain-al-yaqeen*).

The taste of certainty (*haqq-al-yaqeen*) is like the root of a tree and the other two categories are like two branches. Therefore, a full experience of certainty begins with the taste of certainty (*haqq-al-yaqeen*). The taste of certainty (*haqq-al-yaqeen*) refers to the situation whereby the heart comes into a flat position of absolute silence and absolute stillness. It is a neutral station. There is no increase and there is no decrease. When the heart is in this flat position, it attains the taste of certainty, the taste of death (*haqq-al-yaqeen*).

From this position, the heart can move either towards the essence of certainty (*'ilm-al-yaqeen*), or it can move towards the ornament of certainty (*'ain-al-yaqeen*). If the person gets into the sequence of hearing and then seeing, certainty (*yaqeen*) will move towards eyes (*'ain*). If on the other hand, the person gets into the sequence of seeing and then hearing, certainty (*yaqeen*) moves towards knowledge (*'ilm*). In the latter case, his look will be directed from inside-out, while in the former case, his look will move from outside-in. Consequently, the one with the essence of certainty (*'ilm-al-yaqeen*) falls in the upper rank of worshippers who worship God as though they see Him. The one with the ornament of certainty (*'ain-al-yaqeen*) falls in the second rank of those who worship God and know that He sees them.

Unveiling (*Kashf*) and Certainty (*Yaqeen*)

Unveiling (*kashf*) is the ability to have an immediate perception of the truth by casting away whatever is veiling it. It belongs to the branch of certainty (*yaqeen*) known as the essence of certainty (*'ilm-al-yaqeen*). Knowledge (*'ilm*) is the light, which allows us to see the truth naked without any veils. The faculty by which knowledge is able to accomplish the task of unveiling the truth is known as *furqan*. It is also called perception of knowledge (*baseera*). God says:

> *"Those parables we set forth for people, but only the people of knowledge ('aqI, intelligence) do comprehend them."*
> [Surah Al Ankabut (The Spider) 29:43]

> *"(And unto the evil-doer it is said): You were in heedlessness of this. We have taken away from you your veils, and now your sight is sharp!"*
> [Surah Qaf (Qaf) 50: 22]

Therefore, the first veil that is torn away (*kashf*) by the light of knowledge (*furqan, baseera*) that wells up from your heart is the veil covering your own eyes. Once the light of knowledge has first torn away this veil over your own eyes, it then goes out to tear off other veils that hide other realities. On the other hand, the ornament of certainty (*'ain-al-yaqeen*) also gives you a perception except that it allows you to see through the veil. It does not tear away the veil. These veils are called ornaments because they cover the truth as a decoration so that the gazers (*nadhrun*) are lured inward by these ornaments to take a view of the truth.

The Story of King Solomon

This story in *Surah An Naml*, Chapter 27 of the Qur'an describes how the kingdom of God is established on the foundations of Reverence of God (*Taqwa*) and Seeking pleasure of God (*Ridwan*).

Islam

The first premise on which every kingdom of God is built is called *Islam*. It means the unconditional surrender to the will of God and the unconditional acceptance of God's judgment. If this premise is accepted a priori, the kingdom that is consequently built is termed kingdom of God, and the nation that is formed is the nation of *Islam*. For this reason, the word *Islam* is mentioned four times in the story of Solomon (*Sulaiman*) peace be upon him, in *Surah An Naml*, corresponding with the four corners of the space (*saad*) within which the kingdom is built. Each time *Islam* is mentioned, it corresponds to an unconditional submission to God. These four verses are as follows:

I. *"Exalt not yourselves against me, but come unto me as those who submit."*
[*Surah An Naml* (The Ant) 27:31]

II. "He said: O chiefs! Which of you will bring me her throne before they come unto me, submitting?"
[*Surah An Naml* (The Ant) 27:38]

III. "So, when she came, it was said (unto her): Is thy throne like this? She said: (It is) as though it were the very one. And (Solomon said): We were given the knowledge before her and we had submitted (to Allah)."
[*Surah An Naml* (The Ant) 27:42]

IV. "It was said unto her: Enter the hall. And when she saw it she deemed it a pool and bared her legs. (Solomon) said: Lo! It is a

hall, made smooth of glass. She said: My Lord! Lo! I have wronged myself and I submit with Solomon unto Allah, the Lord of the Worlds."
[*Surah An Naml* (The Ant) 27: 44]

Indeed, every structure that is raised in the name of God must be within a definite space with four corners (or dimensions) so that it has the potential to expand infinitely horizontally and vertically, horizontally through the expansion in the four directions of the four corners, and vertically through the expansion in the upward and downward directions. This brings the total to six dimensions. These six dimensions correspond to the six days of creation (i.e. the six dimensions of periods of creation). This means that whatever we build, it must be built after the greater model built by God. God's model—the six days of creation of the earth, heaven and the space in between—is meant to be an example for us to follow.

"Say (O Muhammad): Travel in the land and see how He originated creation, then Allah brings forth the last creation (new creation). Lo! Allah is able to do all things."
[*Surah Al Ankabut* (The Spider) 29:20]

"Will they not regard the camels, how they are created? And the heaven, how it is raised? And the mountains, how they are firmly fixed, and the earth, how it is spread?"
[*Surah Al Ghashiyah* (The Overwhelming Event) 88:17-20]

In these verses and many others in the Qur'an, God is persistently inciting us to not just look at His creations, but to find out how He created them. If we succeed in finding out how, we will be able to copy His model and create our own after the image of His. Therefore, the kingdom of God must be built according to the Way of God.

The Throne (*'Arsh*)

The throne is mentioned five times in the story of Solomon. Four times represent the four corners of the space and the fifth, or the one, which is odd, represents the central throne. The centre, which is odd (one), implies two separate dimensions - the one above it and the one below it. That brings the total to six dimensions. The centre wherein all the six dimensions converge is the seventh station, or the odd or unity station. In other words, the station of the throne is used with the definite article.

> *"Allah, there is no God but He! Lord of the Throne Supreme!"*
> [*Surah An Naml* (The Ant) 27:26]

This is distinct from the four other thrones, which are marked with an indefinite article, signifying that they are not the final station (*mustaqarr*). The four indefinite thrones are mentioned as follows:

I. *"Lo! I found a woman ruling over them, and she hath been given (abundance) of all things, and hers is a mighty throne."*
[*Surah An Naml* (The Ant) 27:23]

II. *"He said: O chiefs! Which of you will bring me her throne before they come unto me, surrendering?"*
[*Surah An Naml* (The Ant) 27:38]

III. *"He said: Disguise her throne for her that we may see whether she will go aright or be of those not rightly guided."*
[*Surah An Naml* (The Ant) 27:41]

IV. *"So, when she came, it was said (unto her): Is thy throne like this? She said: (It is) as though it were the very one. And (Solomon said): We were given the knowledge before her and we had surrendered (to Allah)."*
[*Surah An Naml* (The Ant) 27:42]

The other two thrones exist in the story by inference, since the central throne must have a dimension above it and a dimension below it. The total of the six thrones thus also represent the six days of creation. The seventh day of the creation or the odd day is the day of the Mighty Throne of God, which is the final station.

The difference between things that are definite and things that are indefinite is that the definite is something that has reached its final station and has taken its final shape. In sum, it has become the truth realized. On the other hand, the indefinite is something that is still struggling on its journey through its temporary stations, and is going through its various formative phases. The definite will last forever while the indefinite is susceptible to change and loss. Therefore, any soul that exists within the six days is still indefinite, both in station and in form. However, any soul that has gone beyond the six days up to the seventh or the odd day, called the Throne Day, is a soul that is definite in station (final station or *mustaqarr*), and firm. It lies beyond the reach of change and regeneration. These are the ones whose vision has turned into reality and the promise made to them by God has come to be true. They truly are truth (*haqq*).

Book

The term *kitab* (book) is applied to any form of writing since the root of the word is "*ktb*" which means to write. It appears three times in the story. Two of these times it means letter.

> "Go with this my letter and throw it down unto them; then turn away and see what (answer) they return (The Queen of Sheba) said (when she received the letter): O chieftains! Lo! There has been thrown unto me a noble letter."
> [*Surah An Naml* (The Ant) 27:28-29]

One time it means book. One with whom was knowledge of the

Book said:

"I will bring it thee before thy gaze returns unto thee. And when he saw it set in his presence, (Solomon) said: This is of the bounty of my Lord, that He may try me whether I give thanks or am ungrateful. Whosoever gives thanks he only gives thanks for (the good of) his own soul; and whosoever is ungrateful (is ungrateful only to his own soul's hurt). For lo! my Lord is Absolute in independence, Bountiful."
[Surah An Naml (The Ant) 27:40]

In the last case, the use of the word *kitab* carries a definite article, while in the former two places where it is used, it occurs with no definite article attached. The implication of the presence or the absence of the definite article (*Al*) means that when the word "book" is used with indefinite article (*kitab*), it is referring to a portion of the book, or part of the word called *"harf."* This is in contrast to when it is used with the definite article described as *Al-Kitab*, which refers to the whole book or the entire word, *kalmah*.

The book therefore in its indefinite aspect, is susceptible to change and transformation, and likewise the word. However, once they reach their definite phase, they are beyond the reach of change and transformation. That book as a whole or the word as a whole is permanent and eternal.

"For them are glad tidings, in the life of the present and in the Hereafter; no change can there be in the words of Allah. This is indeed the supreme triumph."
[Surah Yunus (Jonah) 10:64]

"Those who are left behind will say when you set forth for the gaining of acquisitions: Allow us (that) we may follow you. They desire to change the word of Allah. Say: By no means shall you follow us; thus did Allah say before. But they will say: Nay! You are jealous of us. Nay! They do not understand but a little."
[Surah Al Fath (The Victory) 48:15]

In the Qur'an, God oft-repeatedly denounces those who tend to choose one part of the book or the word, and reject the other part, thereby distorting the meaning of the word or the book as a whole. This practice for some is deliberate and for others it is out of ignorance. The deliberate should repent and the ignorant should learn.

"And because of their breaking their covenant, We have cursed them and made hard their hearts. They change words from their context and forget a part of that whereof they were admonished. Thou wilt not cease to discover treachery from all save a few of them. But bear with them and pardon them. Lo! Allah loves the kindly."
[Surah Al Ma'idah (The Table Spread) 5:13]

"O Messenger! Let not those grieve you who strive together in hastening to unbelief from among those who say with their mouths: We believe, and their hearts do not believe, and from among those who are Jews; they are listeners for the sake of a lie, listeners for another people who have not come to you; they change the words from their places, saying: If you are given this, take it, and if you are not given this, be cautious; and as for him whose temptation Allah desires, you cannot control anything for him with Allah. Those are they for whom Allah does not desire that He should purify their hearts; they shall have disgrace in this world, and they shall have a grievous chastisement in the hereafter." [Surah Al Ma'idah (The Table Spread) 5:41]

The change (*tahreef*) that is mentioned in these verses means to attempt to divest the book or the word of its definite character and give it an indefinite character. Whatever the attempt may be God will complete His word or His book.

"The word of thy Lord doth find its fulfilment in truth and in justice: None can change His words: for He is the one who hears and knows all." [Surah Al An'am (The Cattle) 6:115]

"Fain would they extinguish Allah's light with their mouths, but Allah will not allow but that His light should be perfected, even though the Unbelievers may detest (it). He it is Who has sent His messenger with the guidance and the Religion of Truth, that He may cause it to prevail over all religion, however much the idolaters may be averse."
[Surah At Tawbah (The Repentance) 9:32-33]

"Their intention is to extinguish Allah's Light (by blowing) with their mouths: But Allah will complete (the revelation of) His Light, even though the Unbelievers may detest (it). He it is Who has sent His messenger with the guidance and the religion of truth, that He may make it conqueror of all religion however much idolaters may be averse."
[Surah As Saff (The Battle Array) 61:8-9]

Gratitude (*Shukr*) and Ingratitude (*Kufr*)

The story of Solomon informs us as well regarding the benefits of gratitude (*shukr*) and the ills of ingratitude (*kufr*). We find this contrasted between Solomon (*Sulaiman*) peace be upon him, and the Queen of Sheba. Solomon goes from gain to gain and from increase to increase because he offers gratitude to God and appreciates the favours God has conferred upon him. On the other hand, the Queen of Sheba and her people lose their gains and their wealth in favour of Solomon and his people because of their ingratitude to God and lack of appreciation for His favours upon them. The story presents us with four repetitions of the word gratitude (*shukr*) in text, and twice using substitute terms that carry the meaning of gratitude like praise (*hamd*) in verse 15 and the public acknowledgement of God's favours by Solomon in verse 16:

"And We verily gave knowledge unto David and Solomon, and they said: Praise be to Allah, Who hath preferred us above many of His believing slaves! And Solomon was David's heir. And he said: O mankind! Lo! We have been taught the language of birds, and have been given (abundance) of all things. This surely is

evident favour."
[Surah An Naml (The Ant) 27:15-16]

The other four times gratitude (*shukr*) is mentioned are in verses 19 and 40:

"And (Solomon) smiled, laughing at her speech, and said: My Lord, arouse me to be grateful for Thy favour wherewith Thou has favoured me and my parents, and to do good that shall be pleasing unto Thee, and include me in (the number of) Thy righteous slaves."
[Surah An Naml (The Ant) 27:19]

"One with whom was knowledge of the Book said: I will bring it thee before thy gaze returns unto thee. And when he saw it set in his presence, (Solomon) said: This is of the bounty of my Lord, that He may try me whether I give thanks or am ungrateful. Whosoever gives thanks he only gives thanks for (the good of) his own soul; and whosoever is ungrateful (is ungrateful only to his own soul's hurt). For lo! my Lord is Absolute in independence, Bountiful."
[Surah An Naml (The Ant) 27:40]

This brings the total to six times that the word or meaning of the word gratitude (*shukr*) appears in the story. This also corresponds to the six days or dimensions of creation. The seventh or odd day is indicated in the story by the word '*tardahu*' which means "to be pleased with" and comes from the root word *Ridwan* (God's pleasure or God's face).

"And (Solomon) smiled, laughing at her speech, and said: My Lord, arouse me to be grateful for Thy favour wherewith Thou has favoured me and my parents, and to do good that shall be pleasing unto Thee, and include me in (the number of) Thy righteous slaves."
[Surah An Naml (The Ant) 27:19]

The conclusion drawn from the story is therefore that

whoever gives gratitude to God for a complete cycle of six, he would attain God's *Ridwan* (pleasure) forever, and definitely he is one God is pleased with.

> *"If you reject (Allah), Truly Allah has no need of you; but He likes not ingratitude from His servants: if you are grateful, He is pleased with you. No bearer of burdens can bear the burden of another. In the end, to your Lord is your Return, when He will tell you the truth of all that you did (in this life), for He knows well all that is in (men's) hearts."*
> [Surah Az Zumar (The Crowds) 39:7]

> *"(To the righteous soul will be said:) "O (thou) soul, in (complete) rest and satisfaction! Come back thou to thy Lord, well pleased (thyself), and well-pleasing unto Him! Enter thou, then, among My devotees! Yea, enter thou My Heaven!"*
> [Surah Al Fajr (The Dawn) 89:27-30]

It is worthy of mention here that when God's servant (*abdullah*) completes the cycle of the six days and enters into the final station, which is the seventh day or the odd day also known as the *'Arsh* (Throne) day, he experiences two things:

1) The realization of God's word as a whole; and
2) He directly faces the Face of God and directly experiences the Light of His Face (*wajh*).

Hence, when the entire creation within the six days comes to perish at the blow of the trumpet, he shall be among those who will be exempted from living through the tribulation of that day.

> *"And the Day that the Trumpet will be sounded - then will be smitten with terror those who are in the heavens, and those who are on earth, except such as Allah will please (to exempt): and all shall come to His (Presence) as beings conscious of their lowliness."*
> [Surah An Naml (The Ant) 27:87]

"The Trumpet will (just) be sounded when all that are in the heavens and on earth will swoon, except such as it will please Allah (to exempt). Then will a second one be sounded, when, behold, they will be standing and looking on!"
[Surah Az Zumar (The Crowds) 39:68]

Prostration (*Sujud*)

The word prostration (*sujud*) occurs only twice in the story of Solomon (*Sulaiman*).

"I found her and her people worshipping the sun instead of Allah; and Satan makes their works fair seeming unto them, and debars them from the way (of Truth), so that they go not aright, so that they worship not Allah, Who brings forth the hidden in the heavens and the earth, and knows what you hide and what you proclaim."
[Surah An Naml (The Ant) 27:24-25]

These two refer to the two times we prostrate in each (*raka'a*) of prayer. Furthermore, the two prostrations symbolize the star and the tree. The star in turn symbolizes the lamp with the pure oil from the blessed olive tree. This oil is so pure that it is almost luminous even though untouched by fire. That fire that lights up the lamp comes from this tree.

"Allah is the Light of the heavens and the earth. The Parable of His Light is as if there were a Niche and within it a Lamp: the Lamp enclosed in Glass: the glass as it were a brilliant star: Lit from a blessed Tree, an Olive, neither of the east nor of the west, whose oil is well-nigh luminous, though fire scarce touched it: Light upon Light! Allah guides whom He will to His Light: Allah sets forth Parables for men: and Allah knows all things."
[Surah An Nur (The Light) 24:35]

Therefore, the tree and the star stand for fire and light, and when the two come in contact, they turn into light upon light.

"The stars and the trees prostrate in adoration."
[*Surah Ar Rahman* (The Most Gracious) 55:6]

In various places in the Qur'an, the tree and the star are mentioned together.

"Who has appointed for you fire from the green tree, and behold! You kindle from it."
[*Surah Ya Seen* (Ya Seen) 36:80]

"Do you see the fire which you kindle? Is it you who grow the tree which feeds the fire, or do We grow it? We have made it a memorial (of Our handiwork), and an article of comfort and convenience for the denizens of deserts. Then celebrate with praises the name of thy Lord, the Supreme! Furthermore, I call to witness the setting of the Stars."
[*Surah Al Waqi'ah* (The Inevitable Event) 56:71-75]

The stars offer a light that is cool and white while the light from the tree is green to dark green and hot. When the two mix, they present a light that is neither cool nor hot, and it is neither bright nor faint. Such a light is the most approximate representation of God's Light. It is a whole light that is inextinguishable, given to those who are bound to reach up to God's light and never get misled along the way.

Genuflexion or Bowing Down (*Ruku*)

The story of Solomon only mentions one case of genuflexion (*ruku*), which is the noun in a regular prayer. *Ruku* represents the posture that a person assumes when coming in through the door into God's presence, and after entry, then comes the two prostrations. The genuflexion (*ruku*) presents the opportunity to glorify God and the first prostration draws a person near to God, whereas the second prostration offers him the opportunity to ask from God whatever he wishes because he is close to Him.

> "Nay, Obey not thou him. But prostrate yourself, and draw near (unto Allah)."
> [Surah Al Alaq (The Congealed Blood) 96:19]

> "But fall ye down in prostration to Allah, and adore (Him)!"
> [Surah An Najm (The Star) 53:62]

> "And when My servants question thee concerning Me, then surely I am nigh. I answer the prayer of the supplicant when he cries unto Me. So let them hear My call and let them trust in Me, in order that they may be led aright."
> [Surah Al Baqarah (The Cow) 2:186]

However, it must be noted that *Islam* (unconditional submission to God), is a precondition. Without it your bowing cannot let you pass through the door that leads into God's presence nor could your prostration bring you close to God.

> "The Day that the skin shall be laid bare, and they shall be summoned to bow in adoration, but they shall not be able. Their eyes will be cast down, ignominy will cover them; seeing that they had been summoned aforetime to bow in adoration, while they were whole, (and had refused)."
> [Surah Al Qalam (The Pen) 68:42-43]

The proof of this argument comes in the story whereby the Queen of Sheba is invited to enter through the door of the tower where the floor was made of glass and appeared similar to the waves of water. Due to the unsound state of her heart, as she was not in submission (*Islam*) to God, she could not discern between reflection and reality. She therefore bowed down to lift up the hem of her dress so it would not get wet. She was corrected and then realized her error thereupon she unconditionally submitted to God under the guidance of Solomon. Only then in true submission she crossed the threshold that leads into God's presence:

> "It was said unto her: Enter the hall. And when she saw it she

deemed it a pool and bared her legs. (Solomon) said: Lo! It is a hall, made smooth of glass. She said: My Lord! Lo! I have wronged myself, and I surrender with Solomon unto Allah, the Lord of the Worlds."
[Surah An Naml (The Ant) 27:44]

She then performed her two prostrations called "greetings of God's house" (His presence) and she was drawn near.

Categories of Knowledge ('*Ilm*)

The word knowledge ('*ilm*) also occurs four times in the story of Solomon and these four times represent the four categories of knowledge:

1.Knowledge of different tongues including all human languages, the speech of angels, of jinns, and of species that fly in the air like birds and those that crawl on the earth like ants for they are all nations with their specific languages:

"And Solomon was David's heir. And he said: O mankind! Lo! We have been taught the language of birds, and have been given (abundance) of all things. This surely is evident favour."
[Surah An Naml (The Ant) 27:16]

"Till, when they reached the Valley of the Ants, an ant exclaimed: O ants! Enter your dwellings lest Solomon and his armies crush you, unperceiving."
[Surah An Naml (The Ant) 27:18]

"But the Hoopoe tarried not far: he (came up and) said: I have compassed (territory) which thou hast not compassed, and I have come to thee from Saba with tidings true."
[Surah An Naml (The Ant) 27:22]

All these nations are contributors to the Kingdom of God and therefore, God's vicegerent (*khalifah*) should understand their languages.

2. Knowledge of the book (*'ilm-ul-kitab*) is the second category of knowledge. Details regarding this type of knowledge will come up later when we speak about the man who has knowledge of the book.

3. Knowledge of certainty (*'ilm-ul-yaqeen*) is the third type of knowledge and is attributed to the bird in the story (see verse 27:22 above).

4. Knowledge of the unseen (*ghayb*) called *'ilm-ul-ghayb.*

These four categories of knowledge represent the four corners of our space and the two dimensions above and below, bringing them to a total of six dimensions or six days which completes the cycle of creation. Then emerges the seventh dimension or the odd day in which all the various types of knowledge become one true knowledge that encompasses everything (true certainty, *haqq-al-yaqeen*).

Six Components of the Kingdom of God

We have now come to one of the most important parts of the story where we need to identify the six individuals who play key roles in governance of the kingdom as a whole. These six individuals will be identified with different natural and cosmic phenomena, which they each represent as a concept. Those cosmic phenomena are: 1) night; 2) day; 3) sun; 4) moon; 5) space above called firmament (heaven); and 6) space below called earth. This totals six. All six, except for the sun, are represented in the story by natural beings that share similar characteristics as the cosmic phenomena. The following are the cosmic phenomena and their corresponding natural representation in the story.

1. Day: Represented by the man who has knowledge of the book. Their common characteristic is the speed of daylight, which is

equal to the wink of an eye. We hereby come to the realization that the knowledge from the book is equal in power and speed to the particles of daylight, which are called *'kunnas'*. We can also understand from this that the particles of daylight (*kunnas*) are the cause for blinking our eyes:

"One who had the knowledge of the Book said: I will bring it to you in the twinkling of an eye. Then when he saw it settled beside him, he said: This is of the grace of my Lord that He may try me whether I am grateful or ungrateful; and whoever is grateful, he is grateful only for his own soul, and whoever is ungrateful, then surely my Lord is Self-Sufficient, Honored."
[Surah An Naml (The Ant) 27: 40]

"The stars, which rise and set (kunnas)."
[Surah At Takwir (The Folding Up) 81:16]

2. Night: Represented by *Ifrit*, the *jinn*, who is strong and trustworthy. Their common characteristic is the speed of the night particle, which is equal to the period of time between sitting and standing. The particles of the night light are known as *'khunnas'*:

"So verily I call to witness the planets that recede (khunnas)."
[Surah At Takwir (The Folding Up) 81:15]

While the *kunnas* are swift and resonant, the *khunnas* are slow and silent. The *kunnas* are light whereas the *khunnas* are heavy. The *khunnas* are associated with our power of hearing, while *kunnas* are associated with our power of seeing. The *khunnas* therefore give us the weight that allows us to stand firm, stable and balanced. Its energy is thus magnetic. These are the common characteristics the *ifrit* has strength, which is firmness and stability on one hand, and trustworthiness, which is to keep something and not lose it.

"Said an 'Ifrit, of the Jinns: I will bring it to thee before thou rise from thy council: indeed I have full strength for the purpose, and

may be trusted." [Surah An Naml (The Ant) 27:39]

3. Sun: Represented by itself in the story of Solomon. Its major characteristic is that its light called *"diyaa,"* is ascending by nature, and is also able to uplift others. It levitates and elevates. Also, the sunlight is dry and hot, giving heat and warmth. Thirdly, it has consistency of form because it does not decrease or increase in shape; it is the same all the time.

4. Moon: Represented by the Queen of Sheba. Their foremost common characteristic is their representation of the female principle, while the sun represents the male principle.

"By the Night as it conceals (the light); by the Day as it appears in glory; by (the mystery of) the creation of male and female; verily, (the ends) you strive for are diverse."
[Surah Al Layl (The Night) 92:1-4]

Two other common characteristics represented by the Queen and symbolized by the moon is that it gives a cool and wet light; and the moon changes and transforms as it goes through its monthly cycle of various degrees of shape. This is called *"manajil"* and corresponds to the female monthly cycle. The cycle of the moon represents increase and decrease as the moon increases in size from the beginning of the month until it reaches fullness by the middle of the month, after which it begins to decrease in size till the end of the month. The fourth common characteristic is that moonlight is descending because it is cool and wet:

"And (as for) the moon, We have ordained for it stages till it becomes again as an old dry palm branch."
[Surah Ya Seen (Ya Seen) 36:39]

5. Sky: Represented by the hoopoe bird. Their common characteristic is that both the bird and the sky are held up by air. Birds travel in the air and the sky stands supported by the air. The heaven (sky) is the space with which the angels are

commonly associated.

> *"And how many angels are in the heavens whose intercession avails naught save after Allah gives leave to whom He chooses and accepts."*
> [Surah An Najm (The Star) 53:26]

As well, the angels are associated with wings and fly like birds:

> *"Praise be to Allah, the Creator of the heavens and the earth, Who appoints the angels messengers having wings two, three and four. He multiplies in creation what He will. Lo! Allah is Able to do all things."*
> [Surah Fatir (The Originator of Creation) 35:1]

Furthermore the energy that carries the heavens, the energy that carries the birds and the energy that carries the angels are all the same. That energy is called spirit (*ruh*). The spirit (*ruh*) is the dominant principle in the life of birds and angels. The human spirit joins the rank of birds and angels mainly at sleep when their spirit becomes active and moves freely like angels and birds with wings.

During sleep, the human spirit experiences visions (*ru'ya*) like angels and birds do in their waking. The human being can also attain that level when his or her spirit is successfully disenfranchised from their body.

6. Earth: Represented in the story by the ants. The earth is home for all the creatures that crawl along the face of the earth. They are given the generic name of "*daabah*":

> *"There is no moving creature on earth (daab-batin fil 'ardh) but its sustenance depends on Allah: He knows the time and place of its definite abode and its temporary deposit: All is in a clear Record."*
> [Surah Hud (Hud) 11:6]

"There is not an animal (that lives) on the earth (daab-batin fil 'ardh), nor a being that flies on its wings, but (forms part of) communities like you. Nothing have we omitted from the Book, and they (all) shall be gathered to their Lord in the end."
[Surah Al An'am (The Cattle) 6:38]

"How many are the creatures (daabah) that carry not their own sustenance? It is Allah who feeds (both) them and you: for He hears and knows (all things)."
[Surah Al Ankabut (The Spider) 29:60]

The *daabah* find refuge in the earth as birds find refuge in the air.

"Till, when they reached the Valley of the Ants, an ant exclaimed: O ants! Enter your dwellings lest Solomon and his armies crush you, unperceiving."
[Surah An Naml (The Ant) 27:18]

Daabah are gifted with a very fine sensory perception so that their bodies can detect very minute vibrations communicated by the earth and therefore discern whether the vibrations are positive or negative. This sensory perception is called *"shu'ur"* also called *"khawatir."* The *daabah* share this feature with human beings who have developed this acute sense of feeling. The worms of the earth desist from eating the corpse of such human beings for they perceive them as one of them. The example is Solomon himself, peace be upon him, because when he died, the *daabah* (termites, ants, worms) ate his staff but not his body which was leaning on the staff so that when the staff fell off, his body fell down.

"Then, when We decreed (Solomon's) death, nothing showed them his death except a little worm of the earth, which kept (slowly) gnawing away at his staff: so when he fell down, the Jinns saw plainly that if they had known the unseen, they would not have tamed in the humiliating Penalty (of their Task)."
[Surah Saba (Sheba) 34:14]

At the centre of all these six members or components of the kingdom of God is located the person of Solomon, peace be upon him, like the heart is located at the centre of the human body. Such a person is called the heart (*qalb*), also known as the pole (*qutb*). In Qur'anic terms, this person is called the vicegerent (*khalifah*) or messenger (*rasuul*). On one hand, the commandment comes straight from God into the heart and from the heart it is channeled into the six members. Then from the six it flows back into the heart. The six members are 1) flesh (sense of touch); 2) spirit (sense of breathing); 3) eyes (sense of seeing); 4) ears (sense of hearing); 5) sun (male principle); 6) moon (female principle). In terms of the human body, all six must come together in coordination to maintain a sound heart, which occupies the seventh or the odd position.

The principal model after which everything is built is the one put in place by Almighty Allah. He created the six days or the six dimensions, which are the earth, heavens, day, night, sun, and the moon. In the centre is the throne, which is the heart of the entire universe. In a similar manner, we will see how the six members work together in the kingdom of God to help Solomon realize an objective: to find and bring the people of Sheba, their queen and her throne.

The third of these three, the throne, so far belonged to the realm of the unseen (*ghayb*). Therefore, the first step is to find it in the unseen. That role fell upon two members: the ant and the bird. The ant had the intuitive awareness (*shu'ur*) about the throne. Intuition is solely a function of the body without the participation of the spirit (*ruh*). It is a faculty embedded into the human body prior to the introduction of the spirit (*ruh*).

In order for the kingdom of God to fare well, it must have individuals who possess the faculty of intuition and through their intuitive abilities they are able to have presentiment about things that still lie abstract in the unseen. Intuition therefore constitutes the first stage of the conception. However, without further help, everything will remain at this conceptual stage.

The next step in finding the throne in the unseen is taken by the bird (hoopoe). The bird is endowed with the spiritual power of having vision. What the ant was able to sense intuitively, the bird was able to envision. The object (throne) has now moved from notion to vision. The bird flying in the air and the *daabah* crawling over the earth take two different approaches to reach the same objective, which in this case is the throne. The ant approaches from beneath and the bird approaches from above.

The perception of the spirit also called the angelic perception is known as the vision (*ru'ya*), while the sensory perception through the skin is called intuition. The skin is from creation and the spirit is from commandment. When the two are fused together thereupon emerges a living entity in excellence, a living entity made up of body and spirit, from creation and commandment. This union is often called the union of the two souls, meaning spirit and body. The bird represents the spirit and the ant represents the body.

Ifrit (Jinn)

The next pair to emerge after the body and the spirit is the hearing and the seeing. In cosmic terms, they are the night and the day, created after the creation of earth and heaven. Similarly, hearing and seeing as faculties come into being after the union of body (*dhat*) and spirit (*ruh*). Hearing and seeing are represented in the story by the *ifrit* and the one with knowledge of the book, respectively. The personality of the *ifrit* is the person who is endowed with extraordinary powers of listening so that when something is mentioned about the unseen, he is able to make contact with it at the speed of sound and draw it towards himself using magnetic energy. Such a person is known as trustworthy (*siddiq*) because he is strong (*qawiyy*) since one who is weak cannot be trustworthy in the sense that he is not able to safeguard the trust that is given to him. Therefore, strength and trustworthiness are synonymous, for every person who is trustworthy is strong, and everyone who is strong is trustworthy. The following are the claims made by the *Ifrit*:

An ifrit of the jinn said: "I will bring it thee before thou canst rise from thy place. Lo! I verily am strong and trusty for such work."
[Surah An Naml (The Ant) 27:39]

The character of the trustworthy (*siddiq*) and the nature of night are similar in that both are still and silent. For this reason the remembrance was revealed in the night because it is a time of silence and stillness. These two attributes are necessary for good listening and the ability to maintain whatever is heard. The trustworthy (*siddiq*) collects, gathers and keeps as the night gathers and keeps.

"And by the night and all that it enshrouds."
[*Surah Al Inshiqaq* (The Rending Asunder) 84:17]

The trustworthy one's (*siddiq*) strength and trustworthiness covers and protects as the time of night covers and protects.

"And made the night as a covering."
[*Surah An Naba* (The News) 78:10]

"And He it is Who makes the Night as a Robe for you, and Sleep as Repose, and makes the Day (as it were) a Resurrection."
[*Surah Al Furqan* (The Criterion) 25:47]

Man with Knowledge of the Book

The faculty of sight is characterized in the story by the human being who is endowed with knowledge from the book. Seeing is synonymous with witnessing and knowledge from the book is given to those who are witnesses (*shuhada*). When something is mentioned to those who are witnesses (*shuhada*), they have the ability to see it in the blink of an eye, and have that thing in their presence at the same moment. In comparison, it takes the trustworthy (*siddiq*) a longer time and more effort than the witness (*shahid*) because rising to a standing position requires a longer time and greater effort than merely blinking the eye.

As the particle of daylight is quicker and lighter than the night, even so the journey of the witness (*shahid*) is faster and lighter than the trustworthy (*siddiq*).

"Go forth, light-armed and heavy-armed, and strive with your wealth and your lives in the way of Allah! That is best for you if you but knew." [*Surah At Tawbah* (The Repentance) 9:41]

Besides the qualities of lightness and swiftness produced by knowledge in the heart of the one who has it, it also produces fear of God called "*khashyah*" or "*khawf.*" Knowledge breeds this fear in the heart and this fear in turn quickens the person, making him lighter and swift.

"And so amongst men and crawling creatures and cattle, are they of various colours. Those truly fear Allah, among His Servants, who have knowledge: for Allah is Exalted in Might, Oft-Forgiving."
[*Surah Fatir* (The Originator of Creation) 35:28]

The nexus between knowledge (*'ilm*) and fear (*khashyah*) is witnessing (*shahadah*). For when you witness the majesty of God, that witnessing will produce over-awe in your heart, which in turn will quicken your heart and bring lightness and swiftness into your character. This contrasts with the character of a trustworthy (*siddiq*) who is weighty. This weightiness proceeds from the weight of the trust that he is carrying, called faith (*iman*). It comes from the word trust (*amanah*).

Because of its weight, faith (*iman*) gives balance and endurance to individuals who carry it. It is, for the same reason, why the heaven, the earth and the mountains turned down the offer to carry this trust (*iman*), for fear of failing to bear it. We then find that the trustworthy (*siddiq*) who is entrusted with the burden of faith (*iman*) and the witness (*shahid*) who is a watchman of the knowledge given to him, are complementary in character as a pair.

The trustworthy (*siddiq*) is slow while the witness (*shahid*) is fast. When the two are put together, we get the right speed, which is neither slow nor fast. Furthermore, the witness (*shahid*) is light and the trustworthy (*siddiq*) is heavy and when we put the two together, we get the right weight, which is neither too heavy nor too light. Finally, the *shahid* is characterized by over-awe and the *siddiq* by hope. When the two characters are put together, we get a balanced character that is between fear and hope. That character is known as excellence (*ihsan*):

> "And Allah gave them a reward in this world, and the excellent reward of the Hereafter. For Allah Loveth those who do good."
> [*Surah Al An'am* (The Cattle) 3:148]

At this point, we have now covered the four stages of creation, namely: the body (*dhat*), the spirit (*ruh*), the hearing (*sama'*), and seeing (*basar*). In cosmic terms, they are the earth, the heaven, the night and the day. In terms of characterization, they are the ant, the bird, the *ifrit* and the man.

The next pair to emerge is the sun and the moon. As a pair, they represent the male and female principles, in other words fatherhood and motherhood. The light energy that proceeds from the sun is called solar energy (*diyaa*) while the one that we receive from the moon is known as lunar energy (*nur*). In other terms these are the energy of the male and female principles, respectively. Characteristically, the solar energy (*diyaa*) is dry and it moves upward because of the heat it contains while the lunar energy (*nur*) is wet and moves downward because of the moisture it contains. Both principles are necessary in order to keep balance.

Even though the sun is a symbol of ascent and

permanence and the moon is a symbol of descent and mutation, the sun must not override the moon. In order to avoid living in extremes from extreme ascending to extreme descending, from extreme rising to extreme falling, one must regulate the two energies—solar and lunar. While under the influence of solar energy (*diyaa*), feelings of overjoy, highness and dilation occur. Unless checked with self-control, this turns into an extreme called arrogance (*kibr*). While such conditions of expansiveness prevail, one should not get carried away and become lavish and extravagant to the point of losing the opposite principle, which must in turn click in soon after. Therefore, God says:

> *"The sun is not supposed to override the moon."*
> [*Surah Ya Seen* (Ya Seen) 36:40]

This means that even though the sun is higher and greater, it must not transgress upon the moon. The sun must allow the moon to play the part that God has assigned to it. God created the sun and gave it unbounded existence. And He created the moon but gave it an apportioned existence. He created the male on the basis of the solar principle, and He created the female on the basis of the lunar principle.

The objective is to find the right balance by blending solar and lunar energies. When you are uplifted by the solar energy at the moment when you feel elated that is a time to exercise self restraint by using little of that solar energy and saving up the rest. In turn, when the lunar energy pulls you down and you feel contracted, the solar energy you saved up earlier will counteract the lunar contraction (*taqdir*). Therefore, your contraction and your expansion become equal. Your heart has the right height and the middle position is neither too high nor too low.

Guidance (*Hidayah*)

The term guidance (*hidayah, huda*) occurs four times in the story of Solomon, which refers to the four ways to find guidance. The first way is to be guided through your intuition (*shu'ur, hiss, khaatir*). This type of guidance is the most fundamental and the basis for the subsequent ways of guidance.

Furthermore, the channel for this guidance is the skin which is like a dressing for the organs of the body, whether internal or external. The body and the heart are both covered by a clothing (a membrane), which is the equivalent of a womb for the fetus. The dress that covers the heart (*qalb*) is known as the (*fuad*). If this covering remains soft and transparent, then the heart is able to detect very fine vibrations. This transparency of this covering (*fuad*) and softness of the heart keeps the heart flexible and alive. The heart becomes leveled and well-positioned.

This transparency and softness spread out to the outer skin of the body so that the rest of the organs in the body become soft and well-relaxed in their respective positions. In this way, both heart and body become sound.

"Allah has revealed (from time to time) the most beautiful Message in the form of a Book, consistent with itself, (yet) repeating (its teaching in various aspects): the skins of those who fear their Lord tremble thereat; then their skins and their hearts do soften to the celebration of Allah's praises. Such is the guidance of Allah: He guides therewith whom He pleases, but such as Allah leaves to stray, can have none to guide."
[Surah Az Zumar (The Crowds) 39:23]

This soundness in the heart and body allows both to become aware of very fine vibrations -- like sounds made by worms and insects -- and be able to decipher and comprehend the message of those sounds. This category of speech is known as *"hadith"* which means secret communication. This type of fine communication is mediated through the earth and to things that are close to the earth. The earth on a regular basis sends out its communications (*hadith*) in the form of vibrations (*zalzalah, zabzabah*), which at times is concentrated into quakes.

> *"When the earth is shaken to her (utmost) convulsion, and the earth throws up her burdens (from within), and man cries (distressed): 'What is the matter with her?' On that Day will she declare her tidings: For that thy Lord will have given her inspiration."*
> [*Surah Al Zalzalah* (The Convulsion) 99:1-5]

However, only people who are soft in heart and skin can develop the fine intuition (*khushu', shu'ur, hiss*). It was through this fine intuition (*shu'ur*) that Solomon, peace be upon him, in the story heard the speech of the ant (see *Surah An Naml* 27:18 above). As a vicegerent (*khalifah*) in God's kingdom, it was certainly a part of Solomon's responsibility to look after the welfare of everyone in the kingdom including the nation of ants.

Similarly, it was through intuition (*hiss*) that Jesus, peace be upon him, was able to detect disbelief in the hearts of the audience around him and as a result he picked out the helpers (*hawwaris*).

> *"But when Jesus became conscious of their disbelief, he cried: Who will be my helpers in the cause of Allah? The disciples said: We will be Allah's helpers. We believe in Allah, and bear thou witness that we have surrendered (unto Him)."*
> [*Surah Al Imran* (The Family of Imran) 3:52]

Besides *shu'ur* and *hiss*, this fine intuitive awareness is also known as "*dhann*" meaning thought or idea. It is rather a notion formed or conceived about something on the basis of intuition. (*Dhann*) therefore falls under two categories – well thinking (*husn al-dhann*) and ill thinking (*su'u al-dhann*). These two are the origin of all subsequent conduct and actions.

Thinking well will eventually lead to acting well, and thinking ill will eventually lead to acting ill. Between thought and action there are many stages of transformations. Sometimes ill thinking does not materialize into action in which case no sin is written against the person who thinks ill. This is the same method for well-thinking. If it does not materialize into action, it is accounted as one reward and if it materializes into action, it is counted as ten or more.

We can therefore conclude that well-thinking about God and about creation forms the basis of all goodness and that on the contrary, ill-thinking about God and about creation forms the basis of all evil. Good thinking represents the earliest stage of belief (*iman*) so that when that good opinion gets stronger in the heart, it turns into faith, and if that faith gets stronger, it can mobilize different parts of the body—tongue, hands, legs, into action. Thus, what started as an opinion at first turns into action at last.

"Assuredly Allah knows that which they keep hidden and that which they proclaim. Lo! He loves not the proud. And when it is said unto them: What has your Lord revealed? They say: (Mere) fables of the men of old. Let them bear, on the Day of Judgment, their own burdens in full, and also (something) of the burdens of those without knowledge, whom they misled. Alas, how grievous the burdens they will bear!"
[*Surah An Nahl* (The Bee) 16:23-25]

"And it is said unto those who ward off (evil): What has your Lord revealed? They say: Good. For those who do good in this world there is a good (reward) and the home of the Hereafter will be better. Pleasant indeed will be the home of those who ward off (evil)."
[*Surah An Nahl* (The Bee) 16:30]

Similarly, ill-thinking represents the earliest stages of disbelief (*kufr*) because when that ill opinion gets stronger in the heart, it turns into outright disbelief and that disbelief in turn gets stronger and it can mobilize the rest of the body into action. The ill opinion that remains within the heart is the least degree of disbelief (*kufr*) and the good opinion that remains within the heart is the least degree of faith (*iman*).

"You did not hide yourselves lest your ears and your eyes and your skins should testify against you, but you deemed that Allah knew not much of what you did. That, your thought which you did think about your Lord, has ruined you; and you find yourselves (this day) among the lost."
[*Surah Fussilat* (Expouded) 41:22-23]

If we investigate further the causes of well-thinking and ill-thinking, we find that they go back to the condition of the heart and the skin. A heart that is soft and a skin that is transparent have good intuitions and most likely form good opinions about God and creation. On the other hand, a heart that is hard and a skin that is thick have bad intuitions and have the most likelihood of forming ill opinions about God and creation.

Everyone is born with the sound disposition (*fitrah*), which means with a heart that is soft and a skin that is light. During the course of life, this sound disposition changes into ill disposition as their hearts get harder and their skins get thicker. This hardness of the heart and thickness of the skin triggers ill thoughts, and these ill thoughts result in wicked actions. It is ill-thinking that prompts man to be miserly, thinking that God is miserly and therefore God will not give back to him.

On the contrary, it is good thinking that prompts man to be generous and giving, believing that God will give him back more or equal to what he gave. It is ill-thinking that prompts man to act well in public but act wickedly in private because he thinks God is not present with him in private as He is in public. On the contrary, it is good thinking that prompts one to act well in public and in private, knowing that God is with him wherever he is. The same goes for lying, cheating, hatred and arrogance.

These deviations in conduct and character appear even among nations that had inherited the teachings of the prophets and messengers. It is not the teachings (scriptures) that changed in themselves, but rather that in later generations, the hearts of the people became hard. As a result, the teachings they claim to follow got distorted in their endeavour to make them suit their outlook.

Sometimes this attitude towards the scripture has led to textual revisions of the scriptures affecting both form and meaning as is the case with the Old and New Testaments. And sometimes, the change affects only the meaning and not the form, as is the case with Muslims and the Qur'an.

"But because of their breach of their covenant, We cursed them, and made their hearts grow hard; they change the words from their (right) places and forget a good part of the message that was sent them, nor wilt thou cease to find them- barring a few - ever bent on (new) deceits: but forgive them, and overlook (their misdeeds): for Allah loveth those who are kind. From those, too, who call themselves Christians, We did take a covenant, but they forgot a good part of the message that was sent them: so we estranged them, with enmity and hatred between the one and the other, to the Day of Judgment. And soon will Allah show them what it is they have done."
[Surah Al Ma'idah (The Table Spread) 5:13-14]

"O Messenger! Let not those grieve you who strive together in hastening to unbelief from among those who say with their mouths: We believe, and their hearts do not believe, and from among those who are Jews; they are listeners for the sake of a lie, listeners for another people who have not come to you; they alter the words from their places, saying: If you are given this, take it, and if you are not given this, be cautious; and as for him whose temptation Allah desires, you cannot control anything for him with Allah. Those are they for whom Allah does not desire that He should purify their hearts; they shall have disgrace in this world, and they shall have a grievous chastisement in the hereafter."
[Surah Al Ma'idah (The Table Spread) 5:40]

"Of the Jews there are those who displace words from their (right) places, and say: 'We hear and we disobey' and 'Hear what is not Heard'; and 'Ra'ina'; with a twist of their tongues and a

slander to Faith. If only they had said: 'We hear and we obey' and 'Do hear'; and 'Do look at us', it would have been better for them, and more proper; but Allah hath cursed them for their Unbelief; and but few of them will believe."
[Surah An Nisa (The Women) 4:46]

From the foregoing verses it is clear that the primary causes of all deviations come from hard-heartedness, which is the cause of rigidity and dogmatism, which in turn deprives the heart from its ability to look at the word of God (the scripture) from both inside and outside, from both right and left in order to have a complete view of the truth. This inability to see the truth (word of God) from all angles is the cause of extremism, each group pulling the truth towards their side, which then leads to fragmentation and division between them. It was 71 groups after Moses, 72 after Jesus, and now 73 after Muhammad ﷺ, peace and blessings of God be upon them all.

In order to correct this situation, we must attack the problem from the root, which is hard-heartedness by bringing tenderness to the skin and softness to people's hearts. In this way, the person is predisposed to positive thinking. Like a fertile land, the heart is ready to receive the good word. From a seed, the good word grows into a full-grown tree giving fruits and shade.

"Have you not considered how Allah sets forth a parable of a good word (being) like a good tree, whose root is firm and whose branches are in heaven, yielding its fruit in every season by the permission of its Lord? And Allah sets forth parables for men that they may be mindful."
[Surah Ibrahim (Abraham) 14:24-25]

If the heart, however, is hard and the skin is thick, the good word would be alienated into an evil word. An evil word has no roots in the ground and no branches in the sky.

> "And the parable of an evil word is as an evil tree pulled up from the earth's surface; it has no stability."
> [Surah Ibrahim (Abraham) 14:26]

When a believer with a soft heart and a tender skin hears the remembrance of God, it benefits him by increasing the softness of his heart and the tenderness of his skin, which results in increase in faith (*iman*).

> "And continue to remind, for surely the reminder profits the believers."
> [Surah Adh Dhariyat (Winds That Scatter) 51:55]

On the contrary, when a disbeliever with a hard heart and thick skin hears the remembrance, his heart becomes harder and his skin becomes thicker.

> "And if We willed We could withdraw that which We have revealed unto thee, then wouldst thou find no guardian for thee against Us in respect thereof."
> [Surah Al Isra (The Night Journey) 17:86]

> "The Jews say: Allah's hand is fettered. Their hands are fettered and they are accursed for saying so. Nay, but both His hands are spread out wide in bounty. He bestows as He will. That which has been revealed unto thee from thy Lord is certain to increase the contumacy and disbelief of many of them, and We have cast among them enmity and hatred till the Day of Resurrection. As often as they light a fire for war, Allah extinguishes it. Their effort is for corruption in the land, and Allah loves not corrupters."
> [Surah Al Ma'idah (The Table Spread) 5:64]

> "Say O People of the Scripture! You have naught (of guidance) till you observe the Torah and the Gospel and that which was revealed unto you from your Lord. That which is revealed unto thee (Muhammad) from thy Lord is certain to increase the contumacy and disbelief of many of them. But grieve not for the

disbelieving folk."
[Surah Al Ma'idah (The Table Spread) 5:68]

It is because of the open-mindedness and positive thinking of the believers, due to the softness and tenderness of their hearts and skin, that they are able to recognize the truth when the truth is still strange and obscure.

"Mankind was one single nation, and Allah sent Messengers with glad tidings and warnings; and with them He sent the Book in truth, to judge between people in matters wherein they differed; but the People of the Book, after the clear Signs came to them, did not differ among themselves, except through selfish contumacy. Allah by His Grace Guided the believers to the Truth, concerning that wherein they differed. For Allah guided whom He will to a path that is straight."
[Surah Al Baqarah (The Cow) 2:213]

It is this open-mindedness of the believer and positive thinking that allows the believer to recognize the truth from inside, regardless of its outward manifestation in colour or form, age, gender or language.

"And if We had appointed the Qur'an in a foreign tongue they would assuredly have said: If only its verses were expounded (so that we might understand)? What! A foreign tongue and an Arab? Say unto them (O Muhammad): For those who believe it is a guidance and a healing; and as for those who disbelieve, there is a deafness in their ears, and it is blindness for them. Such are called to from afar."
[Surah Fussilat (Expounded) 41:44]

Book and Faith

The book, which contains God's word and His commandments, is closely related to the belief (*iman*), which is the quality of softness in the heart and tenderness in the skin. The book is of no benefit except to the person who has *iman*.

Therefore, belief (*iman*) is a precondition for comprehending the book.

> *"And thus have We, by Our Command, sent inspiration to thee: thou knew not (before) what was book, and what was Faith; but We have made the (Qur'an) a Light, wherewith We guide such of Our servants as We will; and verily thou dost guide (men) to the Straight Way."*
> [Surah Ash Shuraa (The Consultation) 42: 52]

A heart that is already dyed with the dye of *iman* will get softer and smoother and expand when reading the book. The heart that is not dyed beforehand with *iman* will only get narrower and more constricted when hearing the book. The book, which is meant to be a benefit, turns into harm for such whose heart is ill-disposed with ill-thinking.

Belief (*Iman*) and Submission (*Tasleem*)

While submission (*tasleem*) can be voluntary or involuntary (through divine compulsion), faith (*iman*) can only be voluntary by choice. Therefore, *Islam* includes all of the following: those who choose to believe and those who choose not to believe.

Belief (*iman*) with respect to *Islam* is like a part of the whole, since *Islam* encompasses everyone, voluntary and involuntary submitters. The voluntary submitters—the believers—are those when they hear the majestic and overbearing commandment as it may be, are capable of experiencing within it a touch of tenderness and mercy. This increases their submission and their faith in God. A believer's good thinking about God turns into love for God:

> *"Yet there are among mankind who take (for worship) others besides Allah, as equal (with Allah): They love them as they should love Allah. But those of faith are overflowing in their love for Allah. If only the unrighteous could see, behold, they would see the*

penalty: that to Allah belongs all power, and Allah will strongly enforce the penalty."
[Surah Al Baqarah (The Cow) 2:165]

On the contrary, those whose hearts do not contain any quality of faith (*iman*) like softness (*leen*) or tenderness (*khuni*), whenever they hear the word of commandment, they can only discern the outer message of overbearing and majestic waning. It makes their hearts only harder and their skin only thicker, further alienating them. They only submit out of compulsion.

"It is He Who has sent His Messenger with Guidance and the Religion of Truth, that he may proclaim it over all religion, even though the Pagans may detest (it)."
[Surah As Saff (The Ranks) 61:9]

The believer's love, hope and tenderness are internal and his fear is only outward. The non-believer's fear however is internal and his love, hope and tenderness are only external and therefore will not stand the real test.

"On the day when the hypocritical men and the hypocritical women will say unto those who believe: Look on us that we may borrow from your light, it will be said: Go back and seek a light! Then there will separate them a wall wherein is a gate, the inner side whereof contains mercy, while the outer side thereof is toward the doom."
[Surah Al Hadid (The Iron) 57:13]

In this verse we see two groups: one group consists of believing men and women. The faith inside their hearts permits them to have a soft heart and tender skin that was tender that expands internally without limitations. However, on the outside, they are wary. They only extend themselves outwardly with caution and calculation. The internal abandonment of love and the external measure and justice permits their hearts to find the right position between internal horizontal expansion and external vertical expansion.

On the other hand, the disbelievers have outward love, hope and softness. But inwardly they have fear and wariness. They expand outwardly with the self-abandonment of love and over-optimism while inwardly they are wary and overly pessimistic. Since the outward is limited and fraught with tribulation, their outward expansion brings them into conflict with others, while their internal contraction deprives them of the unlimited potential that the inside offers them. In the end, the believers who were inwardly expanded but outwardly contracted find themselves within the wall, while the disbelievers who were outwardly expanded but inwardly contracted find themselves on the outside of the wall.

"They know but the outer (things) in the life of this world: but of the End of things they are heedless."
[Surah Ar Rum (The Romans) 30:7]

There is also the *hadith* of the Prophet Muhammed ﷺ:

"Jannah (paradise) is surrounded with dislikable things and hell is surrounded with likable things."

This means that Jannah on the outside is full of tribulations, but on the inside is full of mercy. Therefore, in order to get to Jannah, you must believe in it and that belief must be from inside your heart to correspond to the mercy that is inside Jannah. Tenderness, love and smoothness must reside in your heart as a believer. Since the outside is full of tribulations (*fitnah*), you must exercise caution and self-control in order to stay away from the *fitnah* outside. The free self inside compensates that control and limitation outside.

On the contrary, hellfire has tribulation (*fitnah*) inside but desires the outside. The disbeliever whose heart is outwardly expanded partakes of these outward pleasures with unbridled love and self-abandonment. However, in his heart there is fear and wariness of the inner life and therefore inward contraction. He exercises justice and control internally but self-abandonment externally. Because of the choice he made, he remains outside the wall with all its tribulations, and those who chose the inside go inside the wall where there is mercy.

In sum, in the outer life the believer has a controlled and limited outer life but he or she is compensated by unlimited expansion inwardly through his heart. In the next life, the believer lives unlimited life with little control or calculation. Conversely, the disbeliever had an outer life that is without control or limit, but that outer expansion was paired with an inner contraction and control. In the next life, the disbeliever passes in to a life that is abundantly controlled and calculated with a little opening.

> *"He said: You shall sow seven years as usual, but that which you reap, leave it in the ear, all save a little which you eat. Then after that will come seven hard years which will devour all that you have prepared for them, save a little of that which you have stored. Then, after that, will come a year when the people will have plenteous crops and when they will press (wine and oil)."*
> [*Surah Yusuf* (Joseph) 12:47-49]

Two, Three, Four

We notice also the events and characters in the story of Solomon (*Sulaiman*) are all disposed in sets of two, three and four. These three sets of numbers are also the numbers of prayers in the day. *Fajr* is two, *Maghreb* is three, *Isha, Dhuhr and 'Asr* are all four each. The two refers to all the pairs in two—tree and star, day and night, sun and moon, heaven and earth. The three refers to the three darknesses. The four refers to the four corners of a space (*saad* - the Arabic letter). The one, which is unity or single is always assumed to be in the middle.

The Twos in the Story

Sujud is mentioned twice in the story of Solomon. These two stand for the principle of pairs in the story—the heavens and the earth, the hidden and the apparent.

"I found her and her people worshipping (yasjuduudun) the sun instead of Allah; and Satan makes their works fairseeming unto them, and debarrs them from the way (of Truth), so that they go not aright; so that they worship (yasjuduu) not Allah, Who brings forth the hidden in the heavens and the earth, and knows what you hide and what you proclaim."
[*Surah An Naml* (The Ant) 27:24-25]

Things that Come in Threes

1. The word guidance is mentioned three times, since guidance leads through three darknesses.

"I found her and her people worshipping the sun instead of Allah; and Satan makes their works fair seeming unto them, and debars them from the way (of Truth), so that they receive no guidance."
[*Surah An Naml* (The Ant) 27:24]

"He said: Disguise her throne for her that we may see whether she is guided or be of those not rightly guided."
[*Surah An Naml* (The Ant) 27:41]

2. *Wajd* is mentioned three times as well. *Wajd* means "to get" or "to find" and consequently the ecstasy enjoyed by someone who has found the *Haqq*, the truth. Therefore, the word "*wajd*" is synonymous with certainty (*yaqeen*) because when you get something, you are certain of it—it is true and realized. The first *wajd* refers to (*'ain-al-yaqeen*). The second *wajd* refers to (*'ilm-al-yaqeen*).

> "But the Hoopoe was not long in coming, and he said: I have found out (a thing) that thou apprehends not and I come unto thee from Sheba with sure tidings (yaqeen). Lo! I found a woman ruling over them, and she has been given (abundance) of all things, and hers is a mighty throne. I found her and her people worshipping the sun instead of Allah; and Satan makes their works fairseeming unto them, and debars them from the way (of Truth), so that they go not aright."
> [Surah An Naml (The Ant) 7:22-24]

3. The word 'book' also appears three times in the story of Solomon (*Sulaiman*). One refers to the mother of the book (*ummul-Kitaab*). The other refers to knowledge of the book (*'ilm-ul-Kitaab*). The third refers to the book with definite article, which is the whole book.

> "Go with this my letter (kitaabi) and throw it down unto them; then turn away and see what (answer) they return. (The Queen of Sheba) said (when she received the letter): O chieftains! Lo! There has been thrown unto me a noble letter (kitaabun kareem)."
> [Surah An Naml (The Ant) 27: 28-29]

> "One with whom was knowledge of the Book (al-kitaabi) said: I will bring it thee before thy gaze returns unto thee. And when he saw it set in his presence, (Solomon) said: This is of the bounty of my Lord, that He may try me whether I give thanks or am ungrateful. Whosoever gives thanks he only gives thanks for (the good of) his own soul; and whosoever is ungrateful (is ungrateful only to his own soul's hurt). For lo! my Lord is Absolute in independence, bountiful."
> [Surah An Naml (The Ant) 27:40]

4. *Ru'ya* also appears three times. It means to see in the sense of vision and vision entails dreaming.

> "And he sought among the birds and said: How is it that I see not the hoopoe, or is he among the absent?"
> [Surah An Naml (The Ant) 27:20]

"One with whom was knowledge of the Book said: I will bring it Thee before thy gaze (ra'aahu) returns unto thee."
[*Surah An Naml* (The Ant) 27: 40]

"She was asked to enter the lofty Palace: but when she saw it (ra'at-hu), she thought it was a lake of water, and she (tucked up her skirts), uncovering her legs. He said: "This is but a palace paved smooth with slabs of glass." She said: " O my Lord! I have indeed wronged my soul: I do (now) submit (in Islam), with Solomon, to the Lord of the Worlds."
[*Surah An Naml* (The Ant) 27: 44]

5. Lastly, the word 'bird' appears three times.

"And Solomon was David's heir. And he said: O mankind! Lo! We have been taught the lanruage of birds, and have been given (abundance) of all Things. This surely is evident favour. And before Solomon was marshalled his hosts - of Jinns and men and birds, and they were all kept in order and ranks."
[*Surah An Naml* (The Ant) 27:16-17]

"And he sought among the birds and said: How is it that I see not the hoopoe, or is he among The absent?"
[*Surah An Naml* (The Ant) 27:20]

Things that Come in Fours

Islam - submission which goes through all the pillars and makes the fifth as one. Islam (unconditional submission to God)- is the first and the last because it accompanies one through all the stations.

"Exalt not yourselves against me, but come unto me as those who surrender."
[*Surah An Naml* (The Ant) 27:31]

"He said: O chiefs! Which of you will bring me her throne before they come unto me, surrendering?"

[Surah An Naml (The Ant) 27:38]

"So, when she came, it was said (unto her): Is thy throne like this? She said: (It is) as though it were the very one. And (Solomon said): We were given the knowledge before her and we had surrendered (to Allah)."
[Surah An Naml (The Ant) 27:42]

"She was asked to enter the lofty Palace: but when she saw it, she thought it was a lake of water, and she (tucked up her skirts), uncovering her legs. He said: "This is but a palace paved smooth with slabs of glass." She said: "O my Lord! I have indeed wronged my soul: I do (now) submit (in Islam), with Solomon, to the Lord of the Worlds."
[Surah An Naml (The Ant) 27:44]

2. Commandment ('*amr*) also appears four times in two verses:

"She said: O chieftains! Pronounce (*amree*) for me in my case. I decide (*amran*) no case till you are present with me. They said: We are lords of might and lords of great prowess, but it is for thee to command (*amru*); so consider what thou wilt command (*ta'-mureen*)."
[Surah An Naml (The Ant) 27:32-33]

3. Gratitude (*shukr*):

"So he smiled, amused at her speech; and he said: O my Lord! So order me that I may be grateful for Thy favours, which thou hast bestowed on me and on my parents, and that I may work the righteousness that will please Thee: And admit me, by Thy Grace, to the ranks of Thy righteous Servants."
[Surah An Naml (The Ant) 27:19]

"One with whom was knowledge of the Book said: I will bring it thee before Thy gaze returns unto thee. And when he saw it set in his presence, (Solomon) said: This is of the bounty of my Lord, that He may try me whether I (give thanks or am ungrateful).

Whosoever gives thanks he only gives thanks for (the good of) his own soul; and whosoever is ungrateful (is ungrateful only to his own soul's hurt). For lo! My Lord is Absolute in independence, Bountiful."
[Surah An Naml (The Ant) 27:40]

4. To look and discern (*nadhar*) is mentioned 4 times:

"(Solomon) said: We shall see (sananthzuru) whether thou speaks the truth or whether thou art of the liars. Go with this my letter and throw it down unto them; then turn away and see (fanthzur) what (answer) they return."
[Surah An Naml (The Ant) 27:27-28]

"They said: We are lords of might and lords of great prowess, but it is for thee to command; so consider (fanthzurii) what thou wilt command."
[Surah An Naml (The Ant) 27:33]

"But lo! I am going to send a present unto him, and to see (fanaathziratum) with what (answer) the messengers return."
[Surah An Naml (The Ant) 27:35]

"He said: Disguise her throne for her that we may see (nanthzur) whether she is guided or be of those not rightly guided."
[Surah An Naml (The Ant) 27:41]

Knowledge ('*Ilm*) to Differentiate

"And We verily gave knowledge unto David and Solomon, and they said: Praise be to Allah, Who has preferred us above many of His believing slaves! And Solomon was David's heir. And he said: O mankind! Lo! We have been taught the language of birds, and have been given (abundance) of all things. This surely is evident favour."
[Surah An Naml (The Ant) 27:15-16]

"So that they worship not Allah, Who brings forth the hidden in

the heavens and the earth, and knows what you hide and what you proclaim."
[*Surah An Naml* (The Ant) 27:25]

"One with whom was knowledge of the Book said: I will bring it thee before thy gaze returns unto thee."
[*Surah An Naml* (The Ant) 27:40]

"So, when she came, it was said (unto her): Is thy throne like this? She said: (It is) as though it were the very one. And (Solomon said): We were given the knowledge before her and we had surrendered (to Allah)."
[*Surah An Naml* (The Ant) 27:42]

Positive Thinking and Respect (*Ta'dheem*)

The way we treat the Creator and the creation depends on the way we think of them. If we think well of God, we treat Him with regard and respect, and the same goes for the creation of God. On the other hand, ill-thinking leads us to treat God and His creation with disregard and disrespect.

The degree of our regard and respect (*ta'dheem*) for God and His creation depends on the degree of our positive-mindedness and vice versa. However, the primary cause for that well-thinking (*husn-al-dhann*) is the softness of the heart and the transparency of the skin. The softer and smoother the heart and skin become, the greater the scope of our intuitive sense (*hiss, shu'ur, khafir, khushu'*), which makes everything look magnificent to our heart and hence the origin of respect for everything.

As for those who have a hard heart and a thick skin, they tend to belittle everything and then have little or no regard for God or for creation. This minimizing and belittling attitude stems from narrow-mindedness, stemming from a hard heart and thick skin, only allows them to look at things from the outside. The outside by nature of things is narrow and small while the inside is broad and magnificent. If you look at something from the inside, you will see that broadness and magnificence with it. If you look at it from the outside, you would see narrowness and littleness around it. The believer with a heart that is soft and a skin that is smooth develops an inward look by which he sees things from inside first before the outside. The first impression is always the last impression. If you look at something internally before externally, your impression of it will always remain till the end even though there might have been intermittent periods of outside look and transient negative impressions. However, those negative impressions do not last because they are second to the first positive impressions, which remain stronger and permanent.

On the other hand, if the heart is hard and the skin is thick, its first look is always from the outside, and therefore, the first impression about anything is always negative (calculated and aloof). Therefore, the last impression will also be negative even though the first negative impression might be followed by positive impressions in between. What is first will always be last.

Thus emerge two outlooks: the outlook of a believer who sees inside first and then outside after; and the outlook of a non-believer who sees outside first then inside after.

Following this difference in outlook are their attitudes towards life as well which differ because God created two lives: inner and outer. The believer sees the inner life (*akhirah*) first before the outer (*dunya*). Therefore, his impression of the inner life surpasses his impression of the outer life and that determines his overall attitude towards life in general. Whenever he turns to look at something he first develops an attitude of love, compassion, pardon and abandon, and then justice and calculation after. The first dominates the second. On the contrary, the non-believer looks outward first before inward and as a result his outward impression overrules his inward impression. As such, whenever he turns to look at anything, the first attitude he has is justice and judgment (*'adl*) and then love, mercy, and compassion (*'afu*). The first dominates the second. For this reason, the non-believers' outer look is broad and the inner look is narrow, which means that his heart is wide open to the outer life, but open little towards the inner life. The believer conversely has a broad inner look so that his heart is open towards the inner life but closed except for little towards the outer life.

Therefore, his justice (*'adl*) is little and his pardon (*'afu*) is abundant, whereas for the former, his justice (*'adl*) is abundant but his pardon is little.

> "Whatever misfortune happens to you is because of the things your hands have wrought, and for many (of them) He grants forgiveness."
> [Surah Ash Shuraa (The Consultation) 42:30]

> "Or He can cause them to perish because of the (evil) which (the men) have earned; but much does He forgive."
> [Surah Ash Shuraa (The Consultation) 42:34]

As a consequence of their attitude God will judge them accordingly. He judges the believer mildly with abundance of compassion and a little bit of justice. On the other hand, He judges the disbeliever thoroughly with abundance of justice and a little bit of compassion in accordance with the disbelievers' own view. In a prophetic tradition, God says:

> *My mercy outstrips my anger.*

That is, for the one who sees inward first before the outward, he sees the inward closer and the outward farther. Therefore, God's pardon, mercy and love is closer to him than His justice and anger. On the other hand, the disbeliever sees the outer first and the inner after, therefore the outer, which is justice and anger, is closer than the inner, which is mercy and love. Thus, in a non-believer's case, God's justice and anger outstrips His love and mercy.

"The recompense for an injury is an injury equal thereto (in degree): but if a person forgives and makes reconciliation, his reward is due from Allah: for (Allah) loves not those who do wrong."
[*Surah Ash Shuraa* (The Consultation) 42:40]

"But indeed if any show patience and forgive, that would truly be an exercise of courageous will and resolution in the conduct of affairs."
[*Surah Ash Shuraa* (The Consultation) 42:43]

To sum up, your own attitude determines the kind of judgment you will receive.

"Whoever works righteousness benefits his soul; whoever works evil, it is against his own soul: nor is thy Lord ever unjust (in the least) to His servants."
[*Surah Fussilat* (Expounded) 41:46]

Charity and Justice

The system of governance of a community of believers must include justice beside charity. In their due proportions, justice in relation to charity is like salt in relation to food. You put little salt in the food and the food will taste excellent. However, food without salt is hard to eat. And food with too much salt is also hard to eat.

Therefore, justice (*'adl*) and charity (*'afu*) should be blended together as one blends food and salt in proportion. In practical terms, charity (*'afu*) is the norm and justice is the exception. Exception means something that clearly and unambiguously stands out from the norm, and therefore contravenes it. It means that justice applies only to a case, which is obvious, and beyond all reasonable doubt with no attenuating circumstances. If however, the guilt needs to be proven the innocence is the verdict. By this process, the proportion of justice is rendered little and charity abundant. In all circumstances well-thinking needs to be maintained at all times, even when justice is applied. Just disapproval is directed not at the person who is guilty, but rather against the guilt, unless the guilty insists on his guilt until death whereupon justice applies to this person.

"Those who reject Faith, and die rejecting - on them is Allah's curse, and the curse of angels, and of all mankind; they will abide therein: their penalty will not be lightened, nor will respite be their (lot)."
[Surah Al Baqarah (The Cow) 2:161]

Well-Thinking and Excellence

Excellence indeed stems from excellence in thought and deeds are measured by the intention. The Prophet Muhammadﷺ defined excellence as:

"To adore God as though you see Him, otherwise know that He sees you."

The Prophetﷺ speaks of two kinds of perceptions in this hadith: one that gives you the awareness that you are seeing God and the other that gives you the awareness that God is seeing you. The difference between the two is a matter of procedure. The person who sees inwardly before outwardly has the first perception. For the one with the perception of seeing inside first sees God's mercy, love and pardon, all of which rank as qualities of unity and non-differentiation. He therefore sees God from the point of view of unity where boundaries are lifted.

"Do no mischief on the earth, after it has been set in order, but call on Him with fear and longing (in your hearts): for the Mercy of

> *Allah is (always) near to those who do good."*
> [*Surah Al A'raf* (The Heights) 7:56]

On the other hand, the person who sees outwardly first sees God's justice and overbearing qualities of separation and differentiation. He therefore sees God as a witness above him and separate from him. This perception comes from knowledge, while the former perception comes from faith (*iman*).

The proper procedure is to start with the inner perception of (*iman*) faith, which allows you to see God from the point of view of unity, and then follow with the outer perception of (*'ilm*) knowledge which allows you to see Him from the point of view of separation. The first view allows you to draw near to God with openness of heart. The second view allows you to keep the first in check lest that openness becomes excessive and overextended. In this manner, the heart finds the just middle and settles in peace. Each separate perception constitutes half of *taqwa* and to combine both is all of *taqwa*.

> *"Perfected is the Word of thy Lord in truth and justice. There is naught that can change His words. He is the Hearer, the Knower."*
> [*Surah Al An'am* (The Cattle) 6:115]

However, if the procedure is reversed by taking the outer view before the inner view, the result is different. Taking the outer view first we would experience abundant separation as we witness God's justice and overbearing domination over us. Then when we take the inner perception afterwards, we would view God's mercy and pardon that is narrow and small. Thereby we would not find the just middle; since our little unity cannot match the abundant separation. While the contrary is fine - a little separation can counterbalance abundant unity.

The right procedure then is to begin with the inner perception and end with the outer perception so that abundant (*iman*) faith can pair with little knowledge and abundant mercy can pair with little witnessing. We develop this procedure in dealing with God through our dealings with God's creation. Namely, we should first approach creation with the perception of belief (*iman*), which promotes unity, mercy and love. Thereafter, apply the second perception of knowledge (*'ilm*), which allows us to put a check on our expansivity so that it does not turn into transgression. In this way, we establish the balance (*'adl, 'ilm*) against abundant expansion (*'afu, iman*).

We should not reverse the order by putting little expansion against abundant contraction. In other words, the proportion between inward action (contemplation, reflection, and remembrance) and outward action should be like the proportion between faith (*iman*) and knowledge, or between charity and justice.

Therefore we need abundant stillness and little action in order for the heart to settle down in the just middle. If that proportion is altered the heart's balance would be upset. Since outward action falls under justice any excess of justice over charity is an excess of contraction over expansion thereby counteracting excellence (*ihsan*), balance (*mizan*) and peace (*salam*). Therefore, the individual should have alternating moments of stillness and action in the day as in the night. God chooses things that are still. God says:

"*Everything still in the day and the night is for God.*"
[*Surah Al An'am* (The Cattle) 6:13]

"*It is out of His Mercy that He has made for you Night and Day, that you may rest therein, and that you may seek of his Grace and in order that you may be grateful.*"
[*Surah Al Qasas* (The Narrations) 28:73]

"*And among His Signs is the sleep that you take by night and by day, and the quest that you (make for livelihood) out of His Bounty: verily in that are signs for those who hearken.*"
[*Surah Ar Rum* (The Romans) 30:23]

Stillness in the day and night but also seeking God's favours in the day and night is the way of those who are chosen by God. Stillness in day or night amounts to remembering Him (*dhikr*) while seeking His favours amounts to gratitude (*shukr*). Therefore, alternation between the two is a fulfillment of both remembrance and gratitude.

> "And it is He Who made the Night and the Day to follow each other: for such have the will to celebrate His praises or to show their gratitude."
> [*Surah Al Furqan* (The Criterion) 25:62]

This alternation between periods of stillness and remembrance, and then periods of action and gratitude, gives the heart suppleness and resilience on one hand, and protects it from incrustation and stagnation on the other hand.

However, due proportion must be kept between the two sides, so that little action corresponds to abundant stillness. Action is contractive and stillness is expansive. In other words, action has a definite character and stillness has indefinite character. Definition means qualities and characteristics that distinguish one thing from another. Whereas indefinition is the opposite of that, whereby things are one and the same and there is no difference between them.

From the point of view of (*iman*) faith, everything internally is indefinite, one and indifferent. This is perception given by (*iman*) faith. This perception is also called remembrance (*dhikr*). God says:

> "...remember (*dhikr*) Allah abundantly."

The impact of remembrance (*dhikr*), also known as (*iman*) faith, is to soften the heart and the skin, and allow them to expand. This ability of the believer (*mu'min*) to switch from definite into indefinite, and from action into stillness, allows him to counter the schemes of Satan, who attempts to condition him into one outer vision and as a result traps the heart to be restless and continuously wandering.

"Those who fear Allah, when a thought of evil from Satan assaults them, bring Allah to remembrance, when lo! They see (aright)!"
[*Surah Al A'raf* (The Heights) 7:201]

Common Ground

Despite the fact that all the characters in the story of Solomon (*Sulaiman*) have their distinctive qualities, they all share a common ground, which is belief in the unseen (*iman-bil-ghayb*). This common ground unites them despite their individual differences. These differences did not hinder them from working together to achieve their common goals.

As we see through the story of Solomon and the Queen of Sheba, they served as assets rather than liabilities to the community to which they belonged. These differences were strengths rather than weaknesses for the larger community. By using the individual strengths of each of the characters, Solomon, peace be upon him, was able to succeed in his enterprise of bringing the throne from the unseen to the seen, or rather, from the potential plane to the virtual plane. The unseen is all the realm of infinite possibilities, formless and indefinite. In order for a possibility to turn into reality moving from the unseen to the seen, a certain procedure must be followed to success.

The first step in that procedure is to believe in the unseen. In other words, believe in the infinite possibilities within God's power that everything is possible with God. This constitutes the common ground and it connects the believer to the source of those infinite possibilities. That connection is the inner perception before the outer. After this common ground, individual faculties emerge. For the ant, it is intuition; for the bird it is vision; for the jinni it is hearing; and for the man with knowledge of the book it is sight. They all believed that the throne existed in the unseen potentially, and then they differed according to their individual qualities. The ant felt about it, the bird had a vision of it, the jinni heard of it, and the man with knowledge from the book saw it, and thereafter the throne was virtually in the presence of Solomon, peace be upon him.

Even the Queen of Sheba can be credited with some form of belief before her submission because of her well-thinking which is a fundamental characteristic of a believer. We discern this characteristic in her from the way she responded to King Solomon's letter, she called his letter an honourable letter:

"The queen said: "Ye chiefs! Here is delivered to me - a letter worthy of respect."
[Surah An Naml (The Ant) 27:29]

She developed a positive attitude of respect towards the letter even before she ascertained what was the content of the letter. This indeed is the character of a believer, namely to express positive thinking of everything from the start, even before realizing what that thing really is about. By virtue of this attitude, we succeed in turning everything to our good advantage just as everything turned well for the Queen of Sheba in the end.

The beginning determines the ending. She first thought well of the letter and it turned out well for her at the end. God is what you think of Him. If you think well of Him, you will find He is well for you. If you think ill of Him, your ill thought that you conceived at the beginning grows into real harm at the end.

"Wherever you are, death will find you out, even if you are in towers built up strong and high! If some good befalls them they say, This is from Allah; but if evil, they say, This is from thee (O Prophet). Say: All things are from Allah. But what has come to these people, that they fail to understand a single fact? Whatever good, (O man!) happens to thee, is from Allah; but whatever evil happens to thee, is from thy (own) soul, and We have sent thee as

a messenger to (instruct) mankind. And enough is Allah for a witness."
[Surah An Nisa (The Women) 4:78-79]

Similarly, we find positive thinking expressed by the bird, when he spoke about the throne of the Queen of Sheba. He described her throne as magnificent (*ta'dheem*) and added that she was endowed with every kind of favour from God. We see that the bird spoke of the Queen of Sheba with respect and dignity even though she and her people were, at that time, committing the gravest sin of shirk by worshipping the sun in partnership to God, Lord of the Magnificent Throne. The hoopoe deplored their condition and hoped for them that they would come to recognize God as their sole Creator and benefactor.

"I found (there) a woman ruling over them and provided with abundance of all things; and she has a magnificent throne. I found her and her people worshipping the sun besides Allah: Satan has made their deeds seem pleasing in their eyes, and has kept them away from the Path, so they receive no guidance, so that they worship not Allah, Who brings forth the hidden in the heavens and the earth, and knows what you hide and what you proclaim."
[Surah An Naml (The Ant) 27:23-25]

The good opinion that the hoopoe had of the Queen and her people came to materialize when she and her people accepted *Islam* at the end. The ant also demonstrated this well-thinking of others which was attested by the warning she gave to her nation when she sensed Solomon and his hosts approaching. She said:

"...enter your habitations lest Solomon and his hosts crush you when they are unaware."
[Surah An Naml (The Ant) 27:18]

She thought well of Solomon and those with him that they would not deliberately destroy a life even if it is the life of a creature as tiny as an ant. Solomon and his hosts were a nation of believers like the ant and her nation, and the life of one believer is sacred to another. For that reason, a nation of believers cannot attack another nation if that nation is a mixture of believers and non-believers, for fear that harm will come to the believers. For this reason, the Prophet Muhammadﷺ, and his faithful companions, were held back by God from making a forceful entry into Mecca for fear that harm will come to the many believing men and women who still remained in Mecca and could not migrate to Medina for one reason or another.

"They are the ones who denied Revelation and hindered you from the Sacred Mosque and tie sacrificial animals, detained from reaching their place of sacrifice. Had there not been believing men and believing women whom you did not know that you were trampling down and on whose account a crime would have accrued to you without (your) knowledge, (Allah would have allowed you to force your way, but He held back your hands) that He may admit to His Mercy whom He will. If they had been apart, We should certainly have punished the Unbelievers among them with a grievous Punishment."
[*Surah Al Fath* (The Victory) 48:25]

In a similar manner, the ant thought well of Solomon and his army that they would not intentionally bring harm to anyone who is innocent. Solomon was able to hear her speech and he thanked God for not only allowing him to understand the speech of ants, but also for saving him from doing wrong to anyone, even if it was not deliberate.

"Till, when they reached the Valley of the Ants, an ant exclaimed: O ants! Enter your dwellings lest Solomon and his armies crush you, unperceiving. So he smiled, amused at her speech; and he said: O my Lord! So order me that I may be grateful for Thy favours, which thou hast bestowed on me and on my parents, and that I may work the righteousness that will please Thee: And admit me, by Thy Grace, to the ranks of Thy righteous Servants."
[*Surah An Naml* (The Ant) 27:18-19]

We find similar open-mindedness and positive thinking with the *jinni* as well, when he said:

> "I can bring it (the throne) before you rise from your seat, for indeed I am strong and trustworthy to take care of it."
> [Surah An Naml (The Ant) 27:39]

This statement of the *jinni* is not self-praise or boasting. Rather, this is known as thinking well of oneself. After all, thinking well of others comes from thinking well of oneself first, and thinking ill of others comes from thinking ill of oneself. Therefore, the change begins with oneself. If one thinks well of himself, certainly he would think well of God and then of everything and everyone. Similarly, if he thinks ill of himself, he would think ill of God and of everything and everyone. For this reason, the *jinni* spoke of himself as strong and trustworthy. Strength and trustworthiness are qualities of a (*siddiq*) sincere believer. Since these qualities are not always apparent, it was good that the *jinni*, as a (*siddiq*) sincere believer, verbalised it in order that he may use that strength and trustworthiness to help a good cause.

> "Said an 'Ifrit, of the Jinns: I will bring it to thee before thou rise from thy council: Indeed I have full strength for the purpose, and may be trusted."
> [Surah An Naml (The Ant) 27:39]

In a similar manner, Prophet Joseph (*Yusuf*) peace be upon him, expressed to the King of Egypt that he was a good keeper and knowledgeable, two qualities necessary to take good care of the trust of the treasury.

> "(Joseph) said: Set me over the store-houses of the land: I will indeed guard them, as one that knows (their importance)."
> [Surah Yusuf (Joseph) 12:55]

In fact this quality of a good keeper (*hafiz*) is a trust given to him by God, in order that he may use it to help those who are in need of help, in particular to use this quality towards the way of God. If he were to remain silent about it this would amount to hiding it, which would be a breach of trust.

> "O you who believe! Betray not Allah and His messenger, nor knowingly betray your trusts."
> [Surah Al Anfal (The Spoils of War) 8:27]

On the other hand, Prophet Joseph (*Yusuf*) also delivered the witnessing which was given to him as a favour from God. By witnessing we mean knowledge, for every man of knowledge is a witness who stands for God and His commandments. If he were to remain silent about what he knew his silence would be a breach of witnessing. God sternly warns those who hide knowledge and more so who make false witnessing.

> "Allah commands you to render back your Trusts to those to whom they are due; And when you judge between man and man that you judge with justice: Verily how excellent is the teaching which He gives you! For Allah is He Who hears and sees all things."
> [Surah An Nisa (The Women) 4:58]

> "Those who faithfully observe their trusts and their covenants."
> [Surah Al Mu'minun (The Believers) 23:8]

> "And those who respect their trusts and covenants; And those who stand firm in their testimonies."
> [Surah Al Ma'arij (The Ladder Steps) 70:32-33]

Prophet Joseph (*Yusuf*), peace be upon him, was both a trustee and a witness for he was endowed with both knowledge and belief (sincerity). As a (*siddiq*) sincere believer, God has endowed him with strength to keep the trust, and as a witness (*shahid*), he is endowed with judiciousness and circumspection. In these capacities, he combines the faculties of both the *Ifrit* (*jinn*) and the man with knowledge of the book – characters in the story of Solomon. In that story, the *Ifrit* was a (*siddiq*) sincere believer who had the strength to bring the throne of the Queen of Sheba in the period between sitting and standing. The man with knowledge from the book was a (*shahid*) witness who had the might to bring the throne of the Queen within a blink of an eye.

As Prophet Joseph (*Yusuf*), peace be upon him, did in his story, both *jinni* and the man were prompted in delivering their trust and witnessing when Solomon made a request of help. The *jinni* said:

"Said an 'Ifrit, of the Jinns: 'I will bring it to thee before thou rise from thy council: indeed I have full strength for the purpose, and may be trusted.'"
[*Surah An Naml* (The Ant) 27:39]

And the man with knowledge of the book said:

"Said one who had knowledge of the Book: 'I will bring it to thee within the twinkling of an eye!'"
[*Surah An Naml* (The Ant) 27:40]

Their promptness in responding to the request of Solomon testifies to their awareness regarding the consequences of hiding what God had given to them in trust.

"Or do you say that Abraham, Isma'il, Isaac, Jacob and the Tribes were Jews or Christians? Say: Do you know better than Allah? Ah! Who is more unjust than those who conceal the testimony they have from Allah? But Allah is not unmindful of what you do!"
[*Surah Al Baqarah* (The Cow) 2:140]

"If you are on a journey, and cannot find a scribe, a pledge with possession (may serve the purpose). And if one of you deposits a thing on trust with another, let the trustee (faithfully) discharge His trust, and let him fear his Lord. Conceal not evidence; for whoever conceals it, his heart is tainted with sin. And Allah knows all that you do."

[*Surah Al Baqarah* (The Cow) 2:283]

"O you who believe! Stand out firmly for Allah, as witnesses to fair dealing, and let not the hatred of others to you make you swerve to wrong and depart from justice. Be just: that is next to piety: and fear Allah. For Allah is well-acquainted with all that you do."
[*Surah Al Ma'idah* (The Table Spread) 5:8]

"O you who believe! Stand out firmly for justice, as witnesses to Allah, even as against yourselves, or your parents, or your kin, and whether it be (against) rich or poor: for Allah can best protect both. Follow not the lusts (of your hearts), lest you swerve, and if you distort justice or decline to do justice, verily Allah is well-acquainted with all that you do." [*Surah An Nisa* (The Women) 4:135]

As well, it is narrated in a prophetic tradition ﷺ:

"That whosoever hides a knowledge, God will bridle him with a bridle of fire in the hereafter."

It must be noted that strength, as a trust, comes in many forms, including money and children. Therefore, those who hold back money and do not spend it in the way of God, or for those in need have committed a breach of trust and have abused their power as vicegerent (*khalifah*) of God.

"Believe in Allah and His messenger, and spend (in charity) out of the (substance) whereof He has made you heirs. For those of you who believe and spend (in charity) - for them is a great Reward."
[*Surah Al Hadid* (The Iron) 57:7]

On the other hand, the person who has knowledge from God is a *khalifah* of Allah and he must express that knowledge by calling people to be just and upright while he himself walks on the straight path. God mentions both groups of people as parables so that people can reflect:

"Allah sets forth the Parable (of two men) one a slave under the dominion of another; He has no power of any sort; and (the other) a man on whom We have bestowed goodly favours from Ourselves, and he spends thereof (freely), privately and publicly: are the two equal? (By no means;) praise be to Allah. But most of them understand not. Allah sets forth (another) Parable of two men: one of them dumb, with no power of any sort, a wearisome burden is he to his master; whichever way he directs him, he brings no good: is such a man equal with one who commands Justice, and is on a Straight Way?"
[*Surah An Nahl* (The Bee) 16:75-76]

Whosoever fulfills these two obligations has fulfilled all the words of God (*kalimaatullah*).

"Perfected is the Word of thy Lord in truth and justice. There is naught that can change His words. He is the Hearer, the Knower."
[*Surah Al An'am* (The Cattle) 6:115]

Mercy and Knowledge

Of all the divine attributes, the attributes of Mercy and Knowledge are the two most comprehensive and most absolute and the rest of the divine attributes are but their derivatives with various connotations. In various Qur'anic verses God refers to His Mercy and His Knowledge as encompassing everything. God says:

"Those who carry the throne and those who stand around it they glorify and praise their Lord and they believe in Him; they ask forgiveness for those who believe (saying): O' Our Lord your Mercy and your Knowledge comprehend everything. Grant forgiveness to those who have repented and follow your way and safeguard them from the punishment of Hell."
[*Surah Al Ghafir* (The Forgiver) 40:7]

"Indeed your Lord is Allah and there is no other deity except He, His Knowledge comprehends everything."
[*Surah TaHa* (TaHa) 20:98]

"And write for us in this life a goodly reward and in the life hereafter, we have turned to you, He said: My punishment is dealt to whom I wish and My Mercy comprehends everything, I will indeed write it for those who safeguard their sound nature (taqwa) and give alms and those who believe in Our Signs."
[*Surah Al 'Araf* (The Heights) 7:156]

Now if we look through the Qur'an we will find no other attribute of God that is said to comprehend everything except His Mercy and His Knowledge. His Mercy and His Knowledge are manifestations of His two names: 1) *Ar-Rahman* (The All-Merciful), the name attributing to His Mercy, 2) *Allah*, the name attributing to His Knowledge. These two names are linked together as the two from which all other names and qualities are derived. Qur'an states:

"Say (O Muhammad), call (invoke) Allah or invoke Ar-Rahman (All-Merciful) whichever name you invoke Him by, indeed all the excellent names belong to Him; do not call loud your invocations nor make it silent, find a way in between."
[*Surah Al Isra* (The Night Journey) 17:110]

We see in this verse that these two names are taken to be the origin of all the other names and attributes. We still find further evidence about these two names (*Allah, Ar-Rahman*) as the prototypes of all other divine names and attributes in Qur'an, where it says:

"It is He Allah, and there is no God but He, possessor of the knowledge of the unseen (Inner) and the seen (Outer), it is He Ar-Rahman (All-Merciful) the bestower of Mercy (Ar-Raheem). It is He Allah, and there is no God but He, the Ruler, the Holy, the Peace, the Believer, the Over-seer, the Magnificent, the Overwhelmer, the Mighty, He is most exalted beyond, to have partners. It is He Allah, the Creator, the Wholesomer, the Fashioner, the Excellent names belong to Him. All those in the heavens and the earth glorify Him, and it is He the Magnificent and the Most Wise."
[*Surah Al Hashr* (The Gathering) 59:22-24]

With a careful look at the verses we will find that the first attribute that is attached to the name '*Allah*' is Knowledge; Knower of the unseen and the seen. However the name *Ar-Rahman* is given a separate treatment by placing the words 'it is He', therefore, it is He, *Allah*, the Knower and it is He *Ar-Rahman*, the Merciful. The first attribute following *Allah* is Knowledge and the first attribute following *Ar-Rahman* is Mercy. In fact, the names *Ar-Rahman* like *Allah* are both proper names of God and have no equivalent and they are not translatable. To translate it as the All-Merciful is not really accurate, therefore, like *Allah*, *Ar-Rahman* should be quoted verbatim without giving it a translation. Furthermore if we examine the three verses of *Surah Al Hashr* (59:22-24) we will see that the rest of the attributes that came after these two proper names of God: *Allah* and *Ar-Rahman*, are derivatives of these two.

The Perfect Teaching

A perfect teaching, that is a teaching that is universal must consist of Mercy and Knowledge. Mercy (*Rahmah*) gives it grace and beauty; "God is beautiful and loves beauty." Knowledge gives it strength and grandeur; a strong believer is better and dearer to God than a weak one" as narrated in a *hadith*. Therefore, the perfect teacher or the universal teacher must reflect these two qualities of God: Mercy and Knowledge. Otherwise, a teaching that comprises only of mercy, it is like flesh without bones. On the other hand the teaching that consists only of knowledge, it is like bones without flesh. The flesh gives grace and beauty to the body and the bones and muscles give strength and support; the body will not be complete without one or the other. The teaching of a perfect teacher must combine grace and beauty on the one hand with strength and majesty on the other. These were the descriptions given to us in the Qur'an about the teacher assigned to Moses by the All-Mighty Allah. Their story is related in *Surah Al Kahf*, the Chapter of the Cave in verses 60-72. The teacher is described in the following words:

"They (both) found a servant from among our servants, We have bestowed on him a Mercy from Us, and We have given him a Knowledge from our presence."
[*Surah Al Kahf* (The Cave) 18:65]

This servant of God is said to have received mercy and knowledge from God and in this capacity he is fit to be a guide and a teacher. The mercy that he received from his Lord lends grace and beauty to his teaching and the knowledge that he received from Him lends strength and majesty to his teaching as well. He, thus, feeds his disciples a healthy balanced diet made up of cream and honey. Milk or cream lends grace and beauty to our skin and our hair. It gives it smoothness, suppleness and tenderness and allows it to grow and expand. Things that are tender and flexible are able to grow and expand and things that are hard and inflexible are not able to grow and multiply. That growth and expansion is what constitutes strength but that strength comes out of tenderness and gentleness.

As long as that tenderness and gentleness is within a creation, it will continue to live, meaning, to grow and multiply, a living being is nothing but a thing that is growing and expanding. When the core ceases to be tender and gentle then that thing ceases to grow and expand. When it ceases to grow and expand it becomes neither dead nor alive.

For death proper is the state of tenderness and gentleness and life is the state of growth and expansion, therefore, strength and solidity. To be in limbo between death and life is what constitutes the painful condition of suspense or void and emptiness, which is the hell in this world and the Hereafter. God says with regards to those who neither embrace full life nor full death:

"The one who enters into the great fire, and then he neither dies in it nor does he live."
[*Surah Al A'la* (The Most High) 87:12-13]

For if he dies he will be in a state of bliss and if he lives he will also be happy. However, he neither lives, nor does he die. Knowing that death could be a relief, the dwellers of hell beg to die.

"They say, O Malik tell your Lord to reduce us to death, he replies: you are going to stay on."
[*Surah Az Zukhruf* (The Gold Adornments) 43:77]

"Those who were in denial (kafirun) their reward is hell. They are neither put completely to death nor do they get relief from its punishment."
[*Surah Al Fatir* (The Originator of Creation) 35:36]

Death, therefore, is as blissful as life and the state of neither life or death is what is painful. So the condition of pain of those in the hellfire does not result merely from the fire, it rather results from their internal condition of neither death nor life. If we assume that a person in a complete state of death or complete state of life was put in the hellfire he will certainly feel nothing except coolness and peace. Abraham, in the fire, is a parable set by God to illustrate this reality.

The Two Forms of Existence

There are only two forms of existence, or two conditions of actual being. One is called death (*mawt*), the other is called life (*hayat*). The intermediate state that lies between the two is the actual state of non-existence or non-realisation.

It is the being in the void, the state of emptiness, commonly called death for lack of better expression. By death we mean the state of primary creation called *fitrah*, the state of clay and water, which is the state of tenderness and gentleness. Out of this state of tenderness and gentleness from clay and water He brought out life by blowing His Spirit into it. The spirit (*ruh*) was accompanied by His Word, which is called the logos (*kalmah*). The spirit (*ruh*) is a vehicle for the logos. Now we have the clay and the water on the one hand and the spirit and the logos on the other, out of the union of these four comes the perfect human being. God relates to us in the Qur'an that Jesus, like Adam, was created in this way and they are the two prototypes of human creation. Allah says:

"The likeness of Isa (Jesus) in the eyes of God is like the likeness of Adam; He created him out of clay and then called 'be' and he becomes."
[Surah Al Imran (The Family of Imran) 3:59]

Here two things deserve our attention: 1) the fact that God's word 'be' (*kun*) that combines both the word (logos) and the spirit (Holy Spirit, espiritus sanctus), 2) the becoming is not in a simple past tense like 'he said 'be' and he was', rather, 'he becomes' that is the "becoming" is in a progressive tense meaning he is continuously for ever in the becoming, meaning growing, expanding and living forever. This is the state of the perfect human being called *'Bashar'*. Only when a human being rises freshly out of clay and water then he or she is called *'Bashar'*.

In general, he or she is called *'insaan'*, especially when he or she is identified as a creature made up of blood and flesh. From the word *'Bashar'*, comes the word *'Bushra'* and *'Bishara'*, meaning glad- tidings or good news. It means that when the human being is in a state of natural sound condition of clay, water, word and spirit, he is promised the mercy of God and the knowledge from God. God says with regards to the state of *'Bashar'*:

"Among His (God's) signs is that he formed you out of clay and there on you become (Bashar) humans of perfect condition, spreading and multiplying."
[*Surah Ar Rum* (The Romans) 30:20]

It is only in this capacity that the human being is called *'Bashar.'* It is said of the Holy Spirit, when it presented itself to Mary that it was a complete *'Bashar'* or *'Basharan Sawiyyah'*. In the Qur'an Allah says:

"She withdrew herself from them and then We send Our Spirit to her and it appeared to her as a complete human form (Basharan Sawiyyah)."
[*Surah Maryam* (Mary) 19:17]

Indeed being a *'Bashar'*, a human being in his complete disposition, he brought *bishara* (glad-tidings) regarding the birth of a holy child, Jesus. That holy child is a mercy and sign from God:

He said: Even so; your Lord says: It is easy to Me: and that We may

make him a sign to men and a mercy from Us, and it is a matter which has been decreed."
[*Surah Maryam* (Mary) 19:21]

Therefore, Jesus was formed out of clay and water by the hand of God like Adam and then the spirit (*ruh*) and the word (*kalmah*) were introduced into that form of clay and water directly by God Himself and then it was given to the angel to introduce the whole into the womb of the virgin Mary. In the womb of the virgin the child was to take on the human flesh, blood and bones. Unlike other children that are usually born out of desire between blood and flesh, Jesus and Adam were made out of clay and water and the spirit and the word (logos) were blown into that clay form '*Bashar*'. As long as this condition of good natural disposition prevails, the person is promised God's Mercy (*Bishara, Rahmah*) and it continues to shower upon them and if they change this good natural disposition (*fitrah*) the *rahmah* ceases to fall on them and they enter into a state called '*fitnah*' of non-death and non-life. Therefore, God sent the messengers to promise and to warn. They are bringers of glad tidings (*Bashiran*) to their people about the Mercy of God, as long as they keep their natural disposition (of clay, water, word, and spirit). They are warners (*naziran*) against altering the natural disposition given by God, which will invite on them pain and agony of non-life and non-death.

Mercy (*Rahmah*) and Safe-Guarding (*Taqwa*)

Taqwa commonly translated as fear, in fact means to safe-guard, which is an aspect of God's reverence. What is it that we have to safe-guard? It is our divinely given natural disposition that we have to preserve and safeguard. If we safeguard our natural disposition of clay, water, word and spirit, then we are entitled to receive God's Mercy. For this reason, *taqwa* and *rahmah* are closely mentioned together in the Qur'an. God says:

"*And if Qur'an is recited listen to it and be silent perhaps you will*

receive Mercy."
[*Surah Al A'raf* (The Heights) 7:204]

In this verse, while mercy is mentioned literally by the word *'turhamoon'* which is *'rahmah'*, *taqwa* is implied by mentioning its prerequisites namely: listening and silence out of reverence for God. If anyone wishes to safeguard his good natural disposition he should listen well and be silent. By force of silence and listening he or she will eventually hear God speaking to him or her. God says:

"Indeed believers are all brothers, therefore, reconcile between your two brothers and safeguard yourself out of reverence for God (taqwa-llah) perhaps you will receive His Mercy."
[*Surah Hujurat* (The Inner Apartments) 49:10]

Here both *taqwa* and *rahmah* are textually mentioned. God says:

"And His is a book that we have sent down, it is blessed, follow it and have Taqwa (safeguard yourself) perhaps you will receive Mercy (Rahmah)."
[*Surah Al An'am* (The Cattle) 6:155]

"O ye who believe, if you safeguard yourself in reverence of Allah (Taqwa) he will grant you furqan (a light to distinguish truth from falsehood) and he will take away your iniquities and He will transform your wrong deeds into virtuous deeds, for Allah is indeed the Lord of the Magnificent blessing."
[*Surah Al Anfal* (The Spoils of War) 8:29]

Here mercy (*rahmah*) is implied under the name of the magnificent blessing which washes away our iniquities and transforms evil into good. God says:

"O ye who believe, safeguard yourselves out of reverence to Allah and believe in His messenger, He will grant two measures of His Mercy and will give you a light to walk by (Furqan: the light by

which we distinguish truth from falsehood) and he will transform your ill-deeds into virtuous ones for indeed Allah is most forgiving and Merciful."
[Surah Al Hadid [The Iron] (57:28)

"Whoever guards himself out of reverence of Allah, He will make for him an opening (a way out) and provide for him from where he least expects it..."
[Surah At Talaq (The Divorce) 65:2-3]

Here in this verse *taqwa* is mentioned in text and *rahmah* (mercy) is implied by the mention of its effects: 1) the opening of the locks, 2) the provision (*rizq*) coming from where we do not expect. Indeed the '*rahmah*' of Allah is close to those who are gracious. Finally, with regards to *taqwa*, God says:

"O ye Humankind, We have created you out of a single male and female, and we have divided you into nations and tribes that you may identify each other; indeed the most honoured among you is the one who safeguards himself the most out of reverence to Allah."
[Surah Al Hujurat (The Inner Apartments) 49:13]

The Twin Fruits of *Taqwa*

By examining the past verses, we observe that in return for *taqwa*, God promises two things: *rahmah* (mercy) and *furqan* (distinguisher) or *nur* (a light) that means a light by which we can distinguish between true and false. This *furqan* or this *nur* (light) mentioned respectively in *Surah Al Anfal*, verse 29 and *Surah Al Hadid*, verse 28, is none other than Knowledge ('*ilm*). Knowledge is a light by which we can distinguish between true and false. Therefore, *taqwa* bears two kinds of fruits; one is the fruit of mercy, which gives grace, and beauty and other is the fruit of knowledge, which gives us strength and uprightness. God says:

"Every fruit comes in pairs."
[Surah Ar Rahman (The Most Gracious) 55:52]

Therefore, every life in its sound disposition (*taqwa*) is able to receive two lights: 1) the light of knowledge and 2) the light of mercy (*rahmah*). These two lights proceed from the two names *Allah* and *Ar-Rahman*.

Tranquility and Mercy

Tranquility (*sakinah*) is one of the manifestations of mercy. Namely it is the stars of mercy, also known as the stars of revelation of Qur'an. Now the distinctive qualities of these stars among all other luminaries are that in their substance they contain grace, beauty and extreme coolness to the freezing point. It is from the word coolness (*sukoon*) that the name '*sakinah*' is derived. *Sukoon* means coolness, tranquility, and calmness. This is the salient characteristic of these stars. So each time that God wishes to communicate a secret to a dear servant of His, He would command the stars to lower themselves upon the dear servant. This lowering of the stars is known as prostration (*sujud*) of the stars:

> "And the star and the tree bow down in prostrations."
> [Surah Ar Rahman (The Most Gracious) 55:6]

The purpose of this lowering of stars is for two reasons. The first, to bring the servant into a complete state of calmness outwardly, his skin, and inwardly, his heart.

> "Allah is the One who has revealed a record, a book in identical pairs which (at first) causes their skin and their hearts to contract, thereafter, their skin becomes smooth and tender."
> [Surah Az Zumar (The Crowds) 39:23]

This tenderness and smoothness of the skin and the heart is a sign of calmness and relaxation and silence. This servant is well disposed to receive the divine communication without let or hindrance, his entire disposition is level without bump or twist and he therefore absorbs the communication with his entire being. The second purpose of the lowering of the stars is to keep away any disruptive agent from interfering with the process of divine communication. If such agents, like devils, try to meddle they are frozen to a standstill by the stars. Allah says about such alien interferers that:

"They are driven away from listening."
[*Surah Ash Shu'ara* (The Poets) 26:212]

"If We wished We would cause them to be frozen on the spot neither able to go forward or back."
[*Surah Ya Seen* (Ya Seen) 36:67]

Besides foiling the interference, it saves the recipient from any distraction so that the communication goes through completely without anything being missed.

This lowering of the stars is called the descent of the *sakinah*. It is mentioned in the following verses in the Qur'an:

"It is He Who sent down tranquility (sakinah) into the hearts of the Believers, that they may add faith to their faith; for to Allah belong the Forces of the heavens and the earth; and Allah is Full of Knowledge and Wisdom."
[*Surah Al Fath* (The Victory) 48:4]

"Allah was well pleased with the believers when they swore allegiance unto thee beneath the tree, and He knew what was in their hearts, and He sent down peace of reassurance on them, and hath rewarded them with a near victory."
[*Surah Al Fath* (The Victory) 48:18]

"When those who disbelieved harbored in their hearts (feelings of) disdain, the disdain of (the days of) ignorance, but Allah sent down His tranquility on His Messenger and on the believers, and made them keep the word of guarding (against evil), and they were entitled to it and worthy of it; and Allah is Knower of all things."
[*Surah Al Fath* (The Victory) 48:26]

"And their Prophet said unto them: Lo! The token of his kingdom is that there shall come unto you the ark wherein is peace of reassurance from your Lord, and a remnant of that which the house of Moses and the house of Aaron left behind, the angels bearing it. Lo! Herein shall be a token for you if (in truth) ye are believers."
[Surah Al Baqarah (The Cow) 2:248]

"If ye help him not, still Allah helped him when those who disbelieve drove him forth, the second of two; when they two were in the cave, when he said unto his comrade: Grieve not. Lo! Allah is with us. Then Allah caused His peace of reassurance to descend upon him and supported him with hosts ye cannot see, and made the word of those who disbelieved the nethermost, while Allah's Word it was that becamewho disbelieved the nethermost, while Allah's Word it was that became the uppermost. Allah is Mighty, Wise."
[Surah At Tawbah (The Repentance) 9:40]

In all these verses where the word 'sakinah' occurs it means the stars of revelation or the light that proceed from them. In many other verses it is mentioned under the name star, 'najm', for example in *Surah Ar Rahman*, the tree and the star are bowing in prostration (*sujud*). God says:

"Indeed I take oath by the stars when they fall (in sujud) in prostration."
[Surah Al Waqi'ah (The Inevitable Event) 56:75]

In subsequent verses the phenomenon of the prostration of the stars is linked to the revelation of the Qur'an:

"It indeed is a magnificent oath if only you knew, it is the glorious Qur'an. In a book that is well-protected, to be touched only by those who are in a state of purity."
[Surah Al Waqi'ah (The Inevitable Event) 56:76-80]

Internal purity of the heart will allow you to touch the well-guarded knowledge it contains, the outer purity will allow you to recite it and study its exterior. There is again a link between the revelation and the stars:

> "He has written/taught Qur'an, He has created the human being, and He taught him well-articulated speech. The sun and the moon are counting through their movement in their orbit (time). The tree and the star are in prostration."
> [Surah Ar Rahman (The Most Gracious) 55:1-5]

The scenario of the lowering of the stars and the moon and the sun is repeated each time God chooses to communicate His Words to a selected servant of His, such as in the story of Joseph and Abraham. Joseph had a vision of 11 stars, the sun and the moon bowing down in prostration to him. What happened was that the stars lowered themselves upon Joseph for the purposes that were mentioned above because God chose to communicate His commandments to him. The additional presence of the moon and the sun is indicative of him being a Prophet and a Messenger. For the sign of Prophethood is stars, and the sun and the moon symbolize Messengership. Likewise, in the story of Abraham we see the presence of a star signifying Prophethood and the sun and the moon signifying Messengership:

> "Thus did We show Abraham the kingdom of the heavens and the earth that he might be of those possessing certitude: When the night grew dark upon him he beheld a star. He said: This is my Lord. But when it set, he said: I love not things that set. And when he saw the moon uprising, he exclaimed: This is my Lord. But when it set, he said: Unless my Lord guide me, I surely shall become one of the folk who are astray. And when he saw the sun uprising, he cried: This is my Lord! This is greater! And when it set he exclaimed: O my people! Lo! I am free from all that ye associate (with Him). Lo! I have turned my face toward Him Who created the heavens and the earth, as one by nature upright, and I am not of the idolaters."
> [Surah Al An'am (The Cattle) 6:75-79]

In another chapter called the star (*najm*), both the star and the tree called (*sidra*) are mentioned together:

"By the Star when it setteth, your Companion is neither astray nor being misled. Nor does he speak out of desire. It is naught save an inspiration that is inspired, He was taught by one Mighty in Power, one vigorous; and he grew clear to view when he was on the uppermost horizon. Then he drew nigh and came down till he was (distant) two bows' length or even nearer, and He revealed unto His slave that which He revealed. The (Prophet's) (mind and) heart in no way falsified that which he saw. Will ye then dispute with him concerning what he seeth? And verily he saw him yet another time, by the lote-tree of the utmost boundary, Nigh unto which is the Garden of Abode. Behold, the Lote-tree was shrouded (in mystery unspeakable!), the eye did not turn aside, nor did it exceed the limit. Verily he saw one of the greater revelations of his Lord."
[Surah An Najm (The Star) 53:1-18]

Three Modes of Divine Communication

God communicates to those he has chosen to speak to through His Word (*Kalam*) in three ways: 1) by direct intuitive communication '*wahy*' 2) behind a veil '*hijab*' and 3) by the intermediary of an angel. However, before any such communication can take place, one major requirement must be fulfilled; namely that the receiver of the communication must be in a state of *fitrah* - natural sound disposition in which he was first created, meaning clay, water, word and spirit. If the person is born a prophet they always retain their '*fitrah*' (natural sound disposition) and therefore they never undergo any formal disciplining or preparation (*suluk*). If the person is born a non-prophet, then he or she will have to go through a certain amount of disciplining and preparation to regain their lost *fitrah* – natural sound disposition. However, acquired qualities are never like native qualities. Native qualities are unalterable and effortless, while acquired qualities are alterable and come with effort and must be maintained with effort.

Once this condition is fulfilled and the person is called *'Bashar'* meaning a human being freshly raised out of clay and water, then God will communicate to him. God says:

"No Bashar, human being in his fitra, has the right to be spoken to by God through His Word (Kalam) except if it be inspiration (wahy) or from behind a veil, or that he sends a messenger to reveal by his permission what was His wish. Indeed God is most Exalted and most Judicious."
[*Surah Ash Shura* (The Poets) 42:51]

The first mode of communication (*wahy*) is called inspiration. It is the universal speech of God that is addressed to all creation. Those who are alert hear it and those who are not alert miss it. In *Surah An Nahl*, verse 68, God is said to have inspired the bees to build their houses and to collect nectar and pollen and make honey. This kind of inspiration (*wahy*) is general and the bees being alert, meaning in their sound disposition, heard it and obeyed.

The difference between this '*wahy*' and that of the prophet is that the prophet's inspiration is accompanied by the presence of stars for a particular purpose. As for the last two modes of communication, behind the veil and the intermediation, it is strictly restricted to Prophets and Messengers. For Moses, it was mainly the second mode, and for Prophet Muhammad ﷺ it was mainly the third.

The Double Measures of Mercy (*Rahmah*)

God says: "O ye who believe, safeguard yourself in reverence of Allah (Taqwa) and believe in His Messenger, and He will bestow upon you a double measure of His Mercy."
[*Surah Al Hadid* (The Iron) 57:28]

Therefore, mercy has two measures. The first one is the mercy of the Inner world known as *'Akhirah'* or *'Malakut'* that is the inner dimension of God's Kingdom. To this Inner Kingdom belongs the Inner Mercy. The second one is the Outer Mercy and this is the mercy of the Outer world called *'Dunya'* or *'Mulk'*, meaning the outer dimension of God's Kingdom, therefore, this outer dimension is sustained by His External Mercy. So all the blessings of the Inner Kingdom result from the Inner Mercy and all the blessings of the Outer Kingdom result from the Outer Mercy. God says:

"Have ye not seen that God has subjected the heaven and the earth to your service and He has bestowed upon you His blessings outwardly and inwardly..."
[Surah Luqman (Luqman) 31:20]

In total there are a hundred mercies and the proportion of the outer to the inner is one to ninety-nine. Out of the one hundred mercies only one has been spread across the outer world and all the blessings in the physical world have resulted from that single mercy. If there are so many blessings upon the earth how much more would there be in the unseen kingdom.

There are some who seek the blessing of the outer world to the total exclusion of inner blessings. There are others who seek the inner blessings exclusively with absolute disregard of the outer blessings of the Outer Kingdom. The former have no share in the Inner Kingdom, and the latter have no share in the Outer Kingdom. There is however a third group who seek the outer blessings of this Kingdom and the inner blessings in the Coming Kingdom. They say to their Lord:

"O Our Lord grant us a life of excellence in this world and a life of excellence in the Hereafter and safeguard us from the Fire."
[Surah Al Baqarah (The Cow) 2:201]

The 'fire' in the above verse meaning the fire of this world and the next world. They are the people of *taqwa* and they are given the double measure of mercy, the one of the Inner and the Outer Kingdoms. They are the ones who have maintained the balance with neither transgression nor deficiency. They came along with the exact measure of one hundred mercies, ninety-nine of the inward plus the one of the outward.

When this world takes its final spin, then the inner moves outward and the outward moves inward. So this Outer Kingdom sets down and the Inner Kingdom rises up. Those who exclusively dwelled in the interior move up with the Inner Kingdom and those who dwelled exclusively in the exterior move down with the Outer Kingdom. The low becomes high and the high becomes low. Those on the high are the people of the right-hand and those in the low are the people of the left-hand and between the right and left, the high and low, is the middle region called *hijab* because it veils the right side from the left. God says:

"...and between the two (Paradise and Hell) there is a hijab [boundary]..."
[Surah Al A'raf (The Heights) 7:46]

It is sometimes called the boundary or the barrier. The dwellers of this middle region are the ones who have fulfilled the measures of both the Inner and Outer Mercies. From their vantage position they witness the people of Paradise and their bliss and they witness the inhabitants of Hell in their torment.

The Double Measure of Knowledge ('Ilm)

Knowledge ('ilm) like mercy (*rahmah*) has a double measure. One is the knowledge of the Inner and the second is the knowledge of the Outer. The Outer Knowledge is called the '*Dhahir*' and the Inner Knowledge is called '*Akhir*' or '*Batin*'. The Outer Knowledge ('Ilm Az-Zahir) relates to the Outer Kingdom and the Inner Knowledge ('Ilm Al- Akhirah or 'Ilm Al-Batin) relates to the Inner Kingdom. God says:

"They know the Outward life of this world, but yet they are in

forgetfulness regarding the Inner life (the life hereafter)."
[Surah Ar Rum (The Romans) 30:7]

Knowledge, therefore, is of two kinds: 1) one that applies to this world, 2) the other that applies to the next world. People of knowledge are therefore divided into three major groups:

1) Those whose knowledge is exclusively limited to this present outer life without any awareness about the inner life.

2) Those whose knowledge is exclusively limited to the inner life (Malakut) without any awareness about the outer life,

3) The third group are those who combine the knowledge of the outer life and the inner life and they see with two eyes.

The Inner eye sees the Inner life and the Outer eye sees the Outer life. They have a full awareness of both worlds. They keep a fine balance between the two worlds. They fulfill the measures of both lives. They live well in this life and they live well in the next life. God says:

"Whoever performs righteous deeds and has a belief, we will make life a pleasant life (in this world) and reward them with the best (in the next)."
[Surah An Nahl (The Bee) 16:97]

In the same chapter, God says about Abraham (*Ibrahim*):

"We have bestowed upon him a good life in this world and hereafter (Inner Kingdom); he will be among those with righteous deeds."
[Surah An Nahl (The Bee) 16:122]

God says:

"Seek the life hereafter (the Inner Kingdom) with that which God has bestowed upon you, nonetheless, do not forget your share in this life..."

[*Surah Al Qasas* (The Narrations) 28:77]

All these verses prove that the best way is the way of those who partake in both lives without neglecting the one for the other. However, this does not mean that the two measures have equal weight, and that the two types of knowledge have equal worth. For the proportion of the Outer Knowledge to the Inner Knowledge is like the proportion of the Outer Mercy to the Inner Mercy: one to ninety-nine. It must be borne in mind that the ninety-nine cannot be complete without the one, even though ninety-nine is greater in number than one, yet, the figure cannot be rounded to one hundred without the missing one. Therefore, the one is part of the equation and there is no way for the equation to be even without the one. In view of evenness, the one is as important as the ninety-nine. The ninety-nine is not complete without the one and the one is not complete without the ninety-nine.

God is Odd and Loves Odd

In a prophetic tradition it is narrated that the Prophet ﷺ said:

"God is odd and he loves odd."

This hadith makes a succinct statement about the nature of love. For love to exist between two entities the relationship between them must bear the mark of exclusiveness. God is odd, He stands alone and what He loves must be the same way, odd and detached. God created the entire creation together in one lot, and then out of the lot He singled out a few and selected them for Himself. This selection meant that He made them into odds so that He loves them and they love Him:

"Thy Lord does create and choose as He pleases: no choice have they (in the matter): Glory to God! And far is He above the partners they ascribe (to Him)!"
[*Surah Al Qasas* (The Narrations) 28:68]

Those who are thus selected by God cannot entertain evermore a relationship of one to one with any one among God's creation for that would constitute partnership with God. This is why the Prophet ﷺ refused to pick anyone as his one to one friend and he said, "If I was to pick anyone as a one to one friend (*Khalil*) I would have picked Abu Bakr as my friend (*Khalil*), but I am the *Khalil* of the All-Merciful God." Even Abu Bakr, his dearest companion could not be his *Khalil* because you can have many companions but only one *Khalil*, and once you have chosen God as your *Khalil*, you cannot have anyone anymore in that capacity:

"Another one who was selected by God as His one to one friend (Khalil) was Abraham."
[*Surah An Nisa* (The Women) 4:125]

When this one to one relationship (*khullah*) was in the way of getting compromised by Abraham's attachment to whatever tends to become even with Abraham or partner with God. Abraham's reaction was swift; he made up his mind to sacrifice Ishmael (*Ismail*). That making up of his mind did it all, his attachment for Ishmael ended and the undivided love for God returned back in force. The sacrifice in the heart happened and the heart is what mattered to God, the flesh and the blood are of no consequence to God. The physical sacrifice of Ishmael was then called off. God says:

"The flesh and the blood do not get to God (matter to Him), but the purity of your heart gets to Him (taqwa)."
[*Surah Al Hajj* (The Pilgrimage) 21:37]

In a similar manner, God selected Joseph as an one to one friend by detaching him from everything beginning with his father and family, next from the life in the palace and sent him into prison and then in the prison he formed relationships with other inmates. Those links were also broken up by God; one was sent out free, the other was killed. Thus finally, Joseph had no one to be attached to or to lean on. At this point God made him a *Khalil*.

He said,

> "Bring him to me and I shall pick him for myself...."
> [Surah Yusuf (Joseph) 12:54]

Communion Between Odds

Communion (*najwa*) is a private talk between two lovers that does not include a third party. If there is a third party it is not *najwa*. This *khalil* is one who is privileged to face one to one with God, while "*munaji*" is the person who takes counsel with God one to one.

In the story of Joseph when the king summoned him, the king spoke to him directly one to one while before the king spoke to him through messengers. Now when the King (God the Almighty) speaks to you directly on a one to one basis, He intends to empower you. Therefore, when He spoke to Joseph:

> "Today you are in a position of power and trust with Us..."
> [Surah Yusuf (Joseph) 12:54]

He is the King and if He speaks to you He makes you King. In this respect, we see the connection between two words that are made up of the same letters: *Kalam* (Word), *Malak* (to have Dominion) and *Mulk* (King).

God generally is speaking with everything He has created and speaks to everything He created. Also, it is through His presence and His commandment that they are sustained. However, there is a general presence and there is a special presence. As well as, there is a general speech and there is a special speech. General presence and general speech include everything that is created by Him, but special presence and special speech are open only to those who are odd among them. The simple obvious reason being that God is odd and the relationship between odd and odd is certainly more complete and more harmonious than between odd and a non-odd (even).

That consummate-symmetry which is harmony between two sides is the cause of love; the greater the concordance, the greater the love. For this God is odd and loves what is odd and whenever God speaks of His presence, He speaks first to those who are odd:

"Don't you see that God knows what is in the heavens and what is in the earth, and that there is no three (3), taking private counsel, but God is the fourth (1), nor five (5), but God is their sixth (1), and there is none less or more, but He is with them."
[*Surah Al Mujadilah* (The Women Who Dispute) 58:7]

Fourth and sixth indicate special presence; three is odd and one (1) stands for God and so "your hearts matter to Him."
[*Surah Al Hajj* (The Pilgrimage) 22:37]

In a prophetic tradition, the Prophet ﷺ says that God does not look at your bodies and your colours, but at your hearts and your deeds (the intentions of the heart and the actions that are based on those good intentions). Therefore oddness is a state that you can acquire but can lose also, since it is based on the condition of stillness. Anyone who is still in heart and soul, he is odd and once he or she loses that stillness of heart and soul, he or she turns even and the immediate link with God is broken. The stillness of the body without the heart and the soul is not important since God does not relate to us in an immediate way, except through the heart and the soul. In this respect we have three groups of people:

1) Those who are still at heart and soul but alive in flesh and blood (body), they are in God's Presence and live among the people,

2) There are those who are still bodily, but moving in heart and soul, they are neither present with God nor live with people,

3) There are those who are still in heart and soul but still in

body also, they are present with God but not live among people.

Therefore stillness brings oddness and oddness leads to a union with God because of the affinity of odd and odd, this union between man and God is a state of presence and togetherness that does not suggest transmutation or transubstantiation. The compound odd always retains its compositeness (complexity) and the single odd its simplicity like when we add 99 to 1; it becomes a total, which is hundred (100). One stands alone still, the two zeros stand for the two nines (99), or when you add 9 to 1 it becomes ten (10); the one (1) and the zero (0) that stand for the nine. The nine and zero stand for one another for they essentially bear the same significance. The origin of the word nine gives us the clue. The word nine in English and *nuen* in German, *neuf* in French, the word *none* in English, as well as, *noon*, the word *nun* in the Qur'an, *nun* in ancient Egyptian, and the word *nox* in Latin, as well as, *night* in English, *nuit* in French, *nacht* in German, and *noir* in French all express one common idea: darkness, shade, emptiness, nothingness and negation. Therefore, the word no, negation or denial, nine in Sanskrit and Indian languages (Hindi, Urdu) are from the same conception. The nine therefore is a zero that represents the void, the all-rounded space of darkness in the heavens and the earth, the all-rounded emptiness, the absolute stillness, the complete silence on the one-hand, on the other, the one (1) that represents God, the light that brightens the darkness of the heavens and the earth, the presence whose praises fills the all-rounded emptiness of the heavens and the earth and everything that is still, the sole word that fills the hearing of everything in silence. *Be darkness, God will brighten you; be still, God acts through you; be empty, God will fill you; be silent, God will speak to you and through you.* The Prophet ﷺ says, in his supplication:

"*O Allah, praise be unto you, praise that fills the heavens and the earth and everything else according to your pleasure.*"

The Two Hundreds

If the Inner Kingdom has ninety-nine mercies that ninety-nine cannot be a complete hundred and made even without the mercy of the Outer Kingdom. The equation cannot be without either of them. The ninety-nine will not be a complete mercy without the one, nor is the one without the ninety-nine. The two together as a pair make it one hundred mercies even and square.

The same is true about the ninety-nine Inner Knowledge even though as great as they are in number they are incomplete without the one Outer Knowledge, nor is the one Outer Knowledge complete without the ninety-nine Inner Knowledge. Both are indispensable for the equation. If we put the ninety-nine Inner Knowledge together with the one Outer Knowledge the result is one hundred knowledge, even and square.

Now the person who has combined the ninety-nine Inner Mercies with the one Outer Mercy has all the hundred Mercies. He is even and square and his balance is even. He has comprehended all the mercies inward and outward. He enjoys the absolute Mercy of God. On the other hand, the one who combines the ninety-nine Knowledge of the Inner life with the one of the Outer life, his knowledge is complete and his balance is even and square. Few are those who fulfill the hundred measures of Mercy and the few are those who fulfill the hundred measures of Knowledge.

Fewest still are those who fulfill the two hundred measures of both Mercy and Knowledge. To these select few is given the key that opens the door to God's boundless, absolute Knowledge. Some are given one or the other, there are very few who are given both keys.

The Two Greatest Names of God

God has two great names: 1) His great name of Mercy; ninety-nine are hidden and the one outward is the name *Ar-Rahman*. If the one outward name is combined with the ninety-nine inward then the formula is complete and the key is available. 2) His great name of Knowledge; ninety-nine are hidden and one is exterior, this one is the name of *Allah*. If the one outward is combined with the ninety-nine inward the formula is complete and the key that opens the door to the infinite Knowledge of God becomes available. The one who has the two keys has access to both infinite treasures of God: His Mercy and His Knowledge.

The Two Universal Needs

There are two things that are indispensable to the well-being of all creatures: 1) the first is health, 2) the second is sustenance, for that matter, wealth. If we assume that someone is wealthy and has food and drink at his disposal, certainly the food and drink will not earn him well-being as long as he is sick. In fact, food and drink may aggravate the sickness. Likewise, if we assume that someone is healthy but deprived of food and drink or sustenance, certainly his healthy condition will not make him feel well if he is deprived of food and drink.

Therefore, our sense of wellness depends on health, on the one hand, and nourishment on the other. The symbol of nourishment is milk and the symbol of health or healing is honey. Both are extracted from between the waste matter and blood. Both come forth from the bowels of creatures, such as, milk from livestock, for example, goat, sheep, cow and camel, and honey from bees. Both the bees and livestock get, in turn, their sustenance from plants. Bees from pollen and nectar, and livestock from leaves, grass. By the permission of All-Mighty the food they have eaten is processed in their bellies and gets separated into three different constituents: 1) waste or flesh, 2) blood, and 3) milk and honey. One of these produces the finest and purest extract, milk and honey; one being nourishment for humankind and the other being a cure and a healing:

> "And lo! in the cattle there is a lesson for you. We give you to drink of that which is in their bellies, from between the waste and the blood, pure milk palatable to the drinkers...And thy Lord inspired the bee, saying: Choose thou habitations in the hills and in the trees and in that which they thatch; then eat of all fruits, and follow the ways of thy Lord, made smooth (for thee). There cometh forth from their bellies a drink divers of hues, wherein is healing for mankind. Lo! Herein is indeed a portent for people who reflect."
> [*Surah An Nahl* (The Bee) 16:66, 68-69]

However there are qualities that distinguish honey from milk 1) texture: honey is solid and thick while milk is flowing and tender, 2) milk has a uniform colour and honey can have many colours. Following these qualities milk makes our body grow and increase while honey makes it strong and solid. Secondly, honey reflects differences of colour or appearance and unity of taste, which is sweet and non-apparent, while on the other hand, milk shows unity of colour or appearance outwardly (always white) while there is a flat taste inwardly. God, therefore, gives us the parable of milk and honey to show us that out of apparent differences we can create an underlying unity like a bee, collecting nectar and pollen from different plants with different tastes and compound them into essence that is the sweetness. In a like manner our differences of colours and tongues is a positive factor which we can put together to compound one wholesome honey reflecting differences in its colours and unity in its taste. Therefore, an outward difference is an asset if we have an inward unity. The outward varieties enrich the inward unity. In this respect, God says to the Prophet ﷺ:

> "Had you spent all the wealth of the world you could not have united their hearts, but God has united them."
> [*Surah Al Anfal* (The Spoils of War) 8:63]

So, the unity they had was the inner unity, the unity of their hearts, even though, outwardly they were so different in colours, tongues, tribes, clans, and nations. In fact, God says:

"O ye humankind we have created out of a male and a female and we have made you into nations and tribes so that you may recognize each other; indeed the most honoured among you, in the eyes of God, is the one with most 'Taqwa' (the one who safeguards his soul the most); indeed God is most knowing and most informed."
[*Surah Al Hujurat* (The Inner Apartments) 49:13]

After speaking of the differences of tribal, racial, ethnic and national affiliations with the accompanying differences in colours and tongues, then He affirms that the best among all is one who sees the underlying unity behind all these differences and that is the unity of the Creator. The one who sees the differences and sees the unity at the same time is the one with the most 'Taqwa'. It is those who are given knowledge of the unity of God. Those who have that knowledge in the heart will have their hearts united regardless of their outward differences. God says:

"Among His signs is the creations of the heavens and the earth and the differences in their tongues and colours, indeed there are signs in that for those who are endowed with knowledge."
[*Surah Ar Rum* (The Romans) 30:22]

These people of knowledge are those who have the sweetness of knowing God in their heart and that sweetness is universal regardless of outer differences. Those who hold unto universal values are bound to be together. However, those who do not know cannot be united in reality, even though, they may seem to do so outwardly, because the factor of inner unity, meaning the unity of the heart is lacking. God says:

"They would not fight you together except in fortified cities or behind walls, they are ferocious among themselves, you would

assume that they are united yet their hearts are torn apart, and that is because they have no understanding."
[*Surah Al Hashr* (The Gathering) 59:14]

If honey represents knowledge with multiple variations in colours and unity in essences, which is the sweetness, milk represents mercy (*rahmah*). These are the two essential components of Qur'an: the knowledge called *'shifaa'* a healing and mercy (*rahmah)*, which is the nourishment symbolised by the milk. God says:

"We send down out of Qur'an what is a healing and a mercy for the believers, yet, it increases the abusers in their loss."
[*Surah Al Isra* (The Night Journey) 17:82]

"O ye humankind an admonishment has come to you from your Lord and what is a healing for what is in the chest (hearts) a guidance and a mercy for those who believe."
[*Surah Yunus* (Jonah) 10:57]

The Exalted Company

Allah the Almighty mentions four categories of companionship and the respective individuals who carry the characteristics of each category.

> "Whosoever obeys Allah and the Apostle, he will certainly be with the Prophets, the truly sincere ones, the witnesses (martyrs) and the righteous. These are the best to keep as company."
> [Surah An Nisa (The Women) 4:69]

Thus, the verse enumerates four categories of companions who keep the company of God and His apostle. Therefore, whoever obeys God and His apostle shall be assigned a place in the ranks of this exalted company.

According to his personal qualities and dispositions, such a person can belong to one of four groups. The four groups of companions constitute the four supports that hold up the word of God - *La ilaha illAllah* - there is no god but Allah - and the Messenger is the bearer of that word (Muhammad ﷺ is the apostle of God, or Jesus, or Moses, etc.). In other terms, the groups of companions represent the four corners of the kingdom of God with the messenger being at the centre bearing the word of God.

Each of these groups plays a vital role in the welfare of the kingdom of God and therefore each group is replenished with a new member to replace the one who dies. The new recruits are picked from the crude membership of the community of believers and then prepared for their respective roles.

> "Whosoever obeys Allah and His messenger, he certainly would be with those Allah has blessed, including the prophets, the truly sincere, the witnesses and the righteous - these are indeed the best company to keep."

[*Surah An Nisa* (The Women) 4:6]

```
   Saliheen                                    Nabi-yeen
  (righteous                                   (prophets)
     ones)
              ┌─────────────────────────────┐
              │           Allah             │
              ├─────────────────────────────┤
              │         Messenger           │
              └─────────────────────────────┘
   Shuhadaa                                    Siddiqeen
  (witnesses)                                   (sincere
                                                  ones)
```

Each group holds one of the four corners (dimensions) of the word and in each corner resides one of the four elements of the good word in such a way that when all the four elements are united, the word is completed. With completion of the word, the truth (*haqq*) comes to pass and God's commandment becomes supreme.

"And Allah will show the truth to be the truth by His words, though the guilty may be averse (to it)."
[*Surah Yunus* (Jonah) 10:82]

The four elements of the word are as follows:

```
     Hadeed                                     Ayaat
              ┌─────────────────────────────┐
              │      The Complete Word      │
              ├─────────────────────────────┤
              │        The Messenger        │
              └─────────────────────────────┘
     Kitaab                                    Taqwa
```

By comparing the two diagrams above, we find that *ayaat* (clear signs), occupies the same corner as *nabi* (prophet); that *siddiq* (sincere one) occupies the same corner as *taqwa* (balance, wisdom); that *shahid* (witness) occupies the same corner as *kitaab* (book); and finally that *salih* (righteous one) occupies the same corner as *hadeed* (iron).

We therefore conclude that a prophet is a person who receives from God His Signs and also relays them; that a *siddiq* (sincere one) is the custodian of balance (wisdom); that a *shahid* is one who stands as a witness to the book; and finally that a *salih* is one who exercises the function of iron as a tool of warfare but also as an item of great benefit for mankind. Iron, on the one hand repels harm, and on the other brings benefit. The *salih*, the righteous one, is the one who cleanses people and the land from sickness and brings healing and reform.

The Qur'an uses various terms in reference to these four dimensions and the persons who are put in charge of these four dimensions:

Sanctification	Secret Communication (*Hadith*)
Book	Wisdom

> Allah is one Who sent down the best of communication (secret) a book of pairs unlike unto one another. Those who fear Allah their skins contract because of it, but then their skins and hearts relax at the remembrance of Allah.
> [Surah Az-Zumar (The Crowds) 30:22]

We notice here that at the right hand corner of the box (*saad*), the word *ayaat* (signs) has been replaced with *hadith* (secret communication), which sheds further light on the meaning of the word *ayaat* (signs). Therefore, we understand that God's signs are secret communications and the person who receives this secret communication is known as *nabi* (prophet) or *muhaddith* (secret counselor of God). This secret communication can be effected by means of symbols (signs) or by intuition. By symbols or by intuition, God can guide His servant on the right path:

> "By marks (symbols) and by stars they are guided."
> [Surah An Nahl (The Bee) 16:16]

The stars that are above and the symbols that are below are all signs (landmarks) to point out the right direction.

> "He is the One who appointed stars for you so that you can be guided through them in the darkness of the land and the sea. We have detailed Our Signs for people who know."
> [Surah Al An'am (The Cattle) 6:97]

Another example of secret communication through symbols is in the story of Zakariah. When he lost the power of speech, he was reduced to communicating to them through symbols.

> "He came out upon his people from the sanctuary of the temple and signified to them to glorify (the Lord) morning and evening."
> [Surah Maryam (Mary) 9:11]

The Qur'anic word used here to refer to secret communication is "*wahy,*" the word, which is commonly used in the Qur'an. It means secret communication through symbols or by intuitive awareness.

The requirements for becoming a *muhaddith* are to have a lively skin (*jild*) and a lively heart. It means to have a skin that is soft and a heart that is soft. This liveliness in the skin and heart bring them awareness (*shu'ur*) that enables them to pick up on minute sensations and delicate vibrations. In order to attain this, one must exercise a great deal of remembrance (*dhikr*), which brings tranquility (*sukoon*) and softness (*leen*) to the skin and heart. Through that tranquility and softness, the person becomes aware of the secret communication that is inviting him to prostrate and draw near.

> *"As for those who safeguard their souls (taqwa), when they are beset by an attack from Satan, they remember (God) and consequently they perceive clearly."*
> [Surah Al A'raf (The Heights) 7: 201]

This means that when those who have the inward balance are attacked with the evil whisperings of Satan, at first this brings them anxiety, which causes their skin and hearts to contract. But then when they remember God, their skin and hearts soften, and thereupon they find the guidance from God, which is communicated to them by symbols through the stars or intuitive communication.

As for the second category, *siddiqeen* (the sincere ones), we see that the word *sidq* (sincerity) is replaced by terms like *hikmah* (wisdom), *mizan* (balance) or *taqwa* (self-guarding), which means that all these terms explain further the meaning of *sidq*. It means that in order to become a *siddiq*, you must first attain inner contentment, satisfaction and fulfillment called *taqwa*. This will certainly allow your heart to stop oscillating and become still, neither leaning towards one side or another.

However, a heart that is discontented cannot stop wandering this way and that way in search of satisfaction and fulfillment. This wandering in the pursuit of fulfillment and satisfaction must perforce cause the heart to contract and the skin to shrink. These are the causes of imbalance in the heart.

However, the primary cause of a wandering heart is ill-thinking about God, which stems from lack of appreciation of His grandour and magnificence. Once you have truly appreciated His grandour and magnificence (*'dhama*), a sense of satisfaction and fulfillment will settle down in your heart and then your heart will stop wandering. Once your heart has stopped wandering, you have then attained your balance. Balance is power, and that power in practical terms is wisdom that allows you to identify pairs and to assign like unto like so that there is no transgression or shortfall.

A *siddiq* therefore is a wise man whose power lies in his ability to hold things together and preserve them, thus creating unity, which is power. Balance, therefore, is a symbol of unity and unity is power so that whenever the balance is established, there is unity. And whenever balance is disregarded there will be disunity, which is weakness. However, this power that comes from balance is internal and thus the hearts of believers with *taqwa* are united and it is this unity that gives them power. Thus, the believers may have differences outwardly, but they have unity inwardly in all cases, at all times.

If *taqwa* in the heart brings balance and unity, its absence then will cause disunity and sedition known as "*fitnah*". *Fitnah* works in a way that is exactly contrary to *taqwa* (fulfilment or safeguarding your true nature). But when *taqwa* comes into the heart, it stops this process of disintegration in the heart, and puts it together, making one whole. Consequently, the two life currents, which were separated before are joined together into one life known as one soul or a single soul.

"...that he might take rest in her. And when he covered her she bore a light burden, and she passed (unnoticed) with it, but when it became heavy they cried unto Allah, their Lord, saying: If thou give unto us a goodly child we shall be of the thankful."
[*Surah Al A'raf* (The Heights) 7:189]

"It is He Who has produced you from a single being: here is a place of sojourn and a place of departure: We detail Our signs for people who understand."
[*Surah Al An'am* (The Cattle) 6:98]

"O mankind! Be careful of your duty to your Lord Who created you from a single soul and from it created its mate and from them twain has spread abroad a multitude of men and women. Be careful of your duty toward Allah in Whom you claim (your rights) of one another, and toward the wombs (that bare you). Lo! Allah has been a watcher over you."
[*Surah An Nisa* (The Women) 4:1]

"We have created the human from a mixed liquid for the matter of testing him and then We caused him to be hearing, seeing. We then indicated to him the way - he either follows the way of gratitude (shukr) or the way of ingratitude (kufr)."
[*Surah Al Insan* (The Human Being) 76:2-3]

As long as these currents of life mix together there is one life and thus unity and power. If these life currents are segregated, there will be dual life and therefore disunity (*fitnah*) and weakness. In other words, what we know as *fitrah* (sound disposition) comes out of the mixing of the two life currents, so that whenever the two mix, a single powerful life emerges.

"And when the souls are conjugated."
[*Surah At Takwir* (The Folding Up) 81:7]

This means when (two) lives are conjoined into one single life. The word 'soul' and 'life' mean the same in the Qur'an:

"And the soul when He made it even."
[*Surah Ash Shams* (The Sun) 91:7]

This means God created life and compounded it into one even life. While the human life was in that state of unity, God inspired it to know *taqwa* (inner satisfaction through God) which helps keep the heart in balance and preserve its unity on one hand. On the other hand, it was also inspired to know *fujur* (lack of inner satisfaction through God), which causes the heart to wander (*zaigh*). And wandering takes away balance from the heart and brings separation and disunity between the two parts of life (*fitnah*).

The Seventh Day

Through reading verse 7 of *Surah Ash Shams* and *Surah At Takwir*, we should realize that the joining of the two lives takes place in the seventh level, or the seventh day. This day is also called the day of the throne (*'arsh*), since it was the day in which God rendered the throne (*'arsh*) even and allowed His manifestation on the throne.

> *"(Allah) Most Gracious is firmly established on the throne."*
> [*Surah TaHa* (TaHa) 20:5]

In other words, the seventh level is the level of unity so that anything that attains to this level attains unity of life and he becomes one single soul. At that point, it is assigned its throne in the likeness of God's throne. Only such a soul is deemed powerful enough to sustain God's manifestation similar to the one He made on the Throne. The power of such a soul stems from its delicate balance and unity of life. *Surah Al Hujurat* evidences this:

> *"The most honourable among you in the eyes of God is the one with the most taqwa (the one who most safeguards his soul)."*
> [*Surah Al Hujurat* (The Inner Apartments) 49:13]

The one with the most *taqwa* is the one most balanced, and most self-integrated. The best description of such a soul is to be found in *Surah An Najm:*

> *"His gaze did not wander nor did it transgress."*
> [*Surah An Najm* (The Star) 53:17]

This is the best description of a soul in a perfect balance. Indeed, such a soul is deemed fit to sustain God's most great manifestation.

> *"For truly did he see, of the Signs of his Lord, the Greatest!"*
> [*Surah An Najm* (The Star) 53:18]

That soul was indeed the soul of Muhammad ﷺ.

Outer Expansion

Once the foundations are laid inwardly through *iman*

(belief in God's signs) and *taqwa* (inner fulfillment), then seeking outward expansion becomes meaningful and realizable. On the contrary, seeking outward expansion without first making a solid foundation internally would only lead to failure and disappointment. As inner expansion is achievable through the means of *iman* and *taqwa*, outer expansion is achievable through *zakah* (sanctification) and *birr* (piety, innocence). Through innocence (*birr*) and through sanctity (*zakah*), life grows and expands outwardly. Without them, there is no outward expansion. For that reason God reminds us about *zakah* immediately after taqwa.

> "He inspired the soul with taqwa and fujur. Salvation is for those who sanctify it."
> [Surah Ash Shams (The Sun) 91:8]

It means that once a person has achieved inward expansion, he should strive for the outward expansion of his life through *tazkiah* and *birr*. The objective of inward expansion through *iman* and *taqwa* is to attain honour (*karam*) with God, which consists of being enthroned in the presence of His throne. The objective of outward expansion is to attain God's favours (*fadl*) and pleasure (*ridwan*). And this second objective is not realizable without the first one.

> "Then, in their wake, We followed them up with (others of) Our messengers: We sent after them Jesus the son of Mary, and bestowed on him the Gospel; and We ordained in the hearts of those who followed him Compassion and Mercy. But the Monasticism which they invented for themselves, We did not prescribe for them: (We commanded) only the seeking for the Good Pleasure of Allah; but that they did not foster as they should have done. Yet We bestowed, on those among them who believed, their (due) reward, but many of them are rebellious transgressors."
> [Surah Al Hadid (The Iron) 57:27]

However, in order to attain *tazkiah* and *birr*, the person concerned must exercise two things:

1. For *tazkiah*, he or she must exercise manipulation of iron (usage of iron) in some or all its forms because continuous manipulation of iron has a cleansing and healing impact on the heart. It is a tool of remediation (*islah*).

2. For *birr*, he must go out in the way of Allah and tour the earth through land and sea (*siyaha*) including visiting the house of Allah (*Ka'ba*). Those who go out in the way of God (*siyaha, hajj, pilgrimage*), God in return showers over their heads a substance called *birr*, which are highly charged particles that resemble fine hailstones or extremely fine pebbles. As a result, the *birr* is supposed to eliminate all their sins and knots.

Due to the combined effect of iron (*hadid*) and *birr*, they become sound and innocent like a newborn child.

> "We verily sent Our messengers with clear proofs (*bayyinat*), and revealed with them the Scripture (*kitaab*) and the Balance (*mizan*), that mankind may observe right measure; and He revealed iron (*hadid*), wherein is mighty power and (many) uses for mankind, and that Allah may know him who helps Him and His messengers, though unseen. Lo! Allah is Strong, Almighty."
> [*Surah Al Hadid* (The Iron) 57:25]

Islah (tazkiah)		*Iman*
	Those who believe in God's Signs and perform righteous deeds - for them is tuuba and a blissful place of return. [*Surah Ar R'ad* (The Thunder) 13:29] Assist one another in *birr* and *taqwa* and do not assist one another in sinfulness and transgression. [*Surah Al Ma'idah* (The Table Spread) 5:2]	
Birr		*Taqwa*

In fact, it is related in a prophetic tradition that the Prophet ﷺ said: "Whoever performs *hajj* (pilgrimage) without indulging in lewd speech or transgressing against God's commandment, he shall return home like the day he was delivered from the womb of his mother. This rebirth is the reward for *hajj*. Those who are reborn are those who are the innocent (*abrar*) with no speck of ill in them and it is they who are allowed into the Kingdom of God (heaven and paradise).

Similarly, a reference is made to iron in the prophetic tradition where the Prophet ﷺ said:

"When Allah utters Truth in the heaven, it would sound like when a chain of iron drops on a rock whereupon the angels would spread their wings down in servile submission to God."

This *hadith* reveals to us that iron comes down in the company of God's word, which are the truthful utterances.

The role of iron here is similar to an alarm bell that rings at the approach of danger. The purpose of alarming is to induce awakening and alertness. A person who is awake and alert is better prepared to meet what is approaching him. Likewise, when God utters His word of truth, He would send iron ahead of it as a warning, which is supposed to awaken the people and make them alert and attentive. The warning may come down in the day or in the night. If it comes down in the night, it will cause them to rise up from their slumber, or if it comes down in the day, it will cause them to stop playing and start working in earnest. Therefore, slumber gets replaced with wakefulness (vigil), which means replacing forgetfulness (*ghaflah*) with remembrance (*dhikr*). On the other hand, play (*la'ab*) gets replaced with work which means replacing ingratitude (*kufr*) with gratitude (*shukr*), for indeed God has made the night a context for remembrance and the day a context for gratitude.

"And it is He Who made the Night and the Day to follow each other: for such have the will to come to (remembrance) His

> *praises or to show their gratitude."*
> [*Surah Al Furqan* (The Criterion) 25:62]

However, against the original purpose of God, they turned the night into a time of forgetfulness (*lahaw*) and the day into a time of sporting (*la'ab*).

> *"If the people of the towns had but believed and feared Allah, We should indeed have opened out to them (all kinds of) blessings from heaven and earth; but they rejected (the truth), and We brought them to book for their misdeeds. Did the people of the towns feel secure against the coming of Our wrath by night while they were asleep? Or else did they feel secure against its coming in broad daylight while they played about (care-free)? Did they then feel secure against the plan of Allah? But no one can feel secure from the Plan of Allah, except those (doomed) to ruin!"*
> [*Surah Al A'raf* (The Heights) 7:96-99]

Therefore, to sleep through the night is alienating the purpose for which the night was created. God created the night and made it dark and still so that you may find in it rest and tranquility. This tranquility softens your heart and skin, and promotes remembrance and awareness, which in turn promotes belief in God and His signs. Instead, you spent it in slumber and forgetfulness, which came to harden your heart and your skin, and ultimately plunged you into total oblivion (*ghaflah*) and disbelief (*takzeeb*).

In a similar manner, wantonly passing the day is alienating the purpose for which the day was created. God created the day and caused it to be bright so that by daylight you could move around the earth in pursuit of God's favours. God spread His favours around the earth and they are not concentrated in one place. Thus, that constant movement in the way of *Allah* helps increase your vitality in order to draw you out of your stupor and heal you from your sclerosis. This daylight movement in quest of God's favours, and ultimately of His pleasure (*ridwan*), is known as gratitude (*shukr*).

Ingratitude (*kufr*) on the contrary, is to spend the day aimlessly in play and idle pleasures with total disregard for the multitude of God's favours that He spread out all over the earth with the coming of the daylight. In the end, when they reflect back on their life on earth at the time of death, they feel as though they never lived a full day or a full night:

Islah(Zakah)   Iman(Salah)

> Your friend can be only Allah, and His messenger and those who believe, who establish worship and pay the poor-due, and bow down (in prayer).
> [*Surah Al Ma'idah* (The Table Spread) 5:55]

> Successful indeed are the believers who are tender-hearted in their prayers; who turn away from idle talk; who practice alms-giving; and who safeguard their chastity.
> [*Surah Al Mu'minun* (The Believers) (23:1-5)]

Birr(Hajj)   Taqwa(Sawm)

Iman and *Islah*

Through careful perusal of Qur'an, we come to observe that the word "*amanu*" those who believe is always paired with the word "*amilu-al-salihaat*" those who perform righteous deeds.

"By the time of late noon, verily man is in loss, except such as have Faith, and do righteous deeds, and (join together) in the mutual teaching of Truth, and of Patience and Constancy."
[*Surah Al Asr* (The Time) 103:1-3]

"Those who believe in God's Signs and perform righteous deeds, for them is tuuba and a blissful place of return."
[*Surah Ar R'ad* (The Thunder) 13:29]

"As to those who believe and work righteous deeds, they have for

their entertainment the Gardens of Paradise."
[*Surah Al Kahf* (The Cave) 18:107]

Believing (*iman*) and performing righteous deeds (*islah*) are opposite actions, one stemming from yearning and the other from warning. Yearning brings stillness and softness to the heart, which instigates remembrance. The formal expression of that yearning in the heart is the position of prostration (*sujud*). It is a state of longing called *hanaan, raghbah, tamanni* and it transcends all boundaries.

"And tenderness (hanaan) as from Us, and purity: He was devout."
[*Surah Maryam* (Mary) 19:13]

"So We listened to him: and We granted him Yehia: We cured his wife's (barrenness) for him. These (three) were ever quick in emulation in good works; they used to call on Us in longing (raghbah) and in reverence, and humble themselves before Us."
[*Surah Al Anbiyah* (The Prophets) 21:90]

"And verily you used to wish for death (tamannawna almawta) before you met it (in the field). Now you have seen it with your eyes!"
[*Surah Al Imran* (The Family of Imran) 3:143]

On the other hand, warning brings awakening to the heart, causing the individual to be alert and focused. Being fully aware of the approach of truth in the night and majesty heralded by the ringing of the iron, the person is therefore stricken with awe, which is represented by the position of bowing (*ruku'*). Any action of service rendered under the influence of this situation would be classified as a righteous deed (*salih*), hence the meaning of verse 55 of *Surah Al-Ma'idah* about those who perform their prayers and give their alms while in *ruku'*, which means, while they are aware of God's warning from His Majesty.

"Your (real) friends are (no less than) Allah, His Messenger, and

the (fellowship of) believers - those who establish regular prayers and regular charity, and they bow down humbly (in worship)."
[Surah Al Ma'idah (The Table Spread) 5:55]

"And those who dispense their charity with their hearts full of fear, because they will return to their Lord."
[Surah Al Mu'minun (The Believers) 23:60]

Birr and *Taqwa*

Like *iman* and *islah*, *birr* and *taqwa* are also treated as pairs in the Qur'an. They have a relationship of means and ends. *Birr* is the end, which is not attainable except by the means of *taqwa*. In other words, the individual who sets out in quest of *birr* must take with him *taqwa* as his provision on the way. If he leaves without *taqwa*, his quest will remain unfulfilled. Therefore, God admonishes the pilgrims to carry along with them their provisions for the way (*zad*). However, He points out to them that the best provision for the way is that of *taqwa*.

"For Hajj are the months well-known. If any one undertakes that duty therein, Let there be no obscenity, nor wickedness, nor wrangling in the Hajj. And whatever good you do, (be sure) Allah knows it. And take a provision (with you) for the journey, but the best of provisions is right conduct (taqwa). So fear Me, O you that are wise."
[Surah Al Baqarah (The Cow) 2:197]

The Exalted Company and the Messenger

The exalted company comprises of four types of membership and each one has a designated role to play in addition to the duties of the principal personage of the company, which is the messenger.

These four types of membership are:

1. The Nabiyeen (the prophets)

2. The Siddiqeen (the sincere ones)
3. The Shuhadaa (the witnesses)
4. The Saliheen (the righteous ones)

These four are known as the exalted company - "*hasuna ulaika rafeeqan.*"

> "*Whosoever obeys Allah and His messenger, he certainly would be with those Allah has blessed, including the prophets, the truly sincere (in their belief), the witnesses and the righteous these are indeed the best company to keep.*"
> [*Surah An Nisa* (The Women) 4:69]

Saliheen (Righteous Ones)	Allah	*Nabiyeen* (Prophets)
	Messenger	
Shuhadaa (Witnesses)		*Siddiqeen* (Sincere Ones)

These four groups of people constitute the membership of the exalted company, and each group has specific duties to perform. These duties are laid out in *Surah Al Ahzab*:

> "*O Prophet, we have sent you as a witness, a bringer of glad tidings, and a warner; as well as a caller unto Allah by His leave, and to be a lamp spreading light.*"
> [*Surah Al Ahzab* (The Confederates) 33:45-46]

Warning   Renewal

> "O Prophet! Lo! We have sent you as a witness and a bringer of glad tidings and a warner. And as a caller unto Allah by His permission, and to be a lamp spreading light. A caller (da'iyan), a lamp spreading light (siraajam muniraa)."
> [Surah Al Ahzab (The Confederates) 33:45-46]

Witness   Glad Tidings

As God sent down His messenger with His good word - *La ilaha illaAllah* - There is no god but Allah - along with it He sent down remembrance, glad tidings, warning and witnessing. While the messenger himself embodies all these four, God raises with him four groups of people, each group assuming one of these four duties.

I: *Nabiyeen* - The Prophets

The first group is *nabi* or *muhaddith* or prophet or secret communicator. Their duty lies in reminding people about God's signs (*ayaat*), which are spread all around them.

> "For how many signs of God in the heavens as well as in the earth which they pass by unaware?"
> [Surah Yusuf (Joseph) 12:105]

Their purpose therefore is to draw people's attention to God's signs and enkindle remembrance (*dhikr*) in their hearts. In exercising this duty, they achieve three objectives:

1. To initiate those who never remembered before, this means those plunged into complete oblivion.

2. To remind those who have forgotten after remembrance.

3. To increase the level of faith of those who are in remembrance.

> "... remind, for reminding is beneficial to the believers."
> [Surah Adh Dhariyat (The Winds that Scatter) 51:55]

This reminding constitutes the first step in the process of awakening. It is part of the internal awakening. Furthermore, remembrance is always in reference to the past, for a person can remember something only that which he knew in the past and has come to forget. Remembrance therefore consists in renewing his knowledge about what he had already known in the past, but has forgotten. When he is reminded of it, he knows it again.

> "You had known the first creation, won't you remember?"
> [Surah Al Waqi'ah (The Inevitable Event) 56:62]

It means, won't you remember what you had already known before. Here, we see remembrance connected to the first creation - *khalq-al-awwal*:

> "Were We then weary with the first Creation that they should be in confused doubt about a new Creation?"
> [Surah Qaf (Qaf) 50:15]

The purpose of remembrance therefore is to take us back to the beginning (*awwal, bad-u*) when creation first started. The term first (*awwal*) and beginning (*bad-u*) are the cornerstones of remembrance.

> "Say! Travel in the earth (land and sea) and see how creation was started, even so God will create the new creation."
> [Surah Al Ankabut (The Spider) 29:20]

As this verse indicates, it is part of the duty of the prophet/*muhaddith* to draw people's attention to God's numerous signs around them, within themselves and in the horizons which by stages will guide them towards the beginning whereupon they would come to realize how creation started.

That realization as a result breeds faith in the heart, bringing coolness and tranquility to the heart and the skin.

> *"Indeed, through remembrance of Allah do hearts find tranquillity."*
> [*Surah Ar R'ad* (The Thunder) 13:28]

> *"Allah has revealed the most excellent speech, a book in pairs resembling one another - it causes the skin of those who fear God to contract, but thereafter their skins and hearts soften at the remembrance of Allah. Such is the guidance of Allah: He guides therewith whom He pleases, but such as Allah leaves to stray can have no none to guide him."*
> [*Surah Az Zumar* (The Crowds) 39:23]

Their hearts and skins contract when they are warned, but then they are reminded about Allah's signs and memories of the beginning, which cause their hearts and skins to soften and relax. It is therefore clear that the role of the prophet/*muhaddith* is to relay the news about the past and to revive the heart and skin of people through the remembrance of the beginning and in inculcating faith of God in people's hearts.

II: *Saliheen* - The Righteous Ones

The righteous ones are those whose duty it is to warn people and alert them.

> *"All the believers (as a community) are not supposed to go to war. Out of every group, a band should go away in order that they may be instructed in matters of Religion, and when they return, they would warn their people so that they may be alert."*
> [*Surah At Tawbah* (The Repentance) 9:122]

This verse gives a precise description of the credentials of a *salih* as well as his duty. A *salih* (righteous one) should be one who possesses in-depth knowledge of religion (*deen*). That in-depth knowledge of *deen* is known as "*fiqh*". The person who has this knowledge is known as a "*faqeeh*". This kind of in-depth knowledge of deen breeds "*khashiyaa*" (awe, reverence) of God. He is a person who is warned of the majesty of God and knows the consequences of breaking through the boundaries of God. He therefore warns others and awakens them when they are getting on the verge of overstepping God's boundaries. In this respect, their function runs parallel to that of the prophets/*muhaddith* because the awakening of the *saliheen* is external while the awakening of the prophets/*muhaddith* is internal. Another parallel is that the prophets/*muhaddith* draw people's attention internally towards the beginning, while the righteous ones (*saliheen*) draw their attention towards the ending (*akhirah*). The ending consists of resurrection, the Day of Judgment, the separation between those who receive God's goodly reward and His pleasure, and those who receive His judgment and retribution.

In other words, the righteous ones, (*saliheen)* are responsible for reforming the individual and collective lives of people by enjoining them to do what is right, and forbidding them from doing what is wrong. They exhort others to respect God's boundaries and warn them against the repercussions of corruption on the earth. In this way, they bring order in the society, and avert social upheaval as well as natural cataclysms that cause loss of humans and nature. This external reform by the righteous ones counterbalances the internal reform by the prophets so that people are connected to both the beginning and the ending, and their lives expand inwardly and outwardly.

Even though Qur'an has not given us a precise number of prophets, it does however tell us that every nation had a warner and therefore every nation will have a warner.

"We sent you by the truth to be a bringer of glad tidings and a warner; indeed, there was never a nation but had a warner."
[*Surah Al Fatir* (The Originator of Creation) 35:24]

Therefore, every nation must have had a warner (*nazeer*). This is true because every nation needs justice and order for it to live and prosper with regards to the outer life regardless whether they have an inner life or not.

> "God shall not cause a nation to perish even though they ascribe partners to God, as long as the people are righteous."
> [Surah Hud (Hud) 11:117]

The Qur'an gives us the stories of a few righteous men who lived among non-believing people. One example is the story of the man who came to warn Moses regarding a plot to kill him and advised him to depart hence.

> "And a man came from the uttermost part of the city, running. He said: O Moses! Lo! The chiefs take counsel against thee to slay thee; therefore escape. Lo! I am of those who give thee good advice."
> [Surah Al Qasas (The Narrations) 28: 20]

The same man is mentioned again in *Surah Ghafir* wherein he warns his people against the dire consequences of their ill deeds:

> "A believer, a man from among the people of Pharaoh, who had concealed his faith, said: Will you slay a man because he says, 'My Lord is Allah?'- when he has indeed come to you with Clear (Signs) from your Lord? And if he be a liar, on him is (the sin of) his lie: but, if he is telling the Truth, then will fall on you something of the (calamity) of which he warns you. Truly Allah guides not one who transgresses and lies! O my people! Yours is the kingdom today, you being uppermost in the land. But who would save us from the wrath of Allah if it should reach us? Pharaoh said: I do but show you what I think, and I do but guide you to wise policy. And he who believed said: O my people! Lo! I fear for you fate like that of the factions (of old); a plight like that of Noah's folk, and 'ad and Thamud, and those after them, and Allah wills no injustice for (His) slaves. And, O my people! Lo! I

fear for you a Day of Summoning, a day when you will turn to flee, having no defender from Allah: and he whom Allah sends astray, for him there is no guide. And certainly Yusuf came to you before with clear signs, but you ever remained in doubt as to what he brought, until when he died, you said: Allah will never raise a messenger after him. Thus does Allah cause him to err who is extravagant, a doubter. Those who wrangle concerning the revelations of Allah without any warrant that has come unto them, it is greatly hateful in the sight of Allah and in the sight of those who believe. Thus does Allah print on every arrogant, disdainful heart. And Pharaoh said: O Haman! Build for me a tower that haply I may reach the roads. The roads of the heavens, and may look upon the god of Moses, though verily I think him a liar. Thus was the evil that he did made fairseeming unto Pharaoh, and he was debarred from the (right) way. And the plot of Pharaoh led to nothing but ruin. And the man who believed said: O my people! Follow me. I will show you the way of right conduct. O my people! Lo! This life of the world is but a passing comfort, and lo! The hereafter, that is the enduring home. Whoso does an ill deed, he will be repaid the like thereof, while whoso does right, whether man or woman, and is a believer, (all) such will enter the Garden, where they will be nourished without stint.

And O my people! How (strange) it is for me to call you to Salvation while you call me to the Fire! You do call upon me to blaspheme against Allah, and to join with Him partners of whom I have no knowledge; and I call you to the Exalted in Power, Who forgives again and again! Without doubt you do call me to one who is not fit to be called to, whether in this world, or in the Hereafter; our return will be to Allah; and the Transgressors will be Companions of the Fire! Soon will you remember what I say to you (now), My (own) affair I commit to Allah: for Allah (ever) watches over His Servants."
[Surah Al Ghafir (The Forgiver) 40:28-44]

Another example is the story of the man who, like the former, came from the far end of the city to warn his people against the consequences of disobeying the messengers of God.

His words are that of a person who received warning by God and is genuinely concerned about the salvation of his people.

> *"Set forth to them, by way of a parable, the (story of) the Companions of the City. Behold! There came messengers to it. When We (first) sent to them two messengers, they rejected them: But We strengthened them with a third: they said, "Truly, we have been sent on a mission to you." They said. " You are naught but mortals like ourselves, nor has the Beneficent Allah revealed anything; you only lie." They said: Our Lord knows that we are most surely messengers to you. And our duty is only to proclaim the clear Message. (The people of the city) said: We augur ill of you. If you desist not, we shall surely stone you, and grievous torture will befall you at our hands. They said: Your evil augury be with you! Is it because you are reminded (of the truth)? Nay, but ye are forward folk! Then there came running, from the farthest part of the City, a man, saying: O my people! Obey the messengers: Obey those who ask no reward of you (for themselves), and who have themselves received Guidance. It would not be reasonable in me if I did not serve Him Who created me, and to Whom you shall (all) be brought back. Shall I take (other) gods besides Him? If (Allah) Most Gracious should intend some adversity for me, of no use whatever will be their intercession for me, nor can they deliver me. I would indeed, if I were to do so, be in manifest error. It was said (unto him): Enter paradise. He said: Would that my people knew (what I know)! For that my Lord has granted me Forgiveness and has enrolled me among those held in honour!"*
> [Surah Ya Seen (Ya Seen) 36:13-27]

III: **The *Siddiqeen* - The Sincere Ones**

The *siddiqs* constitute the third group in the exalted company. Their function is to bring glad tidings in view of steadying the hearts of believers and uplifting it. Their role is identical to the role of the winds that herald the coming of the rain. The *siddiqs* are therefore the harbingers who bring glad tidings regarding the arrival of the mercy of God. Mercy is like that gentle rain that is preceded by the gentle wind.

"Their Lord brings them glad tidings of Mercy (Rahmah), of God's pleasure (Ridwan) and a garden wherein they shall have abiding bliss." [*Surah At Tawbah* (The Repentance) 9:21]

In this verse, God specifies the three major items, which form the subject of the glad tidings: 1) God's Mercy (*Rahmah*); 2) God's Pleasure (*Ridwan*); and 3) The garden of everlasting abode. A *siddiq* is one who is strengthened with a spirit from God and that spirit is a breath of peace and glad tidings announcing the coming of the good word from God. Thus, the function of a *siddiq* is closely tied with the function of a Prophet and the two are often joined together. If the role of a Prophet/*muhaddith* is to bring remembrance that softens the heart and skin and expand them, the role of the *siddiq* must follow that, which is to steady and strengthen the heart of those who believe.

"Thou will not find any people who believe in Allah and the Last Day loving those who oppose Allah and His Messenger, even though they were their fathers or their sons, or their brothers, or their kindred. For such He has written Faith in their hearts, and strengthened them with a spirit from Himself. And He will admit them to Gardens beneath which Rivers flow, to dwell therein (for ever). Allah will be well pleased with them, and they with Him. They are the Party of Allah. Truly it is the Party of Allah that will achieve success."
[*Surah Al Mujadilah* (The Disputation) 58:22]

Many Prophets are also given the title of *siddiq* (sincere one):

"Remember Ibrahim in the book for he was a siddiq (sincrere believer) and a prophet."
[*Surah Maryam* (Mary) 19:41]

"Remember in the book Idris, for he was a siddiq and a prophet."
[*Surah Maryam* (Mary) 19:56]

These verses indicate the tight connection between *sidq* (being sincere) and *nubuwat* (prophethood). One brings remembrance, which gives life, and the other brings the spirit, which strengthens life. The process through which remembrance revives the soul is called "*dhikr*" and the process through which the soul gets inspired is called "*fikr.*" We have discussed *dhikr* earlier. It is a means of tracing God's signs, leading one to the beginning. The ultimate point of remembrance is to remember the beginning of creation, which is the start of the remembrance known as the greatest remembrance (*dhikr-al-akbar*).

Fikr on the other hand is a discipline concerned with breathing as a means of finding connection with God through His spirit. It is a means of gaining strength and inspiration by drawing on the breath of the All-Merciful (*Ar-Rahman*). The first requirement towards improving your *fikr* is to maintain silence. Hence, the idea of fasting as a means of improving your *fikr* since fasting includes abstaining from food, drink, sexual pleasure and speech. Once a person has given up all these four, God in return will strengthen him with a spirit from Him. As a result of that inspiration, *taqwa* (inner fulfillment) develops in his heart, replacing the pleasures of food, drink, sex, and speech of tongue. People usually seek pleasure as well as strength by means of food, drink, and sexual indulgence besides the pleasure of the tongue. However, being strengthened with God's spirit is better and more fulfilling.

God the Almighty Himself has described Himself as one who utters *sidq*, which means that he conveys glad tidings to the believers in order to strengthen their hearts and souls.

> "*Say: Allah speaks truth. So follow the religion of Abraham, one in his true nature. He was not of the idolaters.*"
> [*Surah Al Imran* (The Family of Imran) 3:95]

> "*Who guides you through the depths of darkness on land and sea, and Who sends the winds as heralds of glad tidings, going*

before His Mercy? (Can there be another) God besides Allah? High is Allah above what they associate with Him!"
[Surah An Naml (The Bee) 27:63]

"Among His Signs is this, that He sends the Winds, as heralds of Glad Tidings, giving you a taste of His Mercy, and that the ships may sail (majestically) by His Command and that you may seek of His Bounty in order that you may be grateful."
[Surah Ar Rum (The Romans) 30:46]

In a similar manner that God sends winds to bring glad tidings of the rain which is about to come, God also sends down His spirit upon the *siddiqs* to bring them glad tidings of His mercy that is about to come. The effect of these glad tidings is to strengthen their faith in God's promise, which must come true - and therefore with diligence and sincerity they endeavour hard to attain it. Herein lies the difference then between the *siddiq*, who is a sincere believer in the glad tidings given by God and the messenger, and the insincere believer (*kaazib*), who does not believe sincerely in glad tidings given by God. The proof of sincerity of the *siddiq* is his earnestness in seeking the mercy of God about which he has received the glad tidings. But the mark of an insincere believer (*kaazib*) is lack of earnestness in seeking the fulfilment of God's good promise.

"Who is worse in wrongdoing then the person who attributes falsehood unto Allah and also takes for a lie the glad tidings when they came unto him? Is there not in hell an abiding place for the ungrateful? As for the one who came along with the glad tidings and sincerely believed in it, such indeed are the people of taqwa (inner fulfillment)."
[Surah Az Zumar (The Crowds) 39:32-33]

In the foregoing verses, God presents to us the pictures of two people: 1) the one who is sincere (*siddiq*); and 2) the other who is insincere (*kaazib* and *kazzaab*). As for the word *sidq* (sincerity), it has two derivatives: one is *sadiq* and the other is *siddiq*. A *sadiq* is such a person who sincerely and truly claims that he has received a spirit of glad tidings from God. He truly claims that he is inspired by God to do such and such. A *siddiq* on the other hand is one who believes the claim made by the *sadiq* is true.

Conversely, the word "*kazb*" (lie, insincerity) has two derivatives: one is *kaazib* and the other is *kazzaab*. A *kaazib* is one who makes false claims that he has received inspiration from God (spirit of glad tidings).

> "Who can be more wicked than one who invents a lie against Allah, or says: 'I have received inspiration,' when he has received none, or (again) who says: 'I can reveal the like of what Allah has revealed'? If thou could but see how the wicked (do fare) in the flood of confusion at death! The angels stretch forth their hands, (saying): 'Yield up your souls: this day shall you receive your reward, a penalty of shame, for that you used to tell lies against Allah, and scornfully to reject of His signs!"
> [*Surah Al An'am* (The Cattle) 6:93]

So he is the opposite of a *sadiq*. As for the *kazaab*, he is one who claims or believes that the true glad tidings from God are false, but however believes the false claims as inspiration that is true.

Wisdom and Balance

Wisdom (*hikmah*) and balance (*mizan*) are two things associated with a *siddiq*. His heart is level and well-balanced due to the expansion of his breath under the influence of the glad tidings of a spirit from God. Through balanced and steady breathing, he develops the faculty of "*marifah*" - the ability to recognize or identify beings and things by their smell as much as a baby recognizes its mother through the smell of her body.

A wise man therefore is one who has balanced breathing which means his breath is neither too cold nor too hot, but rather a goodly mixture of both; and his breathing is neither too fast nor too slow. The words of a wise man take on the quality of his breathing. They are neither too cold to freeze the listener and bog him down, nor are they too hot to overexcite him. The former causes stagnation while the latter causes hysteria. The words of wisdom uttered by a wise man incite the listener to move on gently and smoothly at a pace neither too slow nor too fast, it will be gentle and smooth.

> "And among His Signs are the ships, smooth-running through the ocean, (tall) as mountains. If it be His Will He can still the Wind: then would they become motionless on the back of the (ocean). Verily in this are Signs for everyone who patiently perseveres and is grateful. Or He can cause them to perish because of the (evil) which (the men) have earned; but much does He forgive."
> [Surah Ash Shu'ura (The Poets) 42:32-34]

The same goes for his speaking - his speech will come out gentle and smooth, neither speaking too loud nor too low, if he breathes not too slowly nor too fast.

> "Then exalted be Allah, the True King! And hasten not with the Qur'an ere its revelation has been perfected unto thee, and say: My Lord! Increase me in knowledge."
> [Surah TaHa (TaHa) 20:114]

> "Move not thy tongue concerning the (Qur'an) to make haste therewith."
> [Surah Al Qiyamah (The Resurrection) 75:16]

> "Do not say your prayer too loud nor too low, but find a middle way between them."
> [Surah Al Isra (The Journey by Night) 17:110]

That middle way is the way of *siddiqs* whose words are wise and their steps firm. Their call brings immediate response from God.

> "And the servants of (Allah) Most Gracious are those who walk on the earth in gentleness, and when the ignorant address them, they say, 'Peace!'"
> [Surah Al Furqan (The Criterion) 25:63]

> "Is it a wonder for mankind that We have inspired a man among them, saying: Warn mankind and bring unto those who believe the good tidings that they have a sure footing with their Lord?"
> [Surah Yunus (Jonah) 10:2]

Wisdom (*Hikmah*) and Supplication (*Du'a*)

For any supplication to be successful with God, it must be done with wisdom, which means with a sincere tongue (*lisana sidqin*). God emphasizes in *Surah Al Isra*, verse 110 that the choice of the name, whether it be *Allah* or *Ar-Rahman* (Most Merciful) does not matter. Rather the manner in which the name is called is all that matters:

> "Call Allah or call Ar-Rahman, whichever you call, all excellent names belong to Him."
> [Surah Al Isra (The Night Journey) 17:110]

Then He teaches him the appropriate way of calling Him:
> "Do not say your prayer too loud nor too low; find a middle way between them. This is the just voice which God hears and responds to."
> [Surah Al Muzammil (Folded in Garments) 73:4]

In order to have a just voice, the supplicant must adjust his voice between four things:

> "Call your Lord with a wail and a whisper for surely He does not love transgressors. Do not spread corruption in the earth after it has been reformed; call Him with fear and hope, indeed God's mercy is closest to those who exercise excellence."

[*Surah Al A'raf* (The Heights) 7:55-56]

In light of this verse, a just voice is neither a wail nor a whisper for a wail is too loud and a whisper is too low. It must therefore stand in the middle way between wailing and whispering. This is the first adjustment of the just voice.

The second adjustment is to call with fear and hope. Fear makes the voice too dry and fast while hope makes the voice too wet and slow. The just voice therefore is one that is neither too fast nor too slow. At this point, the voice is twice adjusted. This is the voice by which if you call God, He answers; if you ask Him, He gives to you. This is the true voice of the caller unto God (*da'iah*).

> "And as a caller to Allah's (grace) by His leave, and as a lamp spreading light."
> [*Surah Al Ahzab* (The Confederates) 33:46]

The story of Zakariah is proof of the fact that supplication with a just voice obtains immediate positive response from God. In verse 3 of *Surah Maryam*, Zakariah, peace be upon him, calls his Lord in a whisper. In verse 4, he pleads with his Lord with wailings:

> "He said: My Lord, my bones have become fragile, my head is ablaze with grey. However, I know my Lord that supplicating you has never been a cause of misery for me."
> [*Surah Maryam* (Mary) 20:4]

This is what is a wail (*dara'ah*). Then he expressed his fears in verse 5: "*I have fears regarding successors after me and behold my wife is barren.*" Here he expressed his fears of having no successor unto whom he could hand down his heritage and secondly that his wife was barren and would not bear any children. This expression of his fears fulfills the third condition for a successful supplication.

Lastly, in verses 5-6, Prophet Zakariah expressed his hope in God's mercy and generosity, saying: "O Lord, give me a successor who will inherit from me and from the family of Yaqub (Jacob) and Lord make him one as such would earn your pleasure." With the fourth condition now fulfilled, Zakariah's voice became just and his prayer was answered immediately. The glad tidings were sent to Zakariah ahead of God's mercy like the winds before the rain.

"O Zakariah, we bring you glad tidings of a boy whose name is Yehia (John), for whom we never made a namesake before."
[*Surah Maryam* (Mary) 19:7]

After receiving good news there is a period of waiting for the arrival of the promise. That waiting period is a period of abstention (fasting, *sawm*) from habitual indulgences in order to make room for the mercy of God, which is coming. This is the purpose and philosophy of fasting. In the meantime, those who abstain from the pleasures of food and drink, God will provide for them the provision of *taqwa* (*zad at-taqwa*), and those who abstain from the pleasure of sex, God will provide them with the dress of *taqwa* (*libas at-taqwa*), and those who abstain from the pleasures of the tongue, God will provide them with words of wisdom (*hikmah*), which is a tongue of sincerity (*lisana-siddiqeen*). This was what Zakariah did when he was brought the glad tidings about Yehia:

"He said, O my Lord make a sign for me. He said, Your sign is that you cannot talk to people for three complete nights. Then he came out to his people and signaled to them to glorify (the Lord) morning and evening."
[*Surah Maryam* (Mary) 19:10-11]

We see in these verses how God imposed on Zakariah a three-day period of abstinence (fasting) from speaking to people because the spirit of glad tidings had come to him announcing the imminent arrival of God's mercy. This three-night period of abstinence refers to the three darknesses in which creation takes place.

> "He created you (all) from a single person: then created, of like nature, his mate; and he sent down for you eight head of cattle in pairs: He makes you in the wombs of your mothers in stages, one after another, in three veils of darkness. Such is Allah, your Lord and Cherisher: to Him belongs (all) dominion. There is no god but He: then how are you turned away (from your true Centre)?"
> [Surah Az Zumar (The Crowds) 39:6]

A similar wisdom lies in limiting the period of mourning to three days, which represent the three darknesses. A widow is required to wait four months and ten days, which is four complete periods multiplied by three darknesses (4 x 30 = 120 days) plus 10 complementary days. As stated in the hadith, for forty days man is in the liquid state, another forty days he turns into blood and another forty days he turns into flesh. Then the spirit is blown into him so 120 days equals four months for the formation of the body in the womb and the ten days represents the spirit (*ruh*). The word ten means perfection. It is composed of 3 + 7, which equals 3 days of darkness, 6 days of creation and with the one day it is in reference to the day of the throne.

Likewise in the case of Maryam, mother of Jesus, a similar form of abstention was imposed, namely to abstain from speaking to any human being. Fasting from speaking was imposed on her after she had received the glad tidings about the birth of a sanctified son. When she was going through the pains of contraction, the glad tidings were reinforced and the spirit addressed her saying:

> "God has made a spring of water run for you and a date tree with ripe dates; eat and drink and be cool in your eyes, but do not speak to any human."
> [Surah Maryam (Mary) 19:24-26]

The conclusion we draw from these two stories above is that the presence of the spirit requires silence, which is fasting from speaking, but not necessarily from eating and drinking. This is so because the spirit is a bringer of glad tidings about God's word or mercy that is arriving. The receiver of the glad tidings should therefore desist from speaking in order to be spoken to:

"Do not roll your tongue with it out of haste. It is up to us to collect it and then recite it. When We have recited it, follow then its recitation. Then it is up to Us to explicate it."
[Surah Al Qiyamah (The Inevitable Event) 75:16-19]

On a similar note, God says:

"When Qur'an is being recited, listen to it and be silent that perhaps you would receive God's mercy."
[Surah Al A'raf (The Heights) 7:204]

This means that when Qur'an is recited, the spirit comes down and if those present observe *taqwa* - to listen and be silent - they shall earn God's mercy. We notice here that silence constitutes a major portion of *taqwa*. It means fasting from human speech in order to feast on the divine words brought down by the spirit as the forerunner of God's mercy. Therefore, Qur'an was revealed in the month of fasting because it is the month of feasting on the words of God, the Lord of Mercy (Qur'an is the feast of God).

However, this feasting on the Qur'an is not possible except for those who observe *taqwa* - for them the spirit of strengthening comes down unto them from God with greetings of peace, which in essence is reassurance from God to not fear or grieve. With those words, all fear or grief are swept away from their hearts and their hearts turn sound and peaceful.

"Indeed the friends of Allah have no fear and no grief. They are the ones who bear faith and have taqwa."

[*Surah Yunus* (Jonah) 10:62-63]

Indeed only those with a sound heart are admitted into the feast:

"Peace! A word from a Lord Most Merciful."
[*Surah Ya Seen* (Ya Seen) 36:58]

This means He sends the word of peace ahead of His mercy. That word of peace is a spirit from Him that strengthens the hearts of believers by removing fear and grief, and filling the heart with happiness and confidence. When their hearts are strengthened with the spirit of peace, they are sure to achieve the mercy they seek.

The spirit of peace is therefore sent by God to take away *fitnah* and bring peace. *Fitnah* comprises all things that cause fear and grief for people while peace on the contrary takes fear and grief away from the hearts of people. The act of removing fear and grief from the heart constitutes strengthening, since these two (fear and grief) weaken the heart (*da'f*) and enfeeble it (*wahn*). *Wahn* (feebleness) is caused by fear and it means the unsteadiness of the heart swaying from side to side. *Da'f* (weakness) on the other hand is caused by grief and it means the inability of something to stand upright. And since it can't stand straight, it creeps along the ground.

Peace however strengthens the heart so that it is not swayed from side to side but rather stands square and is able to stand up and be straight.

Those who practice alms-giving >*Islah*	Those who are tender-hearted in their prayers >*Iman*
"Successful indeed are the believers who are tender-hearted in their prayers; who turn away from idle talk who practice alms-giving; and who safeguard their chastity." [Surah Al-Mu'minoon (The Believers) 23:1-5]	
And those who safeguard their chastity>*Birr*	Those who turn away from idle talk>*Taqwa*

This chart gives us further evidence regarding the connection between *taqwa* and controlling the tongue. Those who turn away from idle or foul talk are those who have *taqwa*. In return for idle or foul talk, they say 'peace'.

"And when they hear vain talk, they turn away therefrom and say: To us our deeds, and to you yours. Peace be to you: we seek not the ignorant."
[Surah Al Qasas (The Narrations) 28:55]

Their hearts are free from fear and grief and therefore their words inspire peace in the hearts of those who hear it. In consequence, their prayers are answered because they proceed from hearts in peace.

IV: *Shuhadaa* - The Witnesses

The fourth category of people among the exalted company of God and His messenger are known as the witnesses.

"Those who believe in Allah and His messenger are the Siddiqeen (sincere ones), and the Witnesses are with their Lord. They have their reward and their Light."
[*Surah Al Hadid* (The Iron) 57:19]

The witnesses are those who carry the knowledge of the book in their hearts. They are the witnesses of the word of unity.

"Allah bears witness that there is no god but He, and so do the angels and the people of knowledge, standing in uprightness. There is no god but He, the Most Wise the All-Mighty."
[*Surah Al Imran* (The Family of Imran) 3:18]

"From among the community of believers God would choose witnesses."
[*Surah Al Imran* (The Family of Imran) 3:140]

"And from each people shall We draw a witness, and We shall say: "Produce your Proof" then shall they know that the Truth is in Allah (alone), and the (lies) which they invented will leave them in lurch."
[*Surah Al Qasas* (The Narrations) 28:75]

"One Day We shall raise from all Peoples a Witness: then will no excuse be accepted from Unbelievers, nor will they receive any favours."
[*Surah An Nahl* (The Ant) 16:84]

"And (bethink you of) the day when We raise in every nation a witness against them of their own folk, and We bring thee (Muhammad) as a witness against these. And We reveal the Scripture unto thee as an exposition of all things, and a guidance and a mercy and good tidings for those who have surrendered (to

Allah)."
[*Surah An Nahl* (The Ant) 16:89]

"How then if We brought from each people a witness, and We brought thee as a witness against these people!"
[*Surah An Nisa* (The Women) 4:41]

From these verses quoted above, we understand that in every nation there is a witness as well as a warner. The warner is given a distinction called "*furqan*" also called "*fiqh*" from the word "*faraq*" which means to distinguish or to separate. And *fiqh* is from the word "*faqaha*" - to hatch, to split. A warner is an awakener who tears away the veil of slumber in which the people are enshrouded in and awakens them to the danger that lies ahead of them. He enjoins people to do right, to achieve salvation and forbids them from doing wrong by which they upset the balance which calls for Divine justice. Therefore, a nation, whether Islamic or non-Islamic, cannot fare without a warner. Similarly, in every nation there are witnesses who carry the knowledge of the book. They are witnesses for God and over men. By the light of knowledge, which they have been given, they walk straight among human beings judging among them with justice. To play the sincere role of a witness and just judge, one must be totally impartial and non-aligned. That impartiality and non-alignment is what constitutes their uprightness. They are bound by their duty to deliver their witnessing whenever they are called upon. They are forbidden to hide the knowledge over which God made them a witness.

"Who is worse in wrongdoing than one who hid the witnessing which he had with him?"
[*Surah Al An'am* (The Cattle) 6:21; *Surah Al A'raf* (The Heights) 7:37; *Surah Yunus* (Jonah) 10:17]

A witness is therefore one whom God has permitted to encompass something from His knowledge. He is witness over what he knows and he must not hide what he knows. If he hides knowledge, he has breached his witnessing. In this respect, in the story of King Solomon, peace and blessings of God be upon him, we comprehend the position of the man who had knowledge of the book as a witness. He came forward offering his services to the *khalifah* (Solomon) when the latter asked for help. As a witness who had knowledge from the book, it was his duty to use that knowledge to help those who are in the way of God and are struggling to promote the word of God. Here is King Solomon who wanted to promote the word of God - *La ilaha illa Allah* – in the nation of Sheba and part of that effort was to bring thethrone of the Queen into the presence of Solomon.

Two persons offered their help to King Solomon. One was a *siddiq* and the other a *shahid*. The *siddiq* (sincere one) was bound to deliver the trust that God had given him which translates into the strength God had given the *siddiq* by infusing him with his spirit.

"A strong one among the jinns said: 'I will bring it (the throne) before you rise up from your seat. I am strong and trustworthy.'"
[*Surah An Naml* (The Ant) 27:39]

Strength and trust go hand in hand, for only the strong can uphold a trust. The strength he had was a trust God had given him and whenever there is an opportunity to promote the word of God, he must use that strength. However, if he held it back, he would indeed have cheated that trust. Similarly, the witness (*shahid*) said:

"I can bring it (the throne) to you before you return your gaze."
[*Surah An Naml* (The Ant) 27:40]

The man of knowledge was similarly called upon to deliver his witnessing, which he did. The throne was immediately in Solomon's presence. The appearance of the throne of the Queen of Sheba in the presence of Solomon was not due to the effort of any one character in the story. Rather, it was due to the accumulated effort of all four characters, representing the four members of the exalted company of God and His messenger, who was Solomon in this case.

	Solomon	
Ant		Hoopoe bird
One who had knowledge from the book		Ifrit from the Jinns

"Solomon's army of jinns, of humans, and of birds were gathered up until when they came into a valley, an ant said: O' ants, enter your homes lest Solomon and his army crush you unaware."
[*Surah An Naml* (The Ant) 27:18]

"He inspected the birds and said: 'Why do I not see the hoopoe or is he among the absentees? I will punish him severely or I will slaughter him unless he brings me a clear proof. Shortly the hoopoe came and said: 'I have encompassed in knowledge what you have not; I have brought to you from Sheba a certain news. I found a woman who governed them. She was provided with everything and she has a magnificent throne." [*Surah An Naml* (The Ant) 27:20-23]

These companions are:

1. The bird, who is the bringer of news (remembrance), hence the role of an angel, with similarities between the wings of angels and the wings of birds.

2. The ant, who is a warner, and warned others about the coming of Solomon and his hosts into their valley. He warned

them to stay inside their homes to avoid getting crushed. A warning as a rule relates to something in the future. Therefore it is opposite of remembrance which relates only to the past. So the bird represents the past and the ant represents the future.

3. The *ifrit* from the *jinns*, who was a *siddiq*, represents the inspired ones strengthened with the spirit of God. They are those who propagate the glad tidings about the upcoming mercy of God. They are the carriers of the word of peace that banish fear and grief from the hearts of people, and bring love and yearning for God and His mercy.

4. The man with knowledge from the book, who then is a witness over that knowledge. He is required to deliver his witnessing whenever he is called upon. Whatever is witnessed is what is written and what is written is confirmed, binding and abiding. Hence, the book is divided into "*ummul-kitaab*" which is the interior of the book; and "*'ilm-ul-kitaab*" which is the exterior of the book.

Those who relate to the interior of the book are called '*ummi*' or *siddiq* and their role has been described above. They are those whose hearts have been cleared for *taqwa* - *taqwa* as a provision, as a dress and as a word. The counterpart of '*ummul-kitaab*' is '*ilm-ul kitaab*' which is the exterior of the *kitaab*. Those who are charged with the exterior of the book are known as *shuhadaa* - witnesses or '*ulamaa*. They command people to justice and they stand upright. They are also called '*abrar*' from the word '*birr*' - the pious ones whose dwelling place is in '*illiyyina*.

> "Indeed the book of the pious is in ʿilliyyīna. Do you know what ʿilliyyīna is? It is a book that is entrenched only those who were drawn near could witness it."
> [Surah Al Mutaffifeen (The Defrauders) 83:18-21]

In other words, the knowledge of the book is entrenched and immured from viewing except for the *abrar* who are the pious witnesses of God, and who are drawn near unto God. In other terms, the book consists of "*muhkamaat*" and they constitute "*ummul-kitaab*" that is, the interior of the book. The person who knows the interior of the book is known as *ummi* or *siddiq*. The second part of the book consists of *mutashaabihaat*, and they constitute *'ilm-ul-kitaab* which is the exterior of the book. The person who knows this exterior is called *'aalim'* or *'shahid'* or *'kitaabi.'*

> "He (Allah) is the One who sent down the book unto you wherein are signs which are muhkamaat (firm and univocal). They constitute the ummul-kitaab (the interior of the book) and others that are mutashaabihaat (resembling one another which constitutes 'ilm-ul-kitaab)."
> [Surah Al Imran (The Family of Imran) 3:7]

As for those in whose heart there is a lean, they follow the ones that look alike looking for trouble (*fitnah*), and looking for its interpretation and none but Allah knows the interpretation.

> "And those well-established in knowledge say: We believe in the Book, all is from our Lord and none will grasp the message except men of understanding."
> [Surah Al Imran (The Family of Imran) 3:7]

The ones whose hearts are well-guarded are those who are well-rooted in knowledge, with their roots firmly anchored in the earth and the branches towering into the sky. They do not incline towards the interior of the book to the exclusion of the exterior, nor do they incline towards the exterior to the detriment of the interior. But they say we believe that both interior and exterior of the book are from our Lord. We do not discriminate between the two. They have the right attitude, and unto them is given the knowledge of interpretation called "*taweel*." The word comes from "*awwal*" - first or beginning which therefore means to trace something back to its beginning.

Certainly in order to get a full comprehension of something, it would require you to look at it from four different points of view in addition to viewing from below and above.

The Prohibited Tree

The tree that was forbidden to Adam in the garden was a representation of the life of the world in which Adam lived after he came out of the garden. The scriptures (Torah, Bible and Qur'an) all describe the tree as the tree of knowledge of good and evil. In Qur'anic terms it was a tree of mixing (*dhulm*). God says:

> "Do not get close to this tree lest you become part of those who mix (syncretise)."
> [*Surah Al A'raf* (The Heights) 7:19); *Surah Al Baqarah* (The Cow) 2:35]

This mixing is known in other words as duality which is the fundamental principle of this worldly life. Everything is mixed together, wrong and right, good and bad, health and sickness, richness and poverty, joy and pain. This is the nature of this world and it will never change until the end of this world. Due to its dualistic nature its inhabitants always live a polarized life swinging from one extreme to another.

When Adam was created, God placed him first in the other world where everything exists within strict boundaries and no two things mix. Its pain is absolute pain and its pleasure is absolute pleasure, the two never mix. Everything is absolutely pure in its nature and the life that Adam lived in the other world before coming into this one was a life of absolute bliss with no pain, fear and grief. It was a simple life of goodness and he never knew what evil was. The prohibition against eating from the tree was a caution against knowing the nature of this world, which is a mix of good and bad.

In this world of ours, there is nothing, which is absolutely good without a grain of ill in it and there is nothing, which is absolutely evil without a grain of goodness in it. The difference is that somethings contain more good than others while others contain more ill than others, it is a matter of degree and not of kind.

Therefore when Adam was sent down into this world he was surrounded by all those contradictions and confusions, which are inherent to this world and he was left with only a few choices:

1. To repudiate the life of this world as though it never existed. Instead, to live his life entirely in the memory of his former life, which he anticipates returning back to.

2. To repudiate his former life entirely and turn his heart completely to this new life in this new world. There is no more anticipating any life after this worldly life.

3. To accept both, the life of this world and the life of the next world, (previous world) accepting both lives means seeking both of them without risking to lose either of them.

First Choice

Among Adam's descendants there are many who choose to repudiate this world and live on the margin thereof. Their hearts and souls do not live in this world, only their body lives in this world and soon when they die their souls depart to their former home which was the world of Adam before he came into this new world. It is simply called the other world - *akhirah*. Mystics, hermits, monks, nuns, Sufis, *fakeers*, mainly fall into this category. They are known as the people of the right hand.

The Second Choice

The second choice is also made by many of Adam's children who came into this world and with the passage of time, they lost memory of their lives in the former world. They have therefore chosen this life as the only life and repudiated any memory of any other life. Though conscious about the mixed nature of this world they try to make the best out of the good things that they find in it. They enjoy the pleasure of today and suffer the pain of tomorrow. This group represents the majority of Adam's children. They are known as the people of the left side.

The Third Choice

The third choice was the one that Adam made and those among his children who maintain the middle course. This choice is the hardest of all the three for which reason it is avoided by both the former groups: people of the right and the left.

For those who have chosen this middle path called the straight path their first assignment is acceptance. Acceptance means to have a open heart and an open mind to everything in this life based on the understanding that everything in this life contains some good and some bad and therefore nothing should be rejected as a whole and nothing should be embraced as a whole. If something contains more good than bad then sort out the bad and then embrace the remaining good as a whole with absolute pleasure. However if you embrace good mixed with bad the bad will prevent you from having a complete enjoyment of the good.

On the other hand if something contains more bad than good in this case you sort the good out and cast away the bad, which remains. The little good, which you sorted out of the bad will entirely be of perfect goodness to you. In the former it was abundant good admixed with little evil. If that little evil was not separated from the abundant good it has the potential of spoiling the abundant good even though it be very little. Therefore evil must never be underestimated no matter how insignificant it seems to be.

Conversely, the little good that was admixed with abundant evil must not be thrown away with the whole lot of evil, which surrounds it. A good no matter how tiny it is must not be disregarded. That little good has the potential of growing and multiplying into abundant good. In as much as a small evil can destroy abundant good, a small good as well has the capacity of growing into abundant good. Therefore evil, may it be little or abundant must be removed and destroyed as much as good, may it be little or abundant it must be saved and spared, God says:

> *"Say not equal are things that are bad and things that are good even though the abundance of the bad may dazzle thee..."*
> [*Surah Al Ma'idah* (The Table Spread) 5:100]

However, the method of sorting depends on the ratio between good and evil. If good is greater in number then there is no point trying to sort out the good which is greater in number but rather sort out whichever is smaller in number. To sort out the greater in number is taking on unnecessary pain.

Good and bad here are not mere abstractions or philosophical speculations they simply mean what is harmful and what is useful or beneficent to the human in particular and to the world at large. However, as noted above, things that are harmful may contain some benefit in them that benefit should not be cast away with the harmful lot. On the other hand the useful or beneficent things contain some harm in them, which should not be admitted with the greater benefit. The benefit in the greater harm should be sorted out and the harm in the greater benefit should be sorted out. Finally the little good (benefit) in the greater harm once sorted out as well as little harm (evil) in the greater good should be sorted out too then the little good (benefit) should then be added to the greater good (benefit) making up the total sum of good. On the other hand the little evil (harm), which was sorted out should be added up to the greater evil (harm) making up the total sum of evil (harm). Once the total sum of evil is contained and destroyed then there will be no more harm or evil left on earth.

Thus only the good, the beneficent and the righteous shall remain. As Allah says:

"He sends down water from the skies, and the channels flow, each according to its measure: But the torrent bears away to foam that mounts up to the surface. Even so, from that (ore) which they heat in the fire, to make ornaments or utensils therewith, there is a scum likewise. Thus doth Allah (by parables) show forth Truth and Vanity. For the scum disappears like forth cast out; while that which is for the good of mankind remains on the earth. Thus doth Allah set forth parables."
[Surah Ar R'ad (The Thunder) 13:17]

The True and the False

At times in the scriptures the term true and false are used to describe what is good and beneficent and what is evil and harmful. However for something beneficent to be called true it must be permanently beneficent to be called true and similarly for something to be called false it must be permanently harmful. This certainly applies to the period after the sorting out and the aggregation when the little good is sorted out and little evil is sorted out and then the little good is added to the lot of good and little evil added to the lot of evil. Only then is it right to say that the good is truly good and the evil is truly evil.

Distinction and Separation

The process of segregation and aggregation takes place in three steps:

1) The first step consists of the first aggregation in which everything good or bad, harmful or beneficent, is all seen as one. God says:

"...And those who are firmly grounded in knowledge say: We believe in the Book; whole of it is from our Lord..."
[Surah Al Imran (The Family of Imran) 3:7]

Again God says:

> "Wherever you are, death will find you out, even if you are in towers built up strong and high. If some good befalls them, they say, 'This is from Allah but if evil they say, 'This is from thee.' (O Prophet) say: All things are from Allah but what hath come to these people that they fail to understand a single fact."
> [*Surah Al Nisa* (The Women) 4:78]

2) The second step consists of the segregation that follows the first aggregation in which the little good is sorted out of the abundant evil and the little evil is sorted out of the abundant good. God says:

> "Whatever good, (O man!) happens to thee, is from Allah; but whatever evil happens to thee, is from thy (own) soul. And We have sent thee as a messenger to (instruct) mankind. And enough is Allah for a witness."
> [*Surah An Nisa* (The Women) 4:79]

3) The third step consists of the second aggregation after the segregation in which the little good is joined with the abundant good while the little evil is joined to the abundant evil. In this second aggregation it is the union of good only with good and evil only with evil. The measure of good is full and the measure of evil is full. Allah says:

> "So that Allah will turn off from them (even) the worst in their deeds and give them their reward according to the best of what they have done."
> [*Surah Az Zumar* (The Crowd) 39:35]

Allah says:

> "Say: Our Lord will aggregate us together and will in the end segregate us by the truth and justice: and He is the one to decide, the One Who knows all."
> [*Surah Saba* (The City of Saba) 34:26]

Allah says:

> "In order that Allah may separate the impure from the pure, put the impure, one on another, heap them together, and cast them into Hell. They will be the ones to have lost."
> [Surah Al Anfal (The Spoils of War) 8:37]

However in order to apply the rule of the three steps of aggregation - segregation and then aggregation with a net benefit at the end, one must fulfill a precondition without which the three steps cannot yield the desired result of a net benefit. That precondition is known as acceptance commonly termed as surrender (*tasleem*). It means that each time that we are faced with a situation before we look for a solution we must first accept the situation as the will of God. This positive attitude allows us to keep an open heart, which is accepting everything first without judgment. This openness towards the will of God by which things are in the world the way they are, make way for God's light to come into our heart. That acceptance of everything the way they are as the manifestation of God's will allows the first step of the first aggregation to take place. We aggregate all because we accept all as from God.

The second step, which is segregation then kicks in once God's light comes down into our heart which allows us to see and differentiate. Once we can see we are able to segregate between good and bad and beneficent and harmful. There is no way we can sort it out if we have no light and there is no way we can have light if we do not accept all (*tasleem*).

The process of segregation and separation between different parts that make the whole is done in two ways:

1) If we are separating the little evil from the abundant good then we use the method of *kashf*, which means to rip off the little harm out of the abundant good. This method is appropriate because tearing off the little harm out the abundant will not affect the abundant good in any negative way.

2) If on the other hand we are separating the little good out of the abundant evil we use the method of *fath*, which means to open up. This is a gentle and smooth way of extracting the little good out of the abundant evil.

This is a gentle and smooth way of extracting the little good out of a mass of evil. If we try to rip the little good out of the mass of evil we risk losing it all together. This gentle process of opening is dictated by the rules of wisdom (*hikmah*), while the method of forceful tearing is dictated by the commandment ('*amr*). From the point of view of excellence (*ihsan*) each method is appropriate within its area. Whenever there is a little harm, which threatens the abundant good that little harm should be forcibly removed. However in the case where the little good is threatened by abundant evil we must neither try to remove the abundant evil by force which certainly will lead to the destruction of the little good as well nor can we remove the little good with force neither because using force against what is good is wrong in any case. We are therefore left only with one alternative to extract the little good out of the abundant harm with wisdom (*hikmah*) by opening the door of the abundant evil and not by breaking it.

Once we are done with casting every little evil from the abundant good on the one hand we are finished setting the little good out of the mass of evil we then put little good with abundant good and put little evil with abundant evil. When the measure of good is full and the measure of evil is full only then the evil will be judged. As Allah says:

"He sends down water from the skies, and the channels flow, each according to its measure: But the torrent bears away to foam that mounts up to the surface. Even so, from that (ore) which they heat in the fire, to make ornaments or utensils therewith, there is a scum likewise. Thus doth Allah (by parables) show forth Truth and Vanity. For the scum disappears like forth cast out; while that which is for the good of mankind remains on the earth. Thus doth Allah set forth parables."

[*Surah Al Anfal* (The Spoils Of War) 8:37]

Also Allah says:

"They are the ones who denied Revelation and hindered you from the Sacred Mosque and the sacrificial animals, detained from reaching their place of sacrifice. Had there not been believing men and believing women whom ye did not know that ye were trampling down and on whose account a crime would have accrued to you without (your) knowledge, (Allah would have allowed you to force your way, but He held back your hands) that He may admit to His Mercy whom He will. If they had been apart, We should certainly have punished the Unbelievers among them with a grievous Punishment."
[*Surah Fath* (The Victory) 48:25]

The Three Methods in the Story of Moses and the Guide

In *Surah Al Kahf,* verse 60 to 82, there are three episodes and each episode illustrates one of the three methods in segregation.

1) Segregation by means of wisdom (*fath*)
2) Segregation by means of force (*kashf*)
3) Segregation by means of excellence (*ihsan*), which is a combination of both wisdom (*fath*) and force (*kashf*).

In the first episode the guide applied the method of segregation by means of wisdom (*fath*), which is to open and not to break. According to the story the ship they boarded belonged to two poor men who lived off the ship. However the ship risked getting confiscated by the king who had dominion over the area. In order to save the ship the guide decided to make a crack in it. He knew that this was the right way of salvaging the ship rather them battling the king and his forces to save the ship. This episode was a case of little good surrounded by a mass of evil. The only way was to make a little opening for the little good to escape.

In the second episode the guide slew a boy who had faithful parents. This boy, he said, was a threat to his parents if allowed to live, the love his parents had for him would have swayed them off their correct path, therefore, the guide killed the boy. This episode was a case of little harm that is threatening abundant good. The appropriate method for the guide was to forcibly remove the threat by killing (*kashf*).

In the third episode when they come into the city tired and hungry they asked for hospitality but they were denied. As they went about, the teacher noticed a wall that was on the verge of falling he quickly raised it back up. Raising the wall was an act of excellence (*ihsan*), which is a combination of both wisdom and commandment. The wall, which was built using both methods, is the only means by which the full measure of good can be separated from the full measure of evil.

"A *wall was raised between them with a door in it, within was mercy and without was tribulation."*
[*Surah Al Hadid* (The Iron) 57:13]

Land, Sea and the Boundary

From the story of Moses and his guide we deduce other conclusions regarding the nature of the land and sea. These conclusions are that there is more good on the land than in the sea and that there is more evil in the sea than on the land. We deduce these conclusions from the fact that the guide used method of *fath* (opening) in the sea. This method applies only when we have to extract a little good out of a mass of evil.

On the contrary we used the method of *kashf* (tearing) in the land when he slew the boy to save the parents. This method applies only when we have to forcibly remove little harm from abundant good. Thirdly, the city represents a place of meeting between land and sea. The little good of sea meet there with the abundant good of the land on one hand while on the other hand the little evil of the land meets there with the abundant evil of the sea. In the city we need the excellent method, which separates all evil from all good. In other words the city represents the case of the second segregation where all evil is segregated from all good.

In the story we are also informed that there was buried treasure under a wall that belonged to two orphans. If the wall represents excellence (*ihsan*) which separates all evil from all good so that the two never mix, then the treasure under the wall represents *taqwa* (fulfillment) which is the foundation of (*ihsan*) excellence. Indeed one without *taqwa* cannot exercise excellence and indeed one without excellence cannot attain *ridwan* (God's face or pleasure). Allah says:

"Never stand thou forth therein. There is a mosque whose foundation was laid from the first day on piety; it is more worthy of the standing forth (for prayer) therein. In it are men who love to be purified; and Allah loveth those who make themselves pure."
[*Surah At Tawbah* (The Repentance) 9:108]

The Three Methods in the Story of Dhul Qarnain

In *Surah Al Kahf*, verses 83-98, we find the story of Dhul Qarnain, which also contains three episodes. In the first episode he travelled until he reached the setting place of the sun and there he found the sun setting in murky water. Beside the murky water, he found people some of whom were righteous and believing while others who were the majority, were mixed up and muddled. He was authorized by God to punish or reward. In the second episode he travelled till he reached the rising place of the sun and there found some people who were exposed to the naked sun. In the third episode he travelled till he reached the boundary between the setting place and the rising place and there he found people who barely understood language. They requested him to raise a wall between them and

Gog and Magog, which he did.

Like the story of Moses and the guide, the first episode is a reference to life in the sea where there is little good and abundant ill. Through wisdom he was able to salvage the few good people from the West and condemn the vast majority to continuing to live in that confusion and anarchy indicated by the murkiness of water. It is the primitive undeveloped stage of life. Here are the early stages of life or the beginning of creation.

"Say: Travel through the earth and see how Allah did originate creation; so will Allah produce a later creation: for Allah has power over all things."
[*Surah Al Ankabut* (The Spider) 26:20]

It is in this quagmire that creation began, there are creatures who make it out of this quagmire which are those who are guided by their faith, and there are those who remain wallowing, who have no guidance by faith. Dhul Qarnain was authorized by God to salvage the former group and confine the rest to the quagmire.

Another symbol is the setting sun, which represents the descent of the spirit into the domain of creation in order to salvage the soul, which remains in the quagmire of creation. Without the lowering of the spirit from its lofty and exalted station in the commandment down to the low and base station of the soul in the creation the life of excellence would not come into being. It is for the attainment of excellence that the human being was created.

Even though there was no explicit mention of the moon in the story it is however understood. For the relationship of the sun to the moon is the same relationship of the spirit to the soul. As the moon receives its light from the sun, similarly the soul receives its light from the spirit. The moon can be illuminated by the sun as a result of the sun lowering itself on the moon without fully exposing itself to the moon. In a similar manner the spirit is allowed to lower itself down unto the soul but is not allowed to make a full contact since a full contact will result in ending the life of the soul in this world as much as a full contact between the sun and the moon will result in the end of this world.

> "The sun is not allowed to make a full contact with the moon, nor is the night supposed to advance the day they all swim in their respective orbits."
> [*Surah Ya Seen* (Ya Seen) 36:40]

This contact between the soul and the spirit begins when the soul comes to stillness and stops wandering in the quagmire of creation. Immediately when the soul finds stillness the spirit is lowered upon it - illuminating it. This marks the beginning of the journey of the soul out of the creation under the guidance of the spirit. The same relationship between the sun and the moon, this stage by stage extraction of the soul out of creation into commandment is represented by the monthly revolutions of the moon in cycles of growth and decrease until the two finally make the full contact. Allah says:

> "Hast thou not turned thy vision to thy Lord? - How He doth prolong the shadow! If He willed, He could make it stationary! Then do We make the sun its guide; Then We draw it in towards Ourselves, - a contraction by easy stages."
> [*Surah Al Furqan* (The Criterion) 25:45-46]

That full contact between the spirit and the soul is represented by the second episode whereby Dhul Qarnain found the sun rising while the people in that place had no cover between them and the sun. Those people are the souls that have made full contact with the spirit because all veils in between have been torn away. The rising sun recalls the spirit rising in full glory into the commandment and pulling up the soul with it. In ascent or descent one or the other makes the rule. During rising, the soul is subject to the rule of commandment by means of *kashf*, which means that the soul has to let go of all kinds of means; everything is torn away. It is the other way around during descent whereby the rule of the three wisdoms prevails and the spirit has to abide by the rules of measurement and calculation of the law of creation.

Another parallel to that is the stick of Moses. The stick turns into a snake and back. This growth and decrease is similar to the growth and decrease of the moon when it became like a curved stick. Allah says:

"And the Moon - We have measured for her mansions (to traverse) till she returns like the old (and withered) lower part of a date-stalk."
[*Surah Ya Seen* (Ya Seen) 36:39]

The movement of the snake is a perfect duplication of the movement of the moon. It is measured and calculated.

The third episode represents the station of excellence, which stands between creation and commandment. The wall, which he built is the symbol of separation between all evil and all good so that the two cannot mix. Allah says:

"One (such) way he followed, Until, when he reached the setting of the sun, he found it set in a spring of murky water: Near it he found a People: We said: O Dhul-Qarnain! (Thou hast authority), either to punish them, or to treat them with kindness. He said: Whoever doth wrong, him shall we punish; then shall he be sent back to his Lord; and He will punish him with a punishment unheard of (before). But whoever believes, and works righteousness, - he shall have a goodly reward, and easy will be his task as We order it by our Command. Then followed he (another) way, until, when he came to the rising of the sun, he found it rising on a people for whom We had provided no covering protection against the sun. (He left them) as they were: We completely understood what was before him. Then followed he

(another) way, Until, when he reached (a tract) between two mountains, he found, beneath them, a people who scarcely understood a word. They said: O Dhul-Qarnain! The Gog and Magog (People) do great mischief on earth: shall we then render thee tribute in order that thou mightiest erect a barrier between us and them? He said: (The power) in which my Lord has established me is better (than tribute): Help me therefore with strength (and labour): I will erect a strong barrier between you and them: Bring me blocks of iron. At length, when he had filled up the space between the two steep mountain-sides, He said, Blow (with your bellows) Then, when he had made it (red) as fire, he said: Bring me that I may pour over it, molten lead. Thus were they made powerless to scale it or to dig through it. He said: This is a mercy from my Lord: But when the promise of my Lord comes to pass, He will make it into dust; and the promise of my Lord is true."
[*Surah Al Kahf* (The Cave) 18:85-98]

The Three Steps in the Story of Ibrahim

Prophet Ibrahim, peace be upon him, asked God to show him how He brings the death to life. In order to show him how, God instructed him to cut four birds into pieces and mix them up. This mixing represents the first aggregation. Then God told him to divide the meat into four parts and place each part on a mountain, this second step is segregation. God told him to call them and they will come to him in obedience. This third step is the second aggregation whereby all good answer the call and come together from land and sea congregating in the city with the wall as the boundary.

The Three Steps in the Creation of the Universe

The creation of the universe is no exception to the rule of the three steps: aggregation, segregation, aggregation. In fact the creation of the universe serves as the model for all forms of creation. In *Surah Al Anbiyah* (The Prophets) God tells us that at the beginning, the earth and heaven were a single mass in the murky water whence all forms of creation originated. This information is a reference to the first aggregation when the earth and heaven and all the world come forth out of them were all in one undifferentiated lot.

> *"Do not the disbelievers see that the heavens and the earth were joined together then we parted them, from the water we made every living thing, won't they believe then!"*
> [*Surah Al Anbiyah* (The Prophets) 21:30]

This verse points out two major facts: 1) the heavens and the earth were aggregated by God into one undifferentiated mass. 2) That they were extracted out of the murky water simply referred to as the water.

The story of creation pointed out in these verses is that the elements that formed the heaven and earth were at the beginning assembled and aggregated in the murky water by God and rolled into a ball of mass. This ball of mass as it rolled about in the murky water collected and absorbed every substance therein. This is the end of the first aggregation. Then the second step, which is the segregation, began when God cracked the ball punching a hole in it. Then by gentle stages he widened the crack making the ball into two halves a lower half, which is the earth and upper half, which is the heaven. As both halves grew and increased further expansions were initiated. Day and night were brought forth from the heaven and mountains were placed on the earth, as well water and vegetation was brought forth from the earth. This marked the end of step two when everything was segregated according to the rules of wisdom, which applies to the creation. Allah says:

> *"Say: Is it that ye deny Him Who created the earth in two Days? And do ye join equals with Him? He is the Lord of (all) the Worlds. He set on the (earth), mountains standing firm, high above it, and bestowed blessings on the earth, and measure therein all things to give them nourishment in due proportion, in*

> *four Days, in accordance with (the needs of) those who seek (Sustenance)."*
> [*Surah Fussilat* (Explained in Detail) 41:9-10]

At another place Allah says:

> *"What! Are ye the more difficult to create or the heaven (above)? (Allah) hath constructed it:On high hath He raised its canopy, and He hath given it order and perfection. Its night doth He endow with darkness, and its splendour doth He bring out (with light). And the earth, moreover, hath He extended (to a wide expanse); He draweth out there from its moisture and its pasture; And the mountains hath He firmly fixed; - For use and convenience to you and your cattle."*
> [*Surah An Nazi'at* (Those Who Pull Out) 79:27-33]

The third step, which is the second aggregation, began when God summoned the earth and heaven by saying, "Come to me together willingly or unwillingly, they said we have come in willing obedience." This statement of calling them together marks the beginning of commandment after the completion of creation. When they responded to His call positively He lifted them out of water. He stripped the heaven of all veils that may have come up with it from the creation and then extended it from one into seven heavens and placed stars in the lower heaven. In a similar manner He extended the earth from one into seven earths through commandment; this is the second aggregation, which took place in commandment while the first one took place in creation. Consequently, the heavens and the earth that came in the second aggregation will endure forever while the earth and heaven that formed part of the first aggregation and segregation will perish. Allah says:

> *"Moreover He comprehended in His design the sky, and it had been (as) smoke: He said to it and to the earth: Come ye together, willingly or unwillingly. They said: We do come (together), in willing obedience. So He completed them as seven firmaments in two Days, and He assigned to each heaven its duty and command. And We adorned the lower heaven with lights, and*

(provided it) with guard. Such is the Decree of (Him) the Exalted in Might, Full of Knowledge."
[Surah Fussilat (Explained in Detail) 41:11-12]

The Two Extensions

God extended His presence (*istiwaaa*) on the throne twice: first at the end of creation and secondly at the end of commandment. The person who lives in harmony between creation and commandment has attained excellence and he is now endowed with double expansions with *kashf* and *fath*. However the person who lives by either commandment or creation will be granted either *fath* or *kashf*. The person who is granted *fath* is assigned a station under the throne while the person who is granted *kashf* is assigned a station above the throne. The person who attained excellence is neither stationed above nor below the throne, but right in the middle of the throne, they are the ones who are drawn the most close.

This concludes Volume One of the Expansion Series: The Purpose of Creation. Please visit our website: expansions.ca for more information about the forthcoming volumes.

Glossary of Terms

Transliteration	Translation
ʿadl	Justice
ʿafū	Pardon
ahl-l-dhik'ri	People of remembrance
akhbār	News
ākhirah	Hereafter
amanat	Trust
ʿamr	Commandment of God
ʿaql	Understanding
ʿarsh	Throne
awtād	Pegs
barzakh	Boundary
baṣīrat	Sight
basṭ	expansive state
dhikr	Remembrance of God
ḍiyā	Bright light
dunyā	Outer world
farq	Difference
fikr	Reflection
fitnah	Descension
fur'qān	The light to separate truth from falsehood
ghayb	Unwitnessed/Unseen
ghiṭāa	Covering
ḥadīth	Tiding
hafiz	Protector
ḥakīm	Wise
ḥayat	Life
ḥikmah	Wisdom
hiss	Sense
kathīr	Abundant/Most of
khalīfah	Vicegerent
khalq	Creation
khāshiʿa	God-Fearing/Awe

Transliteration	Translation
khayr	Good/Better
kashf	Unveiling
Khunnas	Particles of the Night
Kunnas	Particles of the Day
kibr	Arrogance
kufr	Disbelief
iḥsān	Excellence
ikh'tilāf	Difference of opinion
ʿilm	Knowledge
īmān	Belief
iṣlāḥ	To make right
islām	Submission
madhhab	Methods in Jurisprudence
mazīd	Increase
mawt	Death
mīzān	Balance
mus'taqarr	Permanent Station
muqarrabūn	Those Drawn Near
muq'siṭīn	Those Standing in Uprightness
naba	News
nafs mutmainnah	Tranquil Soul
Nafs Ammara	The Commanding Soul
Nafs Lawwama	The Chiding Soul
Nafs Raadiyah	The soul which is pleased
Nafs Mardiyyah	The soul which is pleased with
nāẓirīn	Gazers
quṭb	The Central Pole
raḥmah	Mercy
ruk'n	Corner Stone
qabḍ	Contractive state
qaḍā	God's Judgment
qadar	God's Dispensation
qalīl	Light less in numbers
qawiī	Strong
qahhar	Overpowering
qisṭ	Uprightness

Transliteration	Translation
raka'a	One unit of prayer
riḍwān	Radiance of God's face which gives pleasure to the beholder
riz'q	Sustenance/Provision
rūḥ	Spirit
ru'yā	Vision
saad	Arabic Alphabet denotes the space within which every created thing is contained
sakīnah	Tranquility
ṣalat	Prayer
sama'	Hearing
shahāda	To Witness
shahīd	Witness/Martyrs
shuhadāa	Witnesses
shukr	Gratitude
shu'ur	Awareness
ṣidq	Sincerity
ṣiddīq	Sincere One
sukūn	Tranquility
ta'dheem	To hold in Reverence
tafrīq	Making factions
taqdīr	God's Dispensation
taqwā	Reverence of God
ṭarīqat	Path
tasawwuf	Sufism
tasleem	Unconditional Submission to God's will
tazkiyyah	Purification of the soul
ṭīn	Dust
ṭugh'yān	Trespassing God's boundaries
'uruj	Ascension
wahdaniyyah	Oneness of God
wajh	Countenance
wasīlat	Means
yaqīn	Certitude
zaki	Pure

www.ingramcontent.com/pod-product-compliance
Lightning Source LLC
Chambersburg PA
CBHW050858160426
43194CB00011B/2199